STONEHAM PUBLIC LIBRARY
431 MAIN STREET
STONEHAM, MA 02180

THIS TROUBLED LAND

THIS
TROUBLED
LAND

Voices from Northern Ireland
on the Front Lines
of Peace

PATRICK MICHAEL RUCKER

BALLANTINE BOOKS • NEW YORK

A Ballantine Book
Published by The Ballantine Publishing Group

Copyright © 2002 by Patrick Michael Rucker

All rights reserved under International and Pan-American Copyright Conventions.
Published in the United States by The Ballantine Publishing Group, a division of
Random House, Inc., New York, and simultaneously in Canada by Random House
of Canada Limited, Toronto.

Ballantine is a registered trademark and the Ballantine colophon is a trademark of
Random House, Inc.

www.ballantinebooks.com

Library of Congress Cataloging-in-Publication Data
is available upon request.

ISBN 0-345-44670-4

Designed by Ann Gold

Manufactured in the United States of America

First Edition: February 2002

10 9 8 7 6 5 4 3 2 1

for my mother and father

Introduction

◫   ◫

We heard the explosion in the middle of the night—a hollow, distant, single, *boom*. It was an unfamiliar sound yet distinct as a thunderclap. It jarred us awake, and we sat up in our sleeping bags. Out there on the streets of Belfast, a bomb had gone off. It was far from where we were sleeping, safe on the floor of a church hall, but it must have been nearby to somebody, somewhere. We wondered what would come next: gunfire, sirens, shouts and rioting, another explosion? We waited a few minutes, but there was nothing but silence and we went back to sleep.

It was the summer of 1991, and we were a group of American students of different religions and races who had come to show the people of Northern Ireland how to get along. The exchange was well intentioned but somewhat naïve and self-indulgent. Our differences were superficial, mediated by a common culture and prosperity. The differences between Protestants and Catholics in Northern Ireland were raw, bloody, and immediate. They were accustomed to hearing bombs.

A friend and I had planned to go jogging in the morning, and we woke up with a destination in mind. East Belfast, where we were staying, is predominantly Protestant, but the bomb had gone off in a small Catholic enclave called the Short Strand, just a few blocks away.

The weather was dreary, cool, and wet. The neighborhood was unpleasant—gray as if it had been washed out like a soggy newspaper and with a bitter odor, somewhere between boiled cabbage and old sneakers. We headed off down the main thoroughfare, the Newtownards

Road, in sweatshirts and shorts looking conspicuously out of place. In a ghetto where exercise was considered a form of deviance, jogging on the road was akin to driving on the sidewalk.

We ran past a butcher's, a bakery, a newspaper shop, and a junk merchant who sat outside of his shop with rusting appliances and tattered furniture, smoking a cigarette and seeming to judge us as something of a novelty or a menace. Little old women wearing head scarves and laden with groceries shuffled along. Children, their faces and shirt-fronts smeared with chocolate, would chase us, laugh, and smile gap-toothed grins. We kept running, past towering steeples (Methodist, Anglican, Presbyterian) past graffiti-scrawled walls ("Our Message to the Irish Is Simple: Hands Off," "Free All Loyalist Prisoners") and past the curbstones that went by in flashes of red, white, and blue until the shops gave way to empty husks, burned-out premises, no-man's-land, and the ten-foot "peace wall" that kept the Protestants and Catholics apart.

We turned left, down Templemore Avenue, then right, down Madrid Street and across the threshold into the Short Strand. It looked like practically the same neighborhood we had just left: children with sugar-rotten teeth swung from the wrought-iron gates in front of their homes; old women hobbled along the pavement. The only real differences were the content of graffiti on the walls ("Up the IRA," "Brits Out!") and the army presence—four-man foot patrols rhythmically traversing the streets. Two soldiers were out front, kneeling and sighting pedestrians with their rifles; the other two would then pass from behind. They would pivot and switch, pumping down the street like a piston. Passersby took no notice, ignored them as if armed men in fatigues were as unremarkable as a mailman swinging a satchel.

We found the bomb site next to a towering police barracks—a motley structure, impenetrable and unsightly. The barracks took up a whole block in the middle of the neighborhood, a red brick and concrete façade splattered with a vandal's paint and pitted by bullets and shrapnel. The roof bristled with cameras and radio antennae; the whole building was covered in a latticework of steel fence running from the roof to the street. It was a blight for everyone but the army and police who were somewhere inside, unseen and safe.

"It was a coffee-jar bomb," one of the neighbors explained, "explosives and nails packed into a tin can." He was alone in the street, casually sweeping up shards of a broken window as if they were autumn leaves. "They threw it on the roof, but it just rolled off the fence and hit the street here across from my house." Scattered glass and a shallow, scorched crater in the road were the only visible damage.

"Does this happen often?" we asked. "Now and again, but not too often," he answered blithely. When we pressed further, his tone changed, as if unexpected guests were commenting on an embarrassing clutter in his living room. He felt the bombing reflected badly on him, personally. "But sure, aren't they all at it—Protestants and Catholics?" he asked dismissively. "One's just as bad as the other. They're all up to something, but most of us just try to get along."

After a few weeks, we flew home and left our erstwhile friends in the same situation that we had found them in, but certain impressions of Northern Ireland stayed with me. The coffee-jar bomb attack was so desperate; it seemed unworthy of the struggle that I had imagined. And everyone that I had met seemed so ordinary; only a few people were involved in violence, while most were trying to lead normal lives. The conflict that I had conceived as being utterly tragic and incomprehensible became a story about commonplace people and, for them, the events that left such an impression on me were commonplace.

The conflict had been going on for over twenty years already, stumbling from shooting, to bombing, to riot. Sometimes violence came briskly; sometimes it hardly came at all. Most of the killings in Northern Ireland had occurred in a one-square-mile corner of Belfast. In those areas, the conflict was just an everyday hazard. Away from such hot spots, it could be as distant as a television news bulletin.

But few people in Northern Ireland used the word *conflict*. If you did, you were considered something of an alarmist. It suggested a condition close to war, which was a word only uttered by the people who were actually involved in the violence. Most people said "the Troubles." It made the everyday madness sound like such a discreet affair. People talked about the Troubles like they groused about bad weather—what could be done?

Anyone in the street would tell you that they wanted peace, but they might also say that they were growing accustomed to the unrest. Most people seemed to live their lives somewhere between these two sentiments. Sometimes they were wrapped so tightly in anxiety and fear that their entire lives were constricted; sometimes they seemed to wear it so loosely that they hardly seemed to be wearing it at all. The Troubles did not demand urgent attention. Society could function; it only required a few adjustments to the everyday way of things before the extraordinary seemed normal.

People who committed political violence were *criminals* and criminals—garden-variety thieves, murderers, rapists, and pedophiles—were known as *ordinary decent criminals*. *Criminals* were easier to convict, but they got better treatment in prison. There were peace talks that year—well, talks about talks about peace. Years of careful negotiations had gone into getting politicians into the same room so they could argue about who should chair their meetings, where the meetings should be held, who would be invited and what they would talk about when they got there. Getting that far was a modest triumph; the talks collapsed after a few months.

That same year, the British prime minister's official residence in London, 10 Downing Street, was mortar bombed by the IRA, and the Belfast City Council tried to have Sinn Fein, the IRA's political wing, "gagged." Six Belfast men who had been convicted of planting bombs in Britain were cleared; meanwhile, so many buildings had been bombed in Northern Ireland that the government stopped building new ones. The total number of deaths, ninety-four, was just about average for the previous fifteen years, as were the hundreds of beatings and shootings.

Then, in the years that I was away, something remarkable happened. The paramilitary groups called cease-fires; the politicians started genuinely talking to one another. There was even mention of peace—and not as a vague abstraction, but as a goal that should be pursued in earnest. The British and Irish governments, local politicians, and paramilitary groups spent two years trying to decide what should be done with the six-county province of Northern Ireland. On Good Friday, 1998, they emerged with a modest proposal to put the insuperable issues of nationality to the side while they set about building a healthy society in Northern Ireland. The most remarkable thing about the agreement was that no one lost. Northern Ireland had achieved a peace yet no one was vanquished.

How did it happen? Why then? There are dozens of scholars and observers who are much more qualified to answer that question than I am, so I will leave it to them. But watching events from the United States, I could see that something exciting had begun. I did not know what would come next—there were sure to be setbacks and obstacles— but I knew that it would only start once and that I wanted to be there.

I returned to Belfast in the fall of 1998 and settled in an apartment on that old, jagged fault line near Madrid Street. On my side of the wall the people were Protestant by religion, British by nationality, and, because they wanted to preserve the union with Britain, unionist by political disposition. Less than a hundred yards away were Catholics— Irish by nationality and, because they hoped to one day see Ireland united, nationalists by political disposition. The people who were zealous enough to consider using violence in pursuit of their goals were further distinguished as loyalists among the Protestants and republicans among the Catholics. Looking past the peace wall that cut across Madrid Street was like peering into some fantastic mirror where everyone looked about like you but they did everything just the opposite.

In the mornings I would buy my paper at the Family Tree newsagent run by David Clelland, a former loyalist paramilitary member who considered himself something of a renaissance man for selling the *Irish News*, a Belfast morning paper favored by Catholics. In the evenings, from my window, I would watch Protestant and Catholic children run rock-throwing sorties up and down the street. Police patrols would often screech past in their gray, three-ton armored vehicles, and in the summer months, Protestant marching bands pounded out a thunderous beat as they approached my street corner to be sure their neighbors over the wall could hear them.

There was a time when east Belfast was the industrial heart of the city. Around the turn of the century, most men from my neighborhood worked at the cigarette factory, the rope works, or the Belfast shipyard that were all nearby. An old man living at the end of my street had been a joiner in the construction of the *Titanic*. Years of industrial decline had already taken their toll before the Troubles came along and finished the neighborhood off. That was what I remembered of the area from my first visit, but by the time I returned, the peace process was driving unemployment to a record low and Belfast was one of the hottest property markets in the British Isles. Army foot patrols had ended, their roadblocks had been removed, and young professionals were snapping up houses and beautifying the neighborhood. The only persistent reminder of the area's turbulent history was the graffiti and murals that covered the walls.

I had not been living in the apartment for long when I started to notice a glass-roofed, double-decker bus passing my window on Thursday and Sunday afternoons around half past one. My desk was tucked into the front of the apartment, so I usually glimpsed the bus while musing on my computer. The top deck of it was about level with the second floor, so I often locked eyes with passengers as the bus slowly drifted past. I looked at them; they looked at me. They'd point; I'd wave; they'd gasp.

The first time I saw the bus, I thought it was lost. When it kept appearing, I wondered why a tour bus was cruising through one of Belfast's most notorious districts and whether my neighbors had noticed it too.

When I went for my Sunday paper one day, Dave Clelland explained, "Sure that's the Belfast bus tour. It goes past the murals here all the time."

It was true, and one day I boarded the bus to get a look at my neighborhood from the other side of the glass. I joined a disparate group of tourists who embarked with some trepidation as if they were going on a wild African safari. "It would be naïve of us to give a tour of Belfast without showing you some of its troubled history," our driver admitted as we passed Madrid Street. Necks craned and flashes popped as we slowed down for some of the scenes.

I was sitting next to an elderly couple from Scotland; they had just crossed over on a ferry that morning and were a bit self-conscious wondering what local people make of tourists roaming through their neighborhood. "Oh, they don't mind," I assured them. In fact, just being there, passing through a blighted area of Belfast like it was an exhibit to a past struggle, was probably the most poignant sign that the Troubles were over. I did not say that but only thought it, because I knew that it was not a unanimous sentiment. The peace process had brought a sudden change of fortune, but the people of Northern Ireland had known too much heartache and disappointment to greet it with unbridled enthusiasm. I heard a funny story that seemed to capture the mood:

Weeks before Northern Ireland went to the polls to ratify the Good Friday Agreement in a popular referendum, every household had received a copy of the exact text. In a move to win public approval, the cover featured the hopeful silhouette of a family gazing upon an ocean sunset. They were looking at the end of a violent era; when they turned around, they would be facing a new dawn. The trouble was, Northern Ireland does not have ocean sunsets. There is no west coast. When it was revealed that the picture was actually taken in South Africa, public cynicism grew. If the photo was a phony, what did that say for the agreement it endorsed?

"Sure, there'll never be peace in this wee country," seemed to be the typical Belfast taxi driver's refrain. "There's too much money in it," some would say, or "There's too much bitterness." The paramilitary groups had been observing a cease-fire for years, and the Good Friday Agreement charted the way ahead; but still, people were faintly optimistic at best, bitterly cynical at worst, and unanimously dissatisfied.

Some things have changed, a skeptic might grudgingly concede. But politicians still bicker; terror groups still exist; the province can still erupt in flashes of unrest. The people of Northern Ireland were so reluctant to admit that life was improving that one might think they preferred to despair than to hope. Despair at least repels disappointment.

But on the streets, long-unutterable questions were being asked. Long-postponed encounters were taking place. "Our John's sorry he killed your Seamus," were a Protestant mother's words of comfort to the Catholic widow left in the wake of her son's heinous murder.

Paramilitary cease-fires and political accords alone will not solve all of Northern Ireland's problems. An ethnic conflict that has slowly simmered for centuries and spent the past thirty years on full boil cannot end abruptly. It will take small acts of redemption and forgiveness over lots of time before long-held grievances are dislodged. In short, it will take reconciliation—a word that even the cynics allow—and that has only just begun.

Maze Prison

◻   ◻

t was a mild summer day when Anthony McIntyre and Steven Rogan bumped into each other outside the Linen Hall Library in the center of Belfast. Rogan was shopping; McIntyre was rushing to work. McIntyre saw Rogan first and ventured a smile of recognition. Rogan smiled back. The two men had not seen one another in about ten years; enough time had passed for them to share a friendly conversation and an ironic laugh at their chance meeting.

When the Troubles erupted in the early seventies, Northern Ireland authorities were short of prison space, so they threw barbed wire around the perimeter of Long Kesh, a 130-acre disused air force base ten miles from Belfast, and held inmates there. The tin huts that had once served as military barracks were recommissioned as prison cells. It was a stopgap measure that worked for a while until, after a few years, the prison population topped three thousand and the authorities reluctantly conceded that, yes, the Troubles would last for a while and they had better make the appropriate arrangements. Eight H-shaped cell blocks were constructed next to the existing huts at Long Kesh and the compound was christened the Maze prison—the most modern and secure prison in Europe.

In 1978, Anthony McIntyre, having gunned down a loyalist paramilitary leader outside a Belfast bar, was beginning a life sentence on one of the IRA wings of the H-blocks. He wore his own clothes, could associate with other prisoners, and did not have to work. Those were the allowances made for the prisoners classed as "special-category"—

jargon for men convicted for political violence. But then the prison authorities decreed that political violence was really only violence and the special category status was being eliminated in favor of a more conventional prison regime.

Anthony McIntyre and the rest of his comrades saw themselves as soldiers fighting a war; they would wear their bedsheets before they would wear a gray prison uniform. And it came to that. Each inmate took one of the three blankets he had been issued, folded it in half, and tied it around his waist like a kilt. If it was cold, he took another blanket, cut a hole in the middle, and wore it like a poncho. The prisoners refused to shave or wash. They did not slop out, but instead smeared their excreta on the walls. Officials hit back, putting prisoners under twenty-four-hour lockdown and taking their books and papers.

McIntyre and his fellow IRA inmates passed the time alone in their fetid cells by singing songs or shouting Irish language lessons down the prison corridors. A game of chess could be organized with a bit of margarine spread on the cell door and torn shreds of the Mass reading stuck to it as pieces. Little luxuries like the contraband parcels of tobacco that were furtively passed during prison visits were savored. But there was no overlooking the foul conditions, not when McIntyre had to sleep in his own filth with maggots crawling across the floor, or the stupefying boredom that was his life in an eight-by-ten-foot cell. It was a grueling, often humiliating existence, but McIntyre tried to keep his spirits up. The protest was a battle of wills, and any time that Anthony McIntyre felt himself overcome with rage or frustration he took all that emotion, his anger against the brutal prison authorities and every hated screw that paced the corridors outside his cell, and turned it into defiance. At night, McIntyre went to bed and dreamed of splashing in a swimming pool or reading a book.

Steven Rogan arrived at the prison the same year that Anthony McIntyre started his protest. The two men were the same age, twenty-one, but instead of a coarse blanket, Steven Rogan wore the sharp blue uniform of a prison officer. It was the money that drew him to the job; Rogan was earning more than twice as much as his friends, but it was exhausting, soul-destroying work. Nine-hour shifts were the norm, but everyone was expected to pull some overtime. It was not uncommon for guards to work thirteen days over two weeks. Rogan saw the prisoners' sallow faces, and he choked on the putrid odor from their cells. Even worse than that was the caustic smell of ammonia used to clean the wings, which could bring a man to his knees. Still, it was enlightening to see the consequence of the violence that was happening on the street. But for the grace of God, Steven Rogan would think, I am on this side of the door.

The officers were paid good money, but they earned it. The novelty of the job soon wore off for Steven Rogan and gave way to tedium at work and fear when he left. The IRA was targeting prison guards for assassination, officers like Agnes Wallace, who had just collected her pay when she was gunned down, and Pacelli Dillon, father of a blind and crippled five-year-old girl, who was shot dead outside his home. Many prison staff just could not cope with the anxiety; their families fell apart or they were ruined by drink. Twenty-nine prison officers were murdered during the Troubles and another fifty committed suicide.

The blanket protest eventually gave way to hunger strikes. When ten men starved themselves to death, prison officials relented and reinstated the privileges. It was around the time that the protests ended that Anthony McIntyre and Steven Rogan met. It might have been when Rogan delivered a meal to McIntyre's cell; maybe it was when Rogan escorted him to the chapel or a prison visit, but the two men started talking. They talked about prison food, the weather, sports—the mundane things at first. Then they shared a few laughs and started talking about prison life and the conflict, what one side was doing to the other outside the prison walls. When the men began to trust one another, they talked about their upbringing, their families, and their plans for the future.

Steven Rogan and Anthony McIntyre knew the rules of the game. McIntyre could not be seen fraternizing with the enemy, and Rogan did not want his bosses to think that he was going soft. But as their friendship grew over the next five years, the two men developed a respect for each other. That mutual respect made it even more awkward when they arrived on that plane of common ground where the only thing left to ask one another was, "So what are we doing here?"

Standing outside the library, the two men reminisced a bit about those days inside the prison and discussed where some of the other prisoners or guards were now. Steven Rogan was working in a youth detention center, but he had earned a degree in psychology and would soon be quitting to start a new career. Who knows? He may even emigrate to Canada. McIntyre had earned a degree too, a Ph.D. in political science. His girlfriend was pregnant and they were living together in west Belfast. It was nice to catch up, but really, both men were in a hurry and should get going. As the two parted, they promised to stay in touch, but they have not seen each other since.

Prisoners

☐   ☐

aturday, October 23, 1993, was an unusually clement day in Belfast. Droves of afternoon shoppers were coaxed out of their homes by the sunshine, and they flooded market areas like the Shankill Road—the city's main Protestant thoroughfare. There, mingled in the crowd and disguised as deliverymen, two young IRA activists went unnoticed as they approached Frizzell's fish shop. Sean Kelly stood guard outside while his accomplice, Thomas Begley, entered carrying a large parcel. Brushing past the customers, he made his way to the counter, set the package on a display refrigerator, turned around, and told the customers to evacuate. The shop was being bombed.

Situated directly above Frizzell's fish shop was an office used by the Ulster Freedom Fighters (UFF), one of Northern Ireland's loyalist paramilitary groups. The bomb was designed to go off during the UFF's weekly meeting and wipe out their leadership, but the IRA was really after Johnny "Mad Dog" Adair—the commander of the Shankill Road brigade of the UFF and the most feared loyalist killer in Northern Ireland.

It had often been said that the IRA maintained a tempo of violence in Northern Ireland that loyalists were never able to match. But Adair created his own momentum; he killed with aplomb and led some of the most audacious murder bids of the Troubles. Police estimate that seventy-two people were killed under Adair's command, a notoriety that he relished. In anonymous newspaper interviews, Adair would brag about his murder prowess and that he could kill at will. Most galling for the IRA, Adair was seemingly indestructible. His small house off the Shankill Road had been turned into a fortress with bulletproof windows, security cameras, a reinforced steel door, and steel shutters. At night, armed UFF members would patrol Adair's neighborhood.

Before that day's bombing there had already been four failed IRA assassination attempts against Adair in 1993. If this one was to be a success, Adair and his colleagues could have no advance warning of the attack. Yet the bombers needed a few minutes if they were to get themselves and civilians out of the shop. As planned, the operation left no margin for error. In fact, the entire plot was flawed.

The UFF meeting had adjourned earlier that morning; the office was empty. The bomb was fixed with a too-short fuse and detonated as soon as it was set down. The shop collapsed, killing Thomas Begley and nine innocent civilians.

In a statement issued hours after the bombing, the UFF swore that the Catholic community would "pay a heavy, heavy price for today's atrocity." Over the next week, innocent Catholics were targeted in a random shooting spree that ended on Halloween night when UFF gunmen raided the Rising Sun bar in the town of Greysteel, shouted "Trick or Treat," and opened fire, killing eight people. In all, twenty people were killed in the Shankill Road bombing and its aftermath. Blood bank reserves were so depleted that technicians had to work overtime to meet the demand.

Sean Kelly was in critical condition after the bombing, but he survived, was tried, and given nine life sentences. And while the IRA never killed Johnny Adair, the police eventually caught up with him. A year after the Shankill Road bombing, Adair was convicted of directing terrorism and given a lengthy prison sentence. If one thing brought comfort to the relatives of those killed by both men, it was the knowledge that they would be spending most of the rest of their lives behind bars. That seemed certain, ironically, until the peace process started.

After twenty-five years of grinding violence, after hundreds of martyrs had been killed, and after so much rhetoric about their righteous cause, republican and loyalist paramilitary groups saw that they would never be defeated, but neither could they win. It was hard to say whether political failure had been a consequence of political violence or whether the reverse was true, but if the conflict was ever going to end there would have to be compromise. That was a matter for the politicians, so the main paramilitary groups had each called a cease-fire by the fall of 1994, less than a year after the Shankill Road bombing, and let them get on with it.

Negotiations leading up to the Good Friday Agreement left paramilitary groups with the dilemma of ending the violence with honor. After all, one might ask, what had the past generation of killing been for if the conflict ended in a draw? That question has yet to find a satisfactory answer, and it must still keep some people from their sleep, but in the end paramilitary groups won one major concession from the Good Friday Agreement: amnesty. No matter what anyone else thought of men like Sean Kelly and Johnny Adair, they considered themselves to be soldiers and freedom fighters. If there was to be peace, they demanded a reprieve, and it was agreed that all political prisoners who backed the accord, regardless of their offenses, would be released from prison within approximately two years of the Good Friday Agreement being ratified.

The image of Northern Ireland's most hardened criminals being released onto the streets en masse caused some consternation among the public, but prisoner release was also an occasion to consider the consequences of the Troubles. What did it say about Northern Ireland society, for instance, that so many people had ended up in prison in the first place? Some people claimed that political prisoners were victims of the Troubles no less than anyone else; they had been brutalized by the conflict, and their paramilitary involvement was an understandable result. It was a hard person who made no allowance for a political prisoner's background when judging his or her later transgressions, but couldn't that argument be taken too far? After all, many people who had seen the worst of the Troubles rejected violence and became advocates for peace.

And it was innocent civilians, not the paramilitary groups or the security forces, that endured the most during the Troubles. Civilian homes were invaded, their cars were hijacked, their businesses were extorted, their families were threatened, and they suffered the most casualties. Paramilitary groups purported to be defending their communities, but those communities bore the greatest brunt of the violence. Civilians were simply used, shifted around like sandbags in a campaign that few supported.

In the end, most people saw prisoner release as a distasteful but necessary step in the peace process. If it meant there would be no more victims, it was worth it. That was an easy rationalization for someone who had not lost a loved one to violence. For the people who had known such a loss there was nothing, no future peace or prosperity that could account for that loved one who was gone. And that fact invited more awkward questions. If everyone was a victim, what was the life of Thomas Begley, an IRA bomber, measured against that of Leanne Murray, a thirteen-year-old casualty of the Shankill Road bombing? When it came to prisoners, what was the life of a man who had forsworn violence and repented for his actions compared to a man who would return to the streets and a life of crime and violence? It was a difficult reckoning and pointless in the end because the peace process removed those old scales of morality, guilt, and consequence. Everyone had to carry their own past and make sense of it any way that they could.

A few days before Christmas, 1998, Michelle Williamson walked over to the exit turnstile of the Maze prison and cuffed herself to its frame. Just beyond, behind concrete walls and observation towers, Northern Ireland's most infamous and brutal killers were being held. That day, 170 of them were to be given a ten-day holiday furlough. Officials said it would prepare inmates for the outside world—an important step on their way to permanent release. All Michelle Williamson knew was that her parents would never have another Christmas because they were dead. The bomb Sean Kelly planted in Frizzell's fish shop had killed them.

While he and other prisoners would be celebrating the New Year,

Michelle would mark another year of her imprisonment, another year without her parents and a year closer to Kelly's release. But before the prisoners could get home to their families or friends, each of them had to walk past Michelle Williamson.

She looked a bit haggard but determined, standing alone in a thin, fleece jacket. In her free hand, she was holding a letter for Sean Kelly. She came to deliver it personally, to tell Kelly face-to-face how he had ruined her life. Inside the letter was the pain and anger of the survivors of violence. It took her eight hours to write and even then, five years after the bombing, her feelings were as fresh and raw as the day her parents were killed. "I will never go away. I will always haunt you. I am never going to let you forget."

Clank. Clank. Clank. The prisoners made their way through the turnstile: Tarlac Connolly was convicted of murdering three police officers and a nun in a two-thousand-pound bomb explosion; Michael Duffy was serving time for his part in six murders; Ciarán Morrison was caught transporting two bombs to Belfast city airport; Thomas McWilliams murdered a Belfast shopkeeper while he served a twelve-year-old boy. As they streamed by, Michelle silently glared. None of them acknowledged her, but turned their faces away. After two hours, Michelle was told that Sean Kelly had been let out through another exit to avoid incident. "I can't believe he would not come through those gates to pass me," she said. "But I always knew he was a coward." Michelle gave prison officers the letter for Kelly; then she went home.

George and Gillian Williamson needed curtains. They had moved into a new house two days earlier and were beginning to decorate. Gillian was a keen seamstress and planned to sew them herself, so the couple drove into Belfast for the material. Their twenty-seven-year-old daughter Michelle stayed at home. She expected her parents back that afternoon.

She thought it was her parents at the door when the police officer arrived around three o'clock that afternoon in 1993. Michelle had been watching the news earlier, and she knew a massive IRA bomb had exploded on the Shankill

Road. Dozens of people were injured, the reporter said; many had been killed.
There had been no warning, no time to clear people away. Michelle could see
people sifting through the rubble where Frizzell's fish shop formerly stood.

Michelle watched the images with a pang of fear that her parents were in-
volved. They were likely to be shopping in that area. "Is this about my parents?"
she asked the officer. Yes. Her parents had been caught in the bombing. Michelle
went numb. Her parents had finished their shopping and were on their way home
when they must have decided to drop in for a piece of fish for that night's dinner.
When Michelle retrieved her parents' car, the curtain cloth was folded in the back.

I visited Michelle a few days after her prison protest. In her early
thirties, she was not living the life of a young woman. After her parents'
death, Michelle stayed on in the modest, attached house where she had
been raised. She shared it with her husband Russell, his eight-year-old
son Craig, and twelve cats. Michelle had one cat before the bombing;
Russell had one, too. The others have been acquired in the years since.
Sitting in her kitchen, Michelle gingerly stroked one of the passing ani-
mals. "They are better than people," Michelle said. "I find comfort in
them."

At home and away from the excitement of the protest, Michelle was
subdued. She had wanted to spark debate about prisoner release. That
at least was a success because the media took fresh interest. Prisoner release was already deeply unpopular. The issue had nearly defeated the
Good Friday Agreement when it went to a public referendum. Only the
much-publicized support among many victims of violence put minds at
ease. If they—the people who had been closest to the pain and trauma
of violence—could accept prisoner release, so should everybody else.
But Michelle proved that that was not a unanimous sentiment.

"It's easy to say forgive and forget, but it is my parents who were
killed," Michelle explained. "I could get on if they were killed in a car
crash, but they were physically murdered. They were not involved in
anything. They were not political. They were just killed for being in the
shop. Now the man who killed them is getting out. He killed nine inno-

cent people, he got nine life sentences, and he will be out in less than seven years. Where is the justice in that?"

Some people have put their lives back together after losing loved ones to violence, but others, like Michelle, have not. She is the first to admit it; she simply cannot cope. Since the bombing, Michelle's life has been crippled by bouts of depression and anxiety attacks. She took medical retirement shortly after the bombing and has not worked since. Russell, too, left his job to take care of Michelle full-time. Now her life is a succession of doctor's visits and psychiatric appointments. "I don't go out anymore in case something happens," she said. "I don't plan ahead."

But anger is blended with her fear. She applied for government compensation after her parents' death. It was denied, officials explained, because she was not dependent on their income and was not a witness to the bombing. "But I have not stopped fighting. I have been a thorn in the government's side," she said with self-assuredness. "I just read where thousands of pounds was spent on prisoner retraining and job placement schemes. Meanwhile, we are living on benefits. The prisoners have their politicians speaking for them, but who is speaking for the victims?

"That is why I always say that the peace process is a fraud," Michelle explained. "I don't think people understand what it is really about. It means that the killers are out and victims are forgotten. Once the prisoners are free, what is stopping them from starting to kill people again? No one asks that question."

Michelle laid a scrapbook out on the kitchen table and leafed through the pages as we spoke. It was a red leather album with clippings, church programs, and letters from the time of the bombing. The book is arranged chronologically. First are the newspaper headlines with accounts of the attack and politicians expressing their outrage. Days later, Michelle and her younger brother are pictured clutching each other at the funeral. One local paper ran Michelle's promise: "I will never forgive."

Then there are the condolence cards from the flower sprays: "In

Loving Memory," "With Deepest Sympathy," "All Our Love." Michelle said she had two more boxes of cards upstairs with other mementos like her mother's jewelry and her father's watch, its hands frozen by the bomb blast.

Michelle vowed that her prison protest was just the beginning. "It took all my courage to go and stand outside the prison, but I know it is not enough. Now I have started a petition to keep the prisoners in jail. I have hundreds of signatures already."

She took heart as other victims, silent for years, came out to support her campaign. There were many more like her who wanted the prisoners kept behind bars. But Michelle only had until July 28, 2000, Sean Kelly's release date, to do something. At that point he would either be free or jailed longer. Until then, she could not stop. But she wished it were over already. She could see how the campaign had distressed her, and she knew the obsession with Kelly had taken over her life. Michelle had a son to raise and a husband to love and did not want to dwell on her anger. But what if she stopped, before she had exhausted every possibility, made every phone call, written every letter?

"This is all part of me getting better," she said, smiling unconvincingly.

Every time she tried to close the door, there was something to bring it all back. Her parents had been standing at the shop counter; did Thomas Begley brush up against them as he walked past? Most of her energy came from those memories and a sense of guilt: Michelle never saw her mother's body before the burial; she owed her parents thirty pounds when they died.

Michelle wants peace, she explained defensively, but not if it is built on the memory of the dead. "I guess I just can't believe that you put two boxes into the ground and then it is all over."

When Gina Murray saw the news footage of Michelle chained to the Maze prison, she phoned her right away. "Why didn't you tell me you were going to do that?" she asked. "I would have been there to support you."

Michelle's determination sparked something in Gina Murray. For an instant, she thought she should join the campaign. On reflection, she realized it was hopeless. No matter how many times they demonstrated or how many letters were written, she knew there was no way to stop the prisoners being released. "We can fight it, but we won't win," Gina said. "We will lose. I know that."

Leanne Murray had just returned from a holiday in the United States when she went shopping that day with her mother and Paul, her mother's companion. They were joking about how much Leanne had grown up in her time away—only thirteen years old, Leanne was nearly her mother's height.

Crossing the Shankill Road, Leanne looked in Frizzell's fish shop. Paul liked willicks, small cocklelike snails, but he said the ones in the window were too small. Leanne said she would get some anyway. She went into the shop and turned to her mother through the glass. We'll be in the grocer's next door, *her mother gestured. As Gina and Paul entered Jackie Phillips and Sons fruit shop, the bomb went off.*

The police said some children had been brought to Dundonald Hospital and that Leanne was probably there. Gina Murray followed the police car, hoping she would find her daughter injured and frightened at worst, but alive and glad to see her mother. Gina wondered why they were taking such a circuitous route to the hospital as they followed the police towards Forster Green Mortuary. There was a mistake, Gina thought, Leanne could not be there. That is where they were taking the dead people.

Medics had found a little girl that could be Leanne, Gina was told. They wanted someone to identify the body, but Gina could not do it. Paul was too upset as well, so his brother went in. He came back and said that it was Leanne, but Gina thought it must be a mistake so she went in. She saw a little girl lying in a plastic bag, zipped up to her neck. Leanne had long dark hair. She wore it draping over her shoulders. She was very particular about her hair. The child in the bag had dark hair too, but it was all matted with dust, speckled stone, and brick. "That's not my Leanne!" Gina said. "Leanne would never let her hair get like that." But the girl had Leanne's Mickey Mouse watch and ring on her finger. "Leanne!" Gina said impatiently. "What have you done with your hair?" Gina

went to unzip the bag so she could take her daughter home. She would not allow
Leanne in a place like that, but the doctors pulled her away sobbing.

Gina explained her method of dealing with the loss. "I'm a good actress. I take my tablets, do what the psychiatrist tells me to do, and then put a smile on my face." But inside Gina is hurt and angry. "I have done well to get this far," she said with some satisfaction. "The only thing is that I drop back." Christmas is hard. Leanne's birthday and the anniversary of the bombing bring it all back again.

When Leanne was killed, Gina was already weighed down with grief. Months earlier, her estranged husband had died of a stroke. Years before that, an infant son was killed in a car accident. Gina's surviving son, Gary, was the only thing that kept her from slipping into complete despair. He needed her, so Gina pulled herself together as best she could.

Gina does not expect to get any better, but she may be able to stop getting worse. It really just involves one challenge: Stop thinking about the past. In that effort, she has good days and bad. The good days are when she looks after Gary's children and her mind is focused. When they leave, and she is alone, her mind wanders.

She remembers the day of the attack with vivid clarity. She can hear Leanne's last words and see her for the last time through the fish shop window. When the bomb went off, Gina and Paul ran out into the street filled with smoke and dust. "Where's Leanne?" they demanded of each other. People were wailing and crying out for help. The wounded were everywhere, but Gina remembers one man looking up at her with his face half blown off. "Help me," he pleaded. Gina stepped around him to look for her daughter, but now that face haunts her. She has gone over the photos and footage of the bomb. She has sifted through the rubble in her mind and tried to picture the man lying there in agony. Was that Sean Kelly?

She can see his bloodied face, and hear his voice, but she cannot tell if he was wearing the bomber's delivery uniform. Gina considered going to a hypnotist to draw the memory out. She thought of getting the police reports to see where Kelly lay. She just wants to know. If that was Sean Kelly, and if she had known, what she would have done to him, she said, "is not printable."

But when she thinks like that, Gina picks up a bit of coloring or cross-stitch. Her therapy class taught her that concentration trick—keep busy hands—but Gina gets upset when she thinks of what could happen when Kelly is released.

While Kelly was in prison, Gina at least had a sense of certainty: She would never have to see him or feel threatened. Now things are unpredictable. Belfast is not a large city; what if Gina passes him in the street or they share a bus? Michelle may know what she wants to say to Kelly, but Gina does not think she could ever face him. The thought nearly brought on another anxiety attack. Gina wanted some official reassurance that Kelly would not be allowed in Belfast, but all she received was impersonal letters from the government's Early Release Scheme: "prisoner Kelly requested parole," "prisoner Kelly has been granted temporary release," "prisoner Kelly will be freed July 28, 2000."

Gina Murray wanted Sean Kelly to remain in prison. It was not a matter of justice; justice would be for her daughter to come back. It was personal. She thought that Kelly should suffer as much as she did. She was not concerned about the politics of prisoner release. She had lost a daughter; there is no equivalent and nothing comparable to that. But she was powerless. Just like hundreds of other victims, she was grieving alone and forgotten.

A girl Leanne's age wrote a poem after watching the news of the Shankill Road bombing: "What are they fighting for; They themselves do not know; I just wish it would all go away; Can't we all just have one day of peace; where the bombs and killings would suddenly cease." Gina carries Leanne's wallet with her everywhere; inside she keeps things like that poem, photos, letters, and a lock of Leanne's hair. The ring Leanne wore is a charm on Gina's necklace.

Gina moved away from the Shankill Road area after Leanne died. She could not watch Leanne's friends grow up. Now living in Bangor, a town situated at the mouth of Belfast Lough, Gina showed me the last

Mother's Day card Leanne had given her. It was a piece of construction paper, hand decorated with "I Love You" written on the back. She treasures that card—Leanne's handwriting gives a trace of her presence.

As we spoke, I recognized a photo on the wall; I had come across it while sifting through archives of the local newspapers. Turning through the issues around the time of the bombing, I had wanted to crumple the pages and somehow stop what I knew was coming next. But there were the scenes and reports from the bombing. Days afterwards, the newspapers were covering the funerals. In one prominent shot, Gina's son Gary was comforting her. In her hand, she clutched a large color photo of Leanne that had been taken during her visit to America, when Leanne visited a petting zoo. She was kneeling on her haunches and smiling as she fed a fawn. Her long dark hair was draped over her shoulders. Gina held the photo at the funeral, and now it was hanging on her wall. Gina noticed me looking at the picture. "That is the way I like to think of her," she said.

Photos mark time, but time is frozen for Thomas Begley. All the photos that decorate his parents' living room were taken around Thomas's current age—his final age. He was only twenty-three when he died, as his thin face and wispy mustache show. In one photo Thomas, dressed in a black coat, is staring blankly towards the camera. In another, he is leaning indifferently towards the lens. The Carrick Hill marching band gave the family an inscribed mirror with one such image. Another photo is set into a hand-wrought wooden Celtic cross— Sean Kelly made that in prison. Thomas does not look like a killer, just a distant and forlorn young man.

Billy Begley was a contract laborer. Work was never regular, but he took it when offered. Sometimes he worked at several different construction sites in a week. Other times he would be at one site for a few months. In October 1993, he was working on Belfast's cross-harbor bridge, a four-lane bypass that would ease traffic across the city's Lagan River.

Billy regularly worked the Saturday shift, and since his wife, Sadie, took Saturday to do her shopping, the couple would routinely meet in town for an afternoon drink. When they got to their usual pub, the place was abuzz with news of a bombing. A waitress told the Begleys what she knew: that the IRA had bombed the UFF headquarters along the Shankill Road. Billy was surprised at the boldness of the attack, but with the recent string of Catholic murders, something like this should have been expected. The Irish News, *Belfast's main Catholic daily paper, called the loyalist attacks a "campaign of genocide against the Catholic community." Just a few weeks earlier, Billy and his son Thomas had been watching the news reports of another Catholic being gunned down. Billy had turned to Thomas and wondered, "What is the IRA doing about all those killings?"*

"Those are just sectarian attacks," Thomas had answered. "The IRA won't stoop to that level."

Around ten o'clock on the night of the bombing, Billy and Sadie Begley took a taxi home and found the security forces going through their house. Billy sent his wife to the neighbor's, walked across the front garden, and pushed his way past the soldiers standing outside the front door. Inside, six police officers had Billy escort them through each room: searching drawers, going through papers, examining anything that could be lifted. One police officer found a letter of placement for Thomas to begin training as a mechanic that Monday. "That should keep him out of trouble," the officer said.

Billy's oldest son John had been planning to go to the disco that night and was having a drink when the police arrived. It was up to him to explain what had happened. "I have something to tell you," he said, pulling his father aside, "Thomas was caught up in that bomb today."

When the local priest arrived, all three men went to the morgue, but there was not enough body to make identification.

When the army searched the house, they found a picture of Thomas Begley, age twelve. The cherubic face was leaked to the *Belfast Telegraph*, where it was augmented and run on the front page. That sort of sensationalism went on for days. By the time of his funeral, Thomas Begley's name was infamous. Anyone who heard it drew to mind each horrible detail of the bombing. The reporters called him evil, but his family knew that was not true. It was easy for others to moralize because they did not know Thomas. He was not their brother or son. Just as the family was growing accustomed to distorted news stories, the press moved on. Thomas Begley had blended into the background with the other thousands of people killed in the Troubles.

Because Thomas Begley was killed in the Shankill Road bombing, the story of his life is left slightly ajar. His family agreed to speak with me, if reluctantly, because their ordeal is largely over. The attention of the bombing has shifted; they are no longer living in its shadow. For Sean Kelly, surviving the attack means living with it. Due largely to Michelle Williamson's campaign, he was still in the media's glare. Kelly steadfastly shunned publicity, and his mother even moved from their old neighborhood. But Begley and Kelly were friends and comrades. A view into one man's life offers insight into the other's. Were it not for the chance events of the day, their fates might have been reversed.

Sadie Begley remembers her son as a quiet lad. The biggest racket he ever caused came from his stereo. He would sit in his room for hours playing records contentedly while the music poured through the house. A painfully quiet woman, she keeps most of her memories of Thomas in a private place where strangers are not welcome. Asked a direct question about her son, she demurred to her husband, who answered politely though warily. Billy Begley was more forthcoming than his wife, though he was careful to preserve his son's memory.

Thomas Begley's parents, like other people who knew him, describe him in few words but none harsh. He was reserved, distant, even a bit melancholic, but also polite, courteous, and kind. He was not an outstanding athlete and did not have an outgoing personality, but neither was he mischievous or defiant. He was distinguished by his utter anonymity. Most of his thoughts were kept to himself.

Thomas was not a very good student, but he did have an inquisitive mind. He dropped out of school when he could and signed on to one of the innumerable governmental vocational schemes that gave young people the skills they would need for jobs that did not exist. Belfast was economically moribund, and Catholic Belfast was grimmer still. There was no expectation of finding work and no shame in taking government benefits. Thomas always took an interest in cars and occasionally helped a mechanic friend with repairs. If there had been work going as a mechanic, he would have taken it, but instead he helped his dad on building sites.

Thomas Begley and Sean Kelly grew up a few doors down from each other. They were best friends through school and shared some of the same indifferences. They were not preoccupied with football or chasing girls. They were disinclined to drinking and were not crazy about the discos. But they both marched in the Carrick Hill Martyr's Flute Band, a Republican pipe and drum brigade.

Thomas played instruments but usually carried the band's colors. They would strike it up for civil rights demonstrations, political and cultural events. In photos, Thomas looks quite comfortable at the head of the procession, leading the march in his green-and-white uniform with the Irish flag held rigidly at the fore. He played with the band for six years and led the first march to Belfast City Hall in 1992. Playing in the band might have offered both Begley and Kelly their first contact with the IRA, but living in the Ardoyne neighborhood of north Belfast meant never escaping the IRA's influence.

North Belfast is a motley patchwork of Catholic and Protestant neighborhoods hemmed together along chaotic seams of roads and row houses. There are dozens of interfaces between the two communities, and so it has always been a perilous place to live. Over a third of the deaths during the Troubles occurred in a one-square-mile area of north and west Belfast, and Ardoyne is situated right between the two. Walking just one block in the wrong direction could mean trespassing on enemy turf.

Sadie Begley spent her childhood in Ardoyne. When she and Billy were married, they raised their own family in the same house. As the Troubles erupted in the late sixties and early seventies, Ardoyne felt like it was under siege. For years, it was heavily patrolled by the security forces and came under sustained attacks by loyalist paramilitaries.

Ardoyne does not inspire great ambitions. Surrounded by Protestant neighborhoods, the small Catholic community is isolated and exposed. Billy Begley guesses that one out of five young men in the area would have been involved in the IRA, and Thomas, he admits, certainly had republican sympathies. It was the British soldiers that drove them to it more than anything, Billy said. Just walking down the street, young men were randomly stopped and harassed by the troops. Mistreatment from the soldiers, combined with the fear of random attacks from Protestant paramilitaries, hardened their attitudes and strengthened their solidarity. The IRA took advantage of those feelings and offered a way for angry young men to vent their frustration and hit back.

Billy and Sadie Begley grieve differently from Michelle Williamson or Gina Murray. Living in Ardoyne, they have always been a family of survivors. The entire community is smudged with the fingerprints of the Troubles; their family has just been sullied worse than others have. Thomas's death, though tragic, is easier to comprehend because he knew what he was doing. He was a young man who had certain beliefs that led him to take certain action. Getting involved with the IRA would be risky, Thomas Begley knew, and he made the decision on his own terms. His parents can understand that. Though the bombing went tragically wrong, their son was doing something he felt was right. In a sense, he walked out of his life rather than having it taken away.

The *Republican News* is the IRA's voice. In Catholic ghettos, the weekly propaganda sheet is sold door-to-door, and everyone buys a copy. Before the cease-fires, columns like "War News" featured a roundup of recent IRA skirmishes with the security forces and photos of armed IRA men on patrol. The IRA still uses the paper for its public pronouncements, and in those pages, the mood of the movement can be found.

After Thomas Begley's death, the *Republican News* eulogized him. An IRA statement revealed that Begley had joined the organization nine months prior to the bombing. He was praised as an eager and dedicated volunteer who "was quick to comprehend the methods and techniques used by his comrades" and who had shown great promise in many prior operations against the security forces.

As an IRA volunteer, Thomas Begley had two loyalties. He was a member of the republican movement and a member of the Begley family. The Begleys lost a son and brother; the republican movement lost a soldier. The two sides are often only joined in death.

Being killed on active service is the greatest martyrdom an IRA volunteer can receive. The funeral procession is a major event. An honor guard watches over the memorial service, and republican dignitaries join as pallbearers—if the family allows it.

Thomas Begley's parents were torn. The son who planted the Shankill Road bomb had been a stranger to them. Yet his IRA involvement was a big part of his life. To ignore that would be to dishonor part of his memory. While most people in Ardoyne would join the family to commiserate over a lost son, others would be there to honor an IRA volunteer.

In the end, Thomas's brother John convinced his parents to allow a republican funeral: It was what Thomas would have wanted. An Irish flag was draped over the coffin with a beret and black gloves folded on top. All the shops on the Falls Road were closed as thousands of mourners marched to the cemetery. Gerry Adams, president of Sinn Fein, shouldered the coffin for one stretch of the procession.

Billy Begley does not know what to make of his son's death, but he does not think it had to happen like it did. He can understand that the IRA wanted to kill Johnny Adair for preying on innocent Catholics. It made sense according to the rules of the game, but the rules were about to change. When Thomas Begley planted the bomb, the IRA had already started secret peace talks. A cease-fire was only ten months away. There would be no more risky IRA bombings after the Shankill Road attack, and Thomas Begley will probably remain the last IRA volunteer to be killed on active service. I asked Billy if he thought his son had been used. That is an opinion he would rather keep to himself, he said.

I first encountered Johnny Adair a week before Christmas, 1999. He had been released from the Maze prison recently after serving less than five years of a twelve-year sentence for directing terrorism. "He is trying to reassert himself along the Shankill Road by assuming his old role in the UFF and getting involved in the drug trade," a senior police officer briefed me. "There is no overstating his influence on a small number of volunteers. If he were sitting in his office and told his henchmen to kill someone while he watched, they would do it. He is a cult figure with disciples. Really, it was only a matter of time before he got involved in drugs. There was no way that he was going to let people make money in his neighborhood without getting in on the action."

It was frustrating for the police to see Johnny Adair back on the streets since it had taken one of their most complicated operations to get him convicted in the first place. The police had known for years that Adair was the leader of the Shankill Road UFF. They knew it, but they could not prove it because Adair was always one step removed from the killings. When police tried to prosecute Adair, they were only armed with suspicion, hearsay, and uncorroborated evidence. Meanwhile, innocent Catholics were being routinely gunned down, so the police were prepared to take some unorthodox steps to catch him.

Adair's chief failing was his irrepressible boastfulness. Under interrogation, Adair was silent; on the street, he was mouthy. Adair routinely bragged to police—sometimes cryptically, sometimes explicitly—that he commanded the province's most fearsome terror unit. Through months of undercover surveillance, police recorded casual conversations with Adair describing past murders, tactics, and possible targets. As a sting operation, the police plan worked perfectly; Adair was convicted largely on the basis of his own words.

I arranged a meeting with Adair through John White. Convicted of the frenzied stabbing murder of Irish senator Paddy Wilson and his female companion in 1972, White was a late convert to the peace process and a leading figure in the Ulster Democratic Party—a nascent political group with close ties to the UFF.

White was initially reluctant to arrange an interview—the press had pursued some unflattering stories about Adair since his release. Some reports had begun to link Adair and White to the local drug trade. Others claimed Adair was organizing a new dissident loyalist group. "Why cooperate with the press when they're coming out with these stories?" was White's thinking. But eventually, and quite suddenly, a meeting was arranged.

It was in the early afternoon—a few hours after an unexpected and abrupt phone conversation with John White—that White, Johnny Adair, and I met at the Loyalist Prisoners' Aid Centre on Belfast's Shankill Road. Immediately, I knew that it was an inopportune time for a candid interview. Standing around the room was an assortment of Adair's most surly comrades, joking and chiding one another. It was like a high school locker room with everyone strutting and posturing for me, the outsider.

I was surprised to find Adair was still so indiscreet. As I—a journalist with a patent interest in the shadier parts of Adair's life—sat five feet away, he chatted openly with fellow loyalists about some recent stories in a local newspaper.

A week earlier, Adair had received an award from the LVF (Loyalist Volunteer Force)—a grisly, breakaway paramilitary group—for his past service to the loyalist cause. He had been proud to receive the award, he said, but the papers had exaggerated the story. Adair wanted to speak openly to the press and refute all the rumors, but he was reluctant, he said, because "the taigs [a derisive term for Catholics] around here know my family and they might have a go at them."

"All right, let's get started," Adair said impatiently, sweeping his hand towards a desk and chair in the back of the office. I sat down while Adair hovered over me restlessly. Through several questions, Adair gave curt, glib replies, and then flashed his comrades a smug look of satisfaction. Often he laughed out loud—a riotous, self-satisfied laugh. The whole situation seemed to tickle him a bit. He was impressed that his renown had drawn the interest of an American journalist.

Heavily built, bald headed, and with a gold hoop in each ear, Adair was almost a caricature of a typical loyalist thug. A thick gold chain with a weightlifter pendant hung around his neck. A large sweatshirt fit snugly around his broad frame; he did not deny rumors of taking steroids.

"The stories going around are just ridiculous," he said.

Adair sighed at charges of drug involvement. "It just sickens me. Of all the lies that have been told about me—that hurts the most. After what our organization did over the years against drugs"—referring to UFF punishment attacks that left dozens of people maimed—"for those people in the media to say that about me, it's just rubbish."

For a moment, Adair sounded genuinely aggrieved. Then he shifted to the allegations that he was organizing another terror squad. He became giddy thinking about his notoriety. "Catholics are scared of me. Mothers tell their children, 'You better get to bed or Johnny Adair is going to get you.' They look at me as the bogeyman," Adair said, through a fit of laughter.

I gave a confused look and recoiled a bit. "I'm laughing because it's funny that they see me that way," he said defensively. "That is not the way I am."

We chatted openly, but I could barely hold Adair's attention. When he could not play to the crowd in the room, he gave short, staccato answers. "I am leaving for the Maze prison in a couple of minutes," Adair abruptly announced, signaling the end of the interview.

I capitulated. "All right. I just wanted to talk to you about the Shankill Road bombing. I understand that you were the intended target of that attack. What do you remember about that day? I understand you were not even at the site at the time."

"No, I was not there at the time. I was visiting the prison; I heard about it later on the news," Adair answered blankly. "I was devastated that so many people had been killed. I was devastated that they had destroyed the office. I came down here afterwards, and the street had been destroyed."

"And you were the target, weren't you?" I ventured. "You were the one they were after?"

"The IRA said they were after the UFF leadership," Adair answered evasively. "But no one was in the office at the time."

"Well, I spoke to the Begley family," I said, watching for a reaction in Adair's face. "And they said their son and Sean Kelly were after the men—you specifically—who had been killing so many Catholics in the previous few months."

"You spoke to the Begleys?" Adair asked, his eyes widening a bit. "What did they say?"

"Just that," I answered plainly, trying to remain impassive. "That Begley and Kelly were after the people who had been killing Catholics in the area."

Adair's interest was piqued; his mind seemed to whir to life. "Who else have you spoken to in Ardoyne?" he asked, now with a mild tone of interrogation.

He was fishing for a name. I knew whom he was thinking of and I paused, and then uttered "Eddie Copeland" as casually as I could.

"You spoke to Copeland?" Adair asked with measured interest. "What did he say?"

I had not planned on mentioning Copeland's name, but now it was out and there was no backtracking. I told Adair a bit about my conversations with Eddie Copeland, a republican of notorious and unsavory renown, and recounted some of the highlights of their feud.

They lived just a few blocks apart in north Belfast, and the area had been the scene of their turf battle. Adair targeted Catholics in Ardoyne just to send Copeland a message. There were reports that Copeland had masterminded the Shankill Road bombing to kill Adair. Back and forth, the two played their bloody game of cat and mouse. Now both men are still alive, but I wondered how many innocent people had been killed in the crossfire of their vendetta.

I gave an account, in some detail, about an encounter Adair and Copeland had had in town several years earlier. I described how, afterwards, UFF gunmen had attacked the home of Copeland's sister. Adair smiled with implicit acknowledgment and then asked in disbelief, "He told you about that?"

Roused out of his stupor, Adair suddenly became animated. "See that?" he asked, lifting his shirt to expose a twelve-inch surgical scar stretching down his midriff. "See that?" he asked again, turning around to show me where a bullet had entered his back. "And that?" This time he pointed to the scar where another bullet had ricocheted off his skull. "Eddie Copeland done those to me."

The rest of the room had become transfixed by our conversation. Adair gave me a curious, penetrating stare. I could feel him trying to unravel what, if anything, I knew. He was puzzled and suspicious. Being an American—a stranger—to Northern Ireland had been an asset in the past. Many people opened up that little bit more, reassured that I would not make the crucial links in their comments that a local journalist could make. I played to that impression and gave Adair a blank, guileless look.

Adair suddenly relaxed, turned to the others, and chuckled. "I can't believe this. It's amazing. I'm sitting here where he was sitting with Copeland."

Adair then took an unexpected interest in me and began asking more questions—what was Copeland like, was he intelligent, did he seem psychotic? Adair wanted to know what Copeland had said—specifically, what Copeland had said about him. He wanted to know what Copeland's scars looked like—because Adair had inflicted them.

I tried to stay calm and described some of my impressions of Copeland without giving away too many details. "You know he was the one behind the Shankill bomb?" Adair asked.

"I heard something like that," I said with diffidence. "But he denies it. Do you think that he was involved?"

"I don't think," Adair answered with conviction. "I know he was. He was responsible for the Shankill bomb. He masterminded it. He does not seem like an evil person, but he is an evil bastard. He did the Shankill bomb and plenty more as well."

How Adair could, without irony, criticize Copeland when he himself had committed some of the most brutal murders of the era was beyond me. Still, I felt Adair was beginning to open up and, not wanting to lose him, suggested we continue the conversation the following day. Adair agreed. "Aye," he said, "we will have a good yarn tomorrow."

Johnny Adair swung through the door with his right arm extended and his left hand bracing his forearm. He stepped forward, cocked his head, and pointed an imaginary gun at me. "Bang, bang, bang," he said, pulling the trigger. Then he laughed.

It was the next day and I was sitting across the room of the Prisoners' Aid Centre. Not knowing how to take Adair's pantomime, I smiled nervously. It might have been a joke, but his movements were too deliberate and menacing. It seemed he was intentionally mimicking his technique. I was intimidated, which surely pleased him. Other than Adair's bodyguard and a receptionist, we were the only two people in the room. Thankfully, Adair himself seemed to be more settled, lucid and alert.

We spoke about his growing up in the Shankill area. Unlike many paramilitary figures, Adair did not describe any deeply personal experiences that drove him to violence. He had been a street punk and petty thief before getting involved with the UFF, where he quickly rose to the top.

Never having great career ambitions or even steady employment, Adair's role as a paramilitary leader was the essence of his life. Once involved, Adair knew there was no retirement. He looked forward to either being killed or spending his life in prison. The peace process turned Adair's world on its head. It came as a shock, maybe even a disappointment that his life was no longer so fated. Earlier rumors claimed that Adair opposed the cease-fires and wanted a return to violence. "Shove your dove," he reportedly told police when the loyalists called their cease-fire. Were those his words?, I asked.

"Over the years there was a long discussion about the cease-fire and about whether we would go ahead. I went into the discussions about a cease-fire with an open mind. We had to work out a lot of nuts and bolts. I asked some questions and wanted to know if the Provos [IRA] were going to stop. Once we decided to go ahead with it, I was completely behind it. They know where I stand, the government. They know there have been some tough times and there would not have been a cease-fire if it were not for this person right here. It nearly would have collapsed. There were times when we had questions, but I always supported the cease-fire."

Adair sounded convincing. Once in prison, Adair probably did support the peace process—after all, it was the only thing that could get him out. But Adair insisted he had not been bought off by early release. Yes, prison had been difficult and getting out was a bonus. "But I was willing," he said, "and we were all willing, to be arrested or killed, so that was not a problem."

And paramilitary prisoners were political prisoners, Adair insisted. He was part of a group of men who were willing to die for their country, to die defending their country. "There is a difference between criminals and soldiers. We were an army. We were soldiers," Adair said. "We had to get out of prison because we were a part of this conflict."

The people loyalists killed, even the innocent Catholics, were part of the conspiracy to destroy Northern Ireland, according to Adair. Now, those people were victims of the conflict, he conceded, but so were the loyalists themselves. Some people have called Adair crazy. He knew that but said, "that if it is crazy to defend your community, there are a lot of crazy people in my community. If it were not for the loyalists, there would have been more killings."

Through most of our conversation, Adair sat impassively. He stared at me coolly as he spoke, or gave me an incredulous smirk when I asked some detail about his past paramilitary involvement. Occasionally, my probing would prompt Adair to ask a question—what, exactly, were some of the stories I had heard about him, and did I believe them? He was not trying to elicit information, I realized, but to unnerve me. He also wanted his ego fed with more incredible tales about his murdering adeptness.

Adair's composure rarely shifted, but just before I left, there was a change when I pushed him on a definition of the "victims" of the Troubles. Surely, there was a difference between the soldiers, as he called them, and the innocent people caught in the middle. What would he say to those people, the relatives of the innocent people he had allegedly killed?

Briefly, Adair broke his stare. He looked towards the wall over my shoulder, not in shame or embarrassment, I suspected, but out of boredom.

"Well, it is sad," Adair said, mustering some sentimentality. "I know it is sad for the people who have lost their loved ones. There have been a lot of people killed. There have been a lot of people who have been killed on all sides, and it is wrong. It is so sad, what happened."

He droned on like that for a minute or two, virtually emotionless. This was the new message Johnny Adair was giving the public, and it was plainly insincere. I imagined, as he spoke, that he had stolen someone else's script. Other former paramilitary activists I spoke to did seem to be truly remorseful. They were remade men who realized that the decades of violence had been pointless and they were now wrestling with the consequences. They spoke with an unmistakable intensity. Johnny Adair was reading those lines, but he was not one of those men.

And yet he used terms like *war* and *soldiers*. To him, there was a rough moral equivalent among loyalists, the IRA, and security forces. But paramilitaries were not involved in a war of convention. It was a siege. It was a backlash. Reason or politics did not guide Johnny Adair and his associates. It was hatred, undiluted and unalloyed, that fueled their murder campaign. His violence was opportunistic. If the Troubles had not been going on, I was sure that he would have found another outlet for violence.

Speaking to friends about Johnny Adair after we met, there was one thing that constantly frustrated me. "It must be a terrible burden for him to live with what he has done," one said. "Everything that he has done will surely come back and haunt him someday," predicted another. But that was nonsense, the kind of comforting thought that allows decent people to sleep at night. It was not true. Johnny Adair has no regrets; he is not sorry. He is not sorry because he does not think that he did anything wrong. More than that, he would do it all over again without hesitation. I just hoped that he would never get the chance.

Clank. Clank. Clank. A metal echo filled the air as, one by one, forty-six IRA prisoners made their way through the turnstile. The Maze prison parking lot, a slab of broken asphalt bordered in corrugated steel panels, was alive with celebrations. Children leapt into their fathers' arms. Lovers embraced. Champagne corks popped. Irish flags waved. Confetti was thrown. It was July 28, 2000, and the final inmates who qualified for early release were going home. Wardens watched the commotion and laughed incredulously. In a few minutes, there would be no one left to guard.

Old IRA veterans, men who had spent most of their lives behind those prison walls, had come back for that day. Many posed for photos, joked and reminisced together. Others stood in silence as a gentle drizzle fell. "This place has been part of people's lives for almost thirty years," Martin Meehan, a venerable IRA activist from Ardoyne, mused. "I can't help but think that most of those lives were ruined."

Loyalist prisoners had been released earlier that morning, part of the careful choreography to avoid confrontation. Johnny Adair, tanned from a recent holiday to Jamaica, was there. He smiled smugly and clapped his former comrades on the back as they walked through the gate. Most of them were looking forward to a quiet, normal life, but Adair was still courting controversy. Not long after he returned to the old neighborhood, fresh UFF graffiti, murals, and other territorial markings had gone up along the Shankill Road—one wall painting featured a skeleton standing over gravestones marked Eddie Copeland and Sean Kelly. For the first time in years, UFF gunmen were seen patrolling the streets around the Shankill Road. Ostensibly, this was part of the UFF campaign to protect the community, but the police knew Johnny Adair was consolidating his drugs empire.

In a sense, things had returned to normal for Adair, but the times had changed. His customary flamboyance was no longer welcome, and a feud broke out between the UFF and other loyalist factions along the Shankill Road, resulting in several murders. Four months after Johnny Adair was congratulating prisoners on their release, he was back behind bars. Under the terms of the Good Friday Agreement, a prisoner's early release can be rescinded, and Adair was rearrested to serve the rest of his original sentence.

Michelle Williamson was not at the prison that day; in fact, she had dropped completely out of sight. Her campaign continued until a few weeks before the prisoners were released. Reality must have then finally pierced her bubble of optimism because, I was told, she left her old house and moved to the country with her family. Michelle always vowed that if her campaign failed she would move so far away that she could never see Sean Kelly.

Gina Murray took measured interest in the prison release. "It has me a bit edgy and short tempered," she explained. But she was not in the best condition anyway, having suffered another breakdown a few months earlier. Feeling stronger, she had stopped taking her medication, but then she slipped back into depression. "It just got the better of me," Gina said, with a forced smile. She had tried to kill herself; took an overdose of her medication. But her partner, Paul, found her lying in the bedroom and revived her. The next time Gina tried that, Paul reproached her, he would send her son Gary in to find her lying there. That scared Gina enough to keep her living.

Gary was there the day I visited, sitting next to his mother, stroking her hand. He did not like to hear her talk about suicide. "You'll not try that again, will you Mum?"

Gina continued. "I don't want Kelly out, but I guess that I just have to put up with it. Maybe this will bring peace. I just don't know." When Gary suddenly got up, clumsily knocked over a teacup that was sitting on the floor, and starting swearing, I remembered how Gina had said that he needed her. "Gary." She sighed.

Clank. Clank. Clank. There were just a few more prisoners to go, and the scrum of camera crews and photographers were jostling for a better view. Padraic Wilson, a former IRA commander in the Maze, leaned against a fence partition and stared down the portal to see who was coming next. "Kells!" Wilson shouted. Sean Kelly, wearing a white T-shirt and with a gold crucifix hanging from his neck, emerged carrying a single bag of belongings. Wilson gestured towards the far end of the parking lot; Kelly nodded acknowledgment.

Sean Kelly would never lead a normal life. He lost his left eye and the use of his left arm in the bombing. There would always be loyalists looking for revenge and, as he told a local republican newspaper shortly after his release, "I know that there are those people who will say that I have no right to talk about victims, but everyone has suffered, including those of us who have been to jail. I lost my close friend Thomas Begley that day; like the other people who died in the bomb he was some mother's son too. We are all victims, we have all suffered, but I just hope and pray that it is all at an end."

Eddie Copeland bustled Kelly through the crowd and across the parking lot to a waiting car. They sped off without a word, heading for Ardoyne, where Thomas Begley's family and the rest of the neighborhood were waiting to welcome Sean Kelly home.

Punishment

◘   ◘

ard drizzle was falling as I stood outside the Royal Victoria Hospital along Belfast's Falls Road. Seeking shelter under the nearby canopy would have given me an obstructed view of the sidewalk, so instead I pulled my coat up around my ears and waited in the rain. Angela and George Cairns were late, and I began to fear that they had reconsidered their offer to let me see their son, Liam. As I scanned around, I recognized Angela Cairns approaching. I had seen her face days earlier in a local newspaper story; she had been holding the blood-soaked pair of jeans Liam was wearing at the time he was nearly beaten to death. Her husband George shook my hand and apologized for being late.

The Royal Victoria Hospital was built in the late nineteenth century, and the original red brick façade disguised the labyrinth of wards within. Several modern additions had been tacked on over the years, and as we wander through the branching corridors, a change in floor tile or paneling marked the joint between an old and new wing. If the family was not there to guide me, I doubted if I could have found my way. "Have you spoken to the hospital administrators about seeing Liam?" George Cairns asked as we walked along. In these circumstances, I explained, it might be better not to ask. "Aye," he agreed. "We'll just say you are a friend of the family if anyone wants to know."

I had heard details about the attack on May 7, 2000, that put Liam Cairns in the hospital, how he had been abducted from his sister's house in Ardoyne by a punishment gang, hooded, strung through a steel fence, and beaten with hammers, nail-studded bats, and a pickax. I had heard the details, but the meeting had been arranged so hastily, I had not bothered to consider what a body that had sustained such a violent attack could look like. But really, nothing could have prepared me for seeing the broken form I found in the intensive care ward.

He was thin and shirtless, so most of the wounds on Liam's battered body were exposed for me to see. Running up and down the length of his arms and legs were the pink scars where surgeons had screwed his fractured limbs together. On the sides of his chest, his forearms, and his legs were deep puncture wounds. His head was braced with steel rods to keep him from moving his neck. His ankles and wrists were wrapped in plaster. I was aghast and looked away rather than betray my shock.

This was three weeks after the attack, and only recently had Liam Cairns been taken off a morphine drip. I wondered for a minute what he must have looked like on the morning he was first admitted to the hospital, when it took seventeen pints of blood and over four hours of emergency surgery to stabilize him. Sitting upright in a chair next to his bed, Liam said the pain was endurable now, as long as he did not move.

The brutality of the attack was revolting, but the inhuman zeal with which it was carried out was almost incomprehensible. I sat on Liam's hospital bed and leaned in to hear him speak, though he did not have much to say. When I asked what had happened, he said simply, "I got beat up." He was still in shock and fearful. I could understand why he did not want to talk to a journalist—telling his story would not ease his pain, and it might just earn another visit from his attackers. Liam's parents were more responsive; they knew that going public with their story was dangerous, but they felt somebody had to speak out.

"They beat him with anything they could get their hands on," George Cairns told me, his son sitting by silently with a distant look on his face. "The doctor thought that he was shot. When they looked at all his wounds, they said it would have been better if he was."

Although he was hooded, Liam guessed that there were fourteen people involved in his abduction and attack. He was passing in and out of consciousness during most of the ordeal, but when the beating stopped and his attackers left him in a vacant lot, Liam was able to free his broken legs from where they had been jammed in the fence. Liam tried to crawl away, but he only got a short distance when he heard laughter and thought he had been found; but in fact, his attackers had returned to beat him once again. Before they finally left, the gang threw garbage cans over Liam's head. A neighbor who had stepped outside for a cigarette found him and phoned an ambulance.

Beating Liam Cairns to within an inch of his life was justice, his attackers probably would have said. The gangs that carried out such beatings were self-styled vigilante enforcers, punishing the criminals and antisocial elements in the community. But the gangs themselves served as judge and jury. The punishments were not dispassionate; they were personal. Liam did not know why he had been singled out. "They said I had burned out a car in the neighborhood, but I had no part in anything like that."

Later, away from their son's side, I spoke with Angela and George about what could have been behind the attack. There was no doubt in their minds as to who was responsible. "Sure, even the dogs in the street know who did this," Angela told me flatly. I was still confused, so George explained.

"A couple days after this happened to Liam, some republicans came around to the house to say that the IRA was not behind this. They said they did not know who was responsible, but that is an insult to my intelligence. Of course it was the IRA. This is what they call community policing. The people who did this live in our area; they know our family. The IRA's military campaign is over, so now they have turned on their own community. They have been fighting a visible enemy for so long, they just have to get their violence out some other way so they beat up on their own people."

Liam Cairns was beaten just hours after the IRA appeared to break a deadlock in the peace process with a plan to dispose of their arsenal of weapons. The plan allowed Northern Ireland's Protestant and Catholic politicians to reconvene their power-sharing Assembly after it had been briefly suspended. From there, local people would chart the future of the province. But while politicians were back in control of the government for a time, paramilitary groups were still masters of the streets.

Through Northern Ireland's Troubles, thousands of people were driven from their homes, beaten, shot, maimed, or killed in paramilitary punishments. Rather than go to the police, communities were encouraged to contact paramilitary leaders about robberies, vandalism, drug dealing, joyriding—anything broadly defined as antisocial behavior. According to paramilitary thinking, vigilante justice was a useful way to tighten their extortionate grip and keep the police out of their areas.

Punishments were always capricious—intimidation, exile, beatings, or "kneecapping" (in the mildest cases, a bullet through the calf; in the most severe, the entire knee is blown away)—but were justified according to paramilitary reasoning. They were brutal but often effective in keeping a lid on petty crime and vandalism. Some communities welcomed the results even if they disapproved of the methods.

But when paramilitary groups called their cease-fires, punishment attacks continued. People began to ask: why? One explanation is that paramilitary groups have nothing else to do. Assaults doubled, and in some areas quadrupled, in the first few years of paramilitary cease-fires. Those numbers have dipped, but punishments are still a regular occurrence; and without the backdrop of political violence, their barbarity stands out more starkly.

The Cairns family was one of many I had met in Belfast that seemed to have suffered so unfairly during the Troubles. Angela Cairns lost a brother and a sister to the violence. Several nephews, too, have been killed or driven out of Belfast by paramilitary groups. Once, a gang of Protestants beat Angela herself. The daily stresses of living in Ardoyne, one of the most violent corners of Belfast, combined with all the personal tragedies, have left her a nervous wreck. She is agoraphobic and spends most of the day in her house with George, who is also on a disability with hearing loss.

I could not understand why the family would draw attention to themselves by speaking out against punishment attacks when they were already facing so many hardships. It was another of the dirty rules of the Belfast ghetto—never publicly criticize the paramilitary group that controls your community. They lived in an insular and suspicious neighborhood; speaking out was seen as betrayal that could earn a brutal reprimand. But George and Angela Cairns did not care. They were disgusted, tired, and had just had enough. Punishment beatings were all too common in Northern Ireland, but so few people had the courage to do anything about it. The Cairns family had that courage. It was something rarely seen in Northern Ireland, and something that I had only witnessed once before.

The IRA had warned Andrew Kearney to keep a low profile. In Twinbrook, west Belfast, they may as well have sent him into a downpour with orders to avoid the raindrops. The housing estate where he grew up was an IRA recruiting ground and almost all his friends were either involved with, or sympathizers of, the republican movement. Still, Andrew Kearney tried to stay away from their bars and hangouts. When his girlfriend, Lisa, had a baby girl, Caitlin Rose, he was too busy to find trouble. A lingering grudge with the IRA seemed to be fading when Andrew got into a bar fight with Eddie Copeland. Andrew fared better in the fracas, and the word was Copeland wanted revenge.

Two weeks later, Lisa's mother arrived from England to visit her new granddaughter. She was flying home on July 19, 1998, so Andrew and Lisa drove her to the airport. Afterwards, they dropped in briefly on Andrew's mother, Maureen, on their way back to Lisa's flat in north Belfast. She was watching Andrew's children from an earlier marriage, and he typically spent most of the day with them. Maureen thought it strange that Andrew did not return later that day. Instead, he stayed at Lisa's flat as if he knew, Maureen later speculated, that he was in danger.

Around midnight that night, Lisa was getting ready for bed. Andrew sat in the living room, eating a chocolate bar and drinking a Coke with the baby on his lap. Andrew told Lisa to get some sleep; he would look after the baby. Suddenly, the front door was kicked off its hinges. An eight-man IRA punishment squad filled the hall. Lisa screamed while one of the men pushed her into the kitchen. "What are you doing?" she pleaded. "Please don't hurt him!"

Lisa heard a voice ordering Andrew to put his hands behind his head before he was carried limp out of the flat without uttering a word. On their way out the door one of the men ripped the phone out of the wall. When they were gone, Lisa rushed to get her child, who had been placed in the nearby stroller. Just then she heard gunshots.

Lisa ran out into the hall looking for Andrew. She knocked on every door in sight, but the flats were either empty or the residents were too frightened to answer. Lisa went for the elevator; it was jammed. She ran down twelve flights of stairs in her

pajamas with her child in her arms. When she got to the ground floor she found An-
drew lying in the elevator, unconscious and shot three times in the leg. His face was
cold and lifeless. She panicked and ran out of the building towards her sister's nearby
apartment. First they called an ambulance; then they called Maureen Kearney.

Maureen had been concerned that something like this might happen to her
son. She and Andrew had talked plainly about his problems with the IRA and
what they might have in store for him. Her nerves were already frayed with worry,
so the news of the shooting was just enough to bring on an angina attack. An am-
bulance was summoned, and she too was brought to the hospital. Maureen was
overwrought thinking about Andrew; attacks like this had been known to cripple
or maim people for life. In her sensitive state, the doctors decided to wait four
hours before telling her that her son was dead.

I first met Maureen Kearney six months after Andrew was killed.
She had launched a personal crusade against punishment attacks that
was finally drawing strong media interest. She appeared on numerous
television programs across Europe and Australia, and was featured on
60 Minutes. The campaign was a catharsis. If Maureen's efforts stopped
other killings, she would be pleased.

We arranged to chat—between television interviews—one afternoon in early January 1999. I took a taxi out to the Kearney home. I
would become familiar with the small terraced house over the next few
months as Maureen and I developed a sort of friendship. Even though, in
my mind at least, I was firstly a writer prying into her life, I developed a
fondness for Maureen that she seemed to reciprocate naturally.

Looking back on that first meeting, I remember being struck by
Maureen's strength. Her friends later told me that the previous months
of grief had taken their toll, though she seemed to be a woman with
ample fortitude. Over sixty years old, Maureen was sanguine and lithe,
with cheerful cheeks and a thatch of white hair. When I came to the
door, she ushered me into the living room with resolve—she had an
important story to tell and wanted me to pay attention.

The mantelpiece was covered with small snapshots of Andrew.
Larger photos were hung on the living room walls. Maureen described

each one to me with a doting, affectionate air. There was one picture of Andrew playing football; another of him with his newborn daughter; another with his family. Andrew was all Maureen wanted to talk about, and through hours of conversation—sometimes weeping, sometimes laughing—I gained a vivid image of Andrew Kearney. I decided that I would have liked him and began to understand her loss.

Andrew was strong-willed, even pugnacious, but he was no bully. Bullies push people around. Andrew preferred to defend people who could not defend themselves. In that way, Andrew was the schoolyard tough everyone wants to befriend—if Andrew was with you everyone else backed off.

"He was no angel, now," Maureen pointed out emphatically. "Don't get me wrong."

He had a mercurial temperament and a complicated character. Andrew's spirited side was always looking for trouble. His nobler side made sure "trouble" meant sticking up for others.

Andrew often played a big-brother role, Maureen remembered. Some people relied on it. She laughed thinking back on one incident. It happened while Andrew was working in the kitchen at the Europa Hotel in central Belfast. Most of the staff was Catholic, but there was one Protestant, Colin, who worked there as well.

Colin was small and meek. The other staff harassed him for that and because of his religion. Colin avoided a beating only by staying away from his colleagues as much as he could. He certainly did not want to socialize with them after work, so when Andrew asked Colin to join the lads for a drink one evening, Colin declined. He and Andrew had always gotten along, but he did not want to see the others. "But, sure, I will be there to look after you," Andrew reassured him.

They were all sitting in Robinson's Bar, across from the Europa, when Andrew went to the bookies next door to check on the results of a horse race. When he got back, he could see Colin was shaking. "What's wrong?" he asked. Colin said it was nothing, but the others told Andrew that they were about to give Colin a good hiding and had told him so. "Is that right?" Andrew asked. "Well then you will have to come through me to do it."

That decided it. Everyone backed off. No one wanted to face Andrew, and Maureen never forgot "that wee titch," Colin, sitting in her living room at Andrew's wake, crying his eyes out as he told that story.

Later, "Big Jim," another friend of Andrew's, came ambling into the house. Standing at over six feet, six inches tall, years of alcohol abuse had diminished Jim's broad frame. He lumbered aimlessly through the door and into the living room looking for Maureen's husband, Tommy. Jim had to give him some money. Tommy was upstairs, Maureen said, and then introduced us. Jim's eyes brightened. He stood up straight and began waving his arms demonstratively through stories of Andrew—what a good friend he had been, how much he was missed. "He treated me like—No, better than a brawther," Jim slurred.

Jim and Andrew had gone to school together. Andrew was not a big drinker, but Jim and a few other friends became alcoholics and Andrew looked after them. When Jim went into extortionate debt to a neighborhood loan shark, Andrew paid off the loan. "I am getting you away from him," Andrew told Jim.

In the new arrangement, Jim owed Andrew, which meant Andrew could keep an eye on him. Every week Jim would hand over some cash. Now, with Andrew gone, his father looks after the account. Jim still arrives occasionally to pay some money or borrow a few pounds.

A week after Andrew was killed, Jim ordered a taxi to bring him up a gallon of gasoline. He was drunk, depressed, and going to torch himself. He missed Andrew. Maureen found out what he was planning and phoned the fire brigade. They found Jim soaked in gasoline but were able to douse him down before he struck a match.

"God, that would have broken my heart," Maureen said. "What were you playing at?" she asked him impatiently.

Jim wandered upstairs sheepishly. She did not mind his visits, Maureen said, becoming tearful. There were just so many reminders of Andrew everywhere, and none of them gave her strength. All his friends were grieving, too. Many of them still broke down, and some women in the neighborhood could not hear Andrew's name without weeping. There was just something inexplicable about his smile and swagger that people had found charming and now missed.

But Andrew's good conscience stood astride fierce pride. He was quick to defend others but just as quick to defend himself. His better judgment often betrayed him when restraint was called for, and any perceived slight was bound to get a reaction. He seemed to relish the indignation that would allow him to lash out.

"He was a hothead," Maureen said dolefully. "Many's the time he could have tried to talk his way out of a conflict. He didn't. He never backed down from a fight."

Most of that intensity was directed into sports. Andrew enjoyed snooker, darts—anything that involved a bit of skill; but football was his favorite. Maureen remembers him earning a string of awards in school: Player of the Year, Highest Goals Scorer, Man of the Match. When he left school, Andrew went on to play in a local semipro league for a while. It seemed he was mentioned in the local paper almost every week.

"At football and the darts and that, he was an awful slagger," Maureen admitted. He taunted and goaded people during a match. Some of them could take it; others could not and it often ended in a fight. "That is how he got into a couple of rows with members of the movement," Maureen remembered.

During one rough football match, Andrew threw a punch at a player he accused of trying to break his leg. The scuffle would not have amounted to much except that the player Andrew hit was involved with the IRA. The whole incident was an overblown schoolyard quarrel, but it was serious. Andrew had challenged an IRA activist, and that had consequences.

After the football incident, the IRA began keeping an eye on Andrew Kearney, and it was not long before he developed a reputation as a "hard nut." It was partly earned one night in a local pub when Andrew had words with a crowd of republicans. The exchange escalated into a shouting match, and Andrew viciously insulted one man who was not going to put up with that sort of talk. He went to the IRA demanding action.

In local parlance, getting a punishment beating is to "get done." To be killed is to "get done right." He insisted that Andrew "get done right," and the IRA began to take serious notice of the troublemaker from Twinbrook.

In almost every way, Andrew was the profile of an ideal IRA activist. He was brawny, clever, and assertive. He came from a republican neighborhood and had no love for the British. Andrew was a perfect recruit but for being proud and headstrong—two traits that precluded his involvement.

The IRA demands complete, unquestioning dedication from their activists, which was something Andrew would never have given. Andrew's energy, if channeled, would have been an asset; his strength, unbridled, was a threat. In other circumstances, the IRA would have welcomed someone like Andrew Kearney into their ranks, but he instead had challenged their power and needed to be dealt with.

At the very least, Andrew Kearney was due for a beating. Depending on who he had annoyed and their clout, he might even be killed. Andrew and Maureen discussed his options. He could either leave the area, or stay and accept the inevitable. Andrew was too close to his family to leave them, and he was too proud to simply accept the attack. Maureen thought there was another way. She felt the whole issue was blown out of proportion and there was still a chance it could be settled without her son being hurt. If she could just speak to the IRA—explain Andrew's circumstances—maybe a reprisal could be avoided.

The republican movement is brutal and arbitrary, but it also has a long memory. Maureen's family had fought and suffered for republicanism, and they were held in some regard. Her father had been decorated in the war for Irish independence; her brother and cousins were some of the first republicans interned without trial in the seventies; her nephew had just served a twenty-year turn in prison. That all had to be taken into account.

Maureen went to her nephew for help, and he agreed to approach the IRA leadership and ask for leniency towards Andrew. He came back with news that Andrew faced one of three punishments. He would have cinderblocks dropped on his hands, a kneecapping, or a severe beating. When they came for Andrew, the IRA promised not to take him from Maureen's home; if, in the end, the IRA did kill Andrew they would not "do him in the head" and prevent an open casket wake. Those were the only assurances that they would give.

Maureen was disgusted. After her family's sacrifice and unwavering support for the republican movement, she could not believe the severe punishment that was being planned for Andrew's minor infractions. She decided to speak to the IRA herself.

The IRA compiles a list of troublemakers at Connolly House—Sinn Fein headquarters in Andersontown, West Belfast. Steadying her nerve, Maureen went to Connolly House and pled for mercy. She was lucky to speak with one of the old guard, someone who would appreciate her family's history, but he said there was nothing he could do. Andrew's name kept appearing on the list, he explained feebly. The wheels were already in motion, and they could not be stopped.

After a pause he gave Maureen one option, then swore he would deny it if asked. There was a well-known priest at the local Clonnard Monastery who served as an IRA intermediary. If Andrew delivered him a letter, humbly asking for forgiveness, there was a chance that the matter could be overlooked.

Maureen and Andrew drafted the letter together. Andrew mustered the contrition and humility that was so uncharacteristic and wrote what the IRA wanted to hear: he was out of sorts facing a failed marriage; he had been drinking on that night he gave offense and things had gotten out of hand; he knew that he had been in fights with members of the republican movement before; he was sorry and promised it would never happen again. Andrew delivered the letter and waited for a reply. He heard nothing. After a few weeks of waiting without word, he wondered what decision had been taken. Nothing was said, and Andrew hoped he would be left alone.

In the meantime, Andrew ended his marriage and took up with Lisa. He was pulling his life together and managed to avoid the sort of confrontations that had dogged him in the past. Before long, Lisa gave birth to their daughter, and Andrew dared hope that his troubles were behind him. Fate then gave him a final prod.

In early July, 1998, Lisa's cousin and her family were heading for Dundalk—a town just over the Irish border. Andrew and Lisa gave them a lift to the train station, but they arrived late and missed their train. Rather than wait at the station, they decided to go for a drink. Andrew, Lisa, Lisa's cousin, her husband, and their son went off to the Red Devil, a newly opened pub along the Falls Road. They took a seat together in the front of the bar. Near the back, Eddie Copeland was having a drink and playing cards with a band of friends and comrades.

It was a terrible coincidence. Copeland and Lisa's cousin had a history of confrontations. Copeland's party began taunting her son and Andrew intervened. "I heard you are a hard man," Copeland said.

"Do you want to see how hard?" Andrew asked. "Or can you only handle women and children?"

Andrew was not going to back down, but neither was Copeland going to let that comment go unchallenged. The two men went outside. Lisa and the others waited inside, fearful that Andrew might be hurt in the brawl but more afraid that he wouldn't. If Copeland won, the matter might be resolved; if Andrew won, he would face Copeland again. After a few minutes, Andrew returned.

Everyone had stood back while he gave Copeland a digging, Andrew said. It was over, but they should leave right away, he thought, before things escalated. As they were going, one of the men who had been sitting with Copeland, an old football mate of Andrew's, approached. "Andy, watch your back," he said. "Copeland has just put out a threat against ye."

Nothing could stop what happened next. That fight, combined with the past incidents, meant it was only a matter of time before the IRA took action. Two weeks later, Andrew Kearney was dead.

Maureen knew the IRA leadership must have sanctioned the attack on Andrew. She wanted to hear them justify Andrew's murder, so she went back to Connolly House and made arrangements for a meeting with IRA leaders. She was taken from her home to an IRA safe house where an inquiry was convened. Maureen sat across a table from men she recognized as the top command. They apologized for Andrew's killing. The attack should never have happened, they admitted. They recognized that it was a personal vendetta but still pointed to Andrew's history of trouble with republicans. They helplessly explained that Andrew's name "kept appearing on the list."

The IRA asked Maureen to leave them a list of her questions; they would interrogate the unit responsible and get back to her. She did, and a few days later she was summoned again.

Andrew had been shot with a 45-caliber revolver, a weapon big enough to take off a limb. A much smaller gun was typically used in such attacks. Maureen wanted to know why they used such a large bore if they only intended to wound Andrew.

The IRA claimed there was too much security that night to go searching for a specific weapon. The attackers went to the nearest arms dump, collected a gun, and carried out the shooting. They used what they could get their hands on. It was just bad luck that the gun happened to be so powerful.

Punishment attacks had become so common that an ambulance was sometimes notified in advance and told where the victim could be found. On the night of Andrew's attack, no ambulance was called. Maureen wanted to know why. The IRA said the men forgot.

They gave similarly unsatisfactory answers to her other questions. Lisa's phone had been yanked out of the wall leaving her unable to reach help. "The men panicked," Maureen was told. The elevator in which Andrew was shot had been jammed. That was unintentional, they said.

The IRA claimed that the attack was a punishment shooting gone awry, that the men had never meant to kill Andrew. Maureen never believed that; she was convinced that her son had been murdered. "That is why I am talking to you," Maureen implored. "If people hear about what is happening—really know what is going on—the IRA will have to respond."

Before Andrew was killed, Maureen admitted with some embarrassment, she had not been fazed by paramilitary punishments. She never wanted to believe stories that the IRA was involved in mindless brutalities or racketeering. When she heard such news reports, she threw her shoe at the television. "How dare you?" she would ask. "Those are the people I have supported all my life!"

She was a republican herself and believed that while the punishments seemed harsh, they must have been measured and fitting. She trusted the IRA to deliberate over individual punishments, but that view changed when Andrew was killed. All the media accusations suddenly seemed credible, and she wondered how the movement could have gone so far astray.

When Maureen started to speak out in the media, the IRA's cooperation evaporated. They had tried to keep her on their side, humoring her outrage if it meant that she kept quiet. When Maureen turned on the IRA, they knew that they had lost control so they ignored her. Suddenly, Maureen no longer heard from Gerry Adams or any of the republican leadership. She was getting some cold looks from neighbors, and Maureen started to worry for her own safety.

"See that?" Maureen asked one day, pointing through the kitchen. An ironing board and chairs were wedged against the back door. "That is our security system. I don't know if they want to keep me quiet, but we put that there in case. It won't stop them from getting in, but it will wake us up if they try."

Andrew Kearney lived according to his own unique code, where apparent recklessness masked his brand of courage and defiance. As I got to know Maureen better, I could see that a streak of her will had been passed on to Andrew and that more than grief or fear, indignation kept her going.

"For the republicans to do this to my son is like my family turning on my son. . . . At first it was like a dagger in my heart to have to speak out against the republican movement, but now I see them for what they are."

Maureen had supported an earlier generation of IRA activists—men she considered to be principled, disciplined, and willing to make sacrifices for their community. The IRA activists who had killed Andrew were something else, a breed of brutal men who were only involved in petty squabbles and turf wars.

Maureen's crusade against paramilitary punishments was compelling, and I wanted to learn more. Had the IRA changed, or had Maureen been naïve from the very beginning? What was the role of the new generation of IRA activists if the political struggle was over? Were punishment beatings the last spasm of a violent era, or were they part of a new story in Northern Ireland? Maureen also wanted these questions answered, and her interest was a kind of command. With just a measure of Maureen's courage, I could find out what we both wanted to know.

In the shadow world of Northern Ireland, Eddie Copeland is an obscure figure. To the police, the army, and many politicians he is known as a ruthless and powerful street enforcer. Yet he has never been convicted of a terrorist offense, so the people who make such claims tend to do so privately. David Trimble, leader of the Ulster Unionist Party and a Nobel Peace Prize laureate, once named Eddie Copeland as a mastermind behind the Shankill Road bombing. As a member of the British Parliament, he could make such a statement without fear of censure. It was the boldest allegation ever made against Copeland. "I don't think anything I said in the House of Commons was news to anybody in Belfast," Trimble said.

Partly in an attempt to shake him, partly out of sheer frustration, the security forces in Northern Ireland harassed Eddie Copeland for years. He has been threatened and humiliated by the army on the streets. His home was frequently searched. An army command once sent Copeland a mock funeral card, and police once fired on his car as it drove past a checkpoint. He did not back down or ignore the incidents, but filed a number of complaints and lawsuits against the security forces and damage claims for the attempts on his life. I arranged to meet Eddie Copeland with the pretense of discussing one such pending decision.

Copeland preferred to keep his own address secret, so we arranged to meet at his mother's house, a small, attached home in the middle of Ardoyne, somewhat garishly decorated with plastic flowers and several glazed porcelain figurines sitting on the shelves. I arrived before Copeland. Carol, his mother, a barmaid at a local republican pub, made me a cup of tea as I waited behind the security cameras and bulletproof glass of the living room window. "We need all of that because of who he is," she explained rather cryptically.

I did not know what to expect from Copeland, whether he would be arrogant and maniacal like Johnny Adair or more cold and distant. As soon as he walked through the door, I could see that Eddie Copeland's reputation did not match the figure he cut. He was young, twenty-eight, tall and fit with red hair. He apologized for being late and sat down on a leather sofa across from me.

When Copeland described the persecution he faced from the security forces, he sounded genuinely aggrieved. He was just an ordinary man with no involvement with the IRA, he said. Later, after further meetings, Copeland also insisted that he had nothing to do with the murder of Andrew Kearney. Yes, the two men had gotten into a fight at the Red Devil, Copeland admitted. "But Kearney was known to start trouble," Copeland said, "and that day, he put his nose into things that did not concern him."

The police questioned Copeland about Kearney's murder, but Copeland was not even in Belfast on that night. He was twenty miles away in the town of Portadown serving as guide for a group of human rights observers. Still, as the police explained to me, it is common for a third party to carry out punishment attacks; it keeps things impersonal. And since Copeland must have guessed that he would be a suspect in any attack against Andrew Kearney, it would only have been prudent to arrange an alibi if he was involved. Copeland's denials, when they came, were rather laconic, as if he had nothing to fear and he was growing weary of the question.

When we would meet at his mother's house, Copeland was generally open, cordial, talkative. Looking at it from my standpoint, he said, he could see how some of the things that had happened to him were notable, and he was rather unguarded in describing them. Copeland discussed his life with patience and frankness. If he did not want to answer a question, he said so. He spoke easily but through an almost inveterate edginess. He gave the small security monitor in the corner of the room occasional glances and strolled to the front window when a clatter in the neighborhood stirred his paranoia.

In time, I developed an ambivalence towards Eddie Copeland. I believed everything that I had heard about him, but I found his candor and courtesy disarming. I also found it fascinating that the man allegedly responsible for Andrew Kearney's murder doted paternally over his young son. Once, when the boy passed us on the way into the kitchen for a soft drink, Copeland told him to "get milk; it's better for you." I was given to an involuntary recognition of Copeland's humanity, a quality, if the stories were true, that Copeland was able to put aside.

At twelve months old, Eddie Copeland's father was shot dead by the British Army outside their home in October 1971. "He was only twenty-three and the Troubles had just started," Copeland told me.

Copeland showed me a faded newspaper clipping from the time. It was one of the few keepsakes he had. In a few hundred words, the story reported the people killed in the previous days of violence. John Copeland was given two lines in the middle of a story that listed a few personal details with the indifference of an obituary. "The Brits said he had a gun," Copeland explained matter-of-factly, "but, back then, they probably just panicked and shot him." With that sort of formative experience, Copeland's later republican involvement is unsurprising. But what did that involvement entail?

Castlereagh detention center is infamous. It is where most paramilitary suspects in Belfast were once interrogated and where, through days of questioning, police meted out systematic abuse. Suspects were woken at all hours, day or night, and then coaxed, cajoled, and threatened into giving a confession. The sessions were brutal but, according to police, very effective. Human rights activists protested for years against the interrogations at Castlereagh, but the police were satisfied when their tactics secured lengthy prison sentences. Many suspects found the pressure too much to bear, broke down, and signed anything that was placed in front of them. Eddie Copeland was held at Castlereagh fourteen times, he explained. He spent hundreds of hours in interrogation but never uttered a word and never signed a thing.

His stamina is frightening. "I just shut down when I was in there. If [the police] were slobbering and yelling, I just ignored them. They would beat you, but nothing that would leave a mark. You just had to ignore that, too," Copeland said flatly. "I just shut down until I was released. Other people signed things; I guess they could not take it."

To loyalist paramilitary activists, and particularly to Johnny Adair, Eddie Copeland is something of a nemesis. Besides his harassment at the hands of the security forces, Eddie Copeland is known for the number of loyalist murder bids he has escaped.

The last attempt on Copeland's life came in December 1996 when a bomb was put under the driver's seat of his car. When he shifted into reverse, the bomb detonated and shrapnel blew through his right calf and arm. Copeland was rushed to the Royal Victoria Hospital where republican comrades, many wearing flak jackets, kept twenty-four-hour watch. The doctors thought they would have to amputate the leg, since most of the muscle mass was lost. The leg was saved, but Copeland once lifted his tracksuit to show me what was left—nothing more than a bone wrapped in skin. These were the scars Johnny Adair had shown such interest in.

Loyalists first tried to kill Copeland when he was just twenty-one years old. A UFF unit stormed his front door one night, but when it would not give way they fired several dozen shots through the windows and ran off. No one was hurt in the attack. Copeland was not even home at the time. He only found out about the incident when he returned from a holiday in Cyprus.

A year later loyalists tried a more elaborate attack. They were going to secure the neighboring house and lay an ambush for Copeland when he arrived home after a night out, but as they were advancing up the footpath, the gunmen touched off the motion detectors. The street was flooded in light; the gunmen panicked, fired into the neighbor's house, and ran away.

A few months later Copeland had a bizarre encounter in town. He was waiting at a traffic light when he happened to look at the adjacent driver. It was Johnny Adair. "He started yelling 'You fenian bastard' and 'I'll kill you,'" Copeland recalled. "But I just stuck up my thumb and drove away."

Hours after the exchange with Adair, gunmen attacked Copeland's sister's Ardoyne home. They fired indiscriminately into the house and fled. No one was hurt, but Copeland knew Adair was responsible.

Eddie Copeland grew up with Thomas Begley and Sean Kelly in Ardoyne; they went to school together, but Copeland was a few years older. Copeland's reputation in the neighborhood would have impressed the two susceptible younger men. While Begley and Kelly met their fate in the Shankill Road bombing, police never apprehended the IRA team that assembled the bomb and planned the attack.

Three days after the Shankill Road bombing, at a memorial service at the Begley home, fellow IRA activists gathered to pay their respects. Copeland was there, as was a visible British Army presence. One army patrol included trooper Andrew Brian Clarke, perched in a jeep. Tensions were high. Despite their armaments and intelligence, soldiers like Clarke had been powerless to prevent the Shankill Road bombing. Clarke had been shown photographs of the Shankill bomb suspects, and Eddie Copeland was among them. He circled the Begley home once, then again; then he opened fire. Eddie Copeland was the target, and he was hit twice in the back while standing in the Begleys' front garden. One bullet exited through his stomach. Copeland fell to the ground. "I've been hit!" he yelled.

A crowd rushed to Copeland's aid while fellow troopers disarmed Clarke. Copeland was taken to the hospital where he spent the next two weeks. His wounds were serious, but he survived. Surgeons removed a yard of intestines, and after nine months of convalescence, he made a recovery. Other than a few digestion problems, his life was back to normal. Copeland received around forty thousand dollars in his settlement with the British Ministry of Defense after the shooting incident—part of the nearly one hundred and fifty thousand dollars he has collected in all of his damages claims.

I could not fathom the single-mindedness it took for Copeland to survive days in Castlereagh, nor the mental strength needed to ignore the day-to-day abuse he faced on the street. And then there were his children, whom Copeland seemed to adore. He was such a complicated contradiction. How did he reconcile such disparate parts of his life? I often left Copeland without any answers, just more questions. But Copeland did not seem to mind my visits, so I got a glimpse into his day-to-day life over my time in Belfast. What I found was rather dull and detached.

Eddie Copeland did not have a steady job. He occasionally worked as a doorman in a club, but that is all. The money from damages and legal settlements helped pay for his car and the furnished house he owns in the middle of Ardoyne. Copeland eventually felt comfortable enough to meet me there, but more often I found him at his mother's house, watching television on the couch or waiting for her to serve dinner. One bright afternoon, I dropped by the house and found Carol sunning herself in a lounge chair situated just over the scorched spot of driveway where her son nearly lost his leg. Copeland had taken up a position like a guard dog, leaning over the front garden wall scanning the streets. Everyone that walked past seemed to acknowledge his authority with a wave. If he saw a car or person that he did not recognize, Copeland would absently mutter something to himself, "They're not from the district."

Why would anyone get involved with the paramilitaries? I often asked myself. It seemed there were many personalities in the IRA. Some people were just angry—they had been aggrieved and were seeking revenge. Others believed they were part of a proud republican tradition. Many had reasons that are now long forgotten.

Copeland seemed to be caught in a cycle of violence that just kept on spinning. He is not a great republican thinker; his world barely stretches outside of Ardoyne. He is a foot soldier completely immersed in a republican culture that defines him. Most of his actions are done on command. The rest—like the fight with Andrew Kearney—are done as a matter of pride. Copeland's personal life, his family, is something apart.

Eddie Copeland was one among a generation of IRA activists who were born into the struggle. He had never known the idealism of the early movement when people made a choice between leading a normal life or getting involved. The people who had made that decision had all expected it would all end soon. But Copeland came of age during the most cynical period of the Troubles. His father was killed in those years.

He grew up under the fear of loyalist attacks and abuse from the security forces. Through the years, he lost many friends and family members to violence. He did not have the chance to dream of a different life.

I last visited Copeland one spring afternoon, just as he was leaving his house to play Gaelic football. He offered to give me a lift back into town. As we passed Carlisle Circus, a junction between Protestant and Catholics neighborhoods in north Belfast, Copeland began to reminisce. "Years ago, when I drove through this area, Protestant kids would throw stones at my car," he laughed.

"But you do think that you are lucky sometimes and wonder why it is that you survived," he said. "I believe in God. I would not be a big churchgoer and I don't believe that priests should be preaching at you. But I do think about the things that happened to me and how lucky I am. I think that someone must be watching over me. But you try not to think about it too much or you might go crazy."

When I asked Copeland what he expected his life would be like in the future, he said, "Things will probably go on about like the same."

Maureen's most ornate memorial to Andrew was hanging behind the main door of the living room. It was a mirror etched with Celtic trim. Joe Doherty, a cousin of Andrew's girlfriend Lisa, had made it in the Maze prison.

"Now he was part of the IRA which I would have supported," Maureen said. "When someone like Joe went to prison in the seventies, it was the neighbors who would pitch in and help the family. It wasn't charity. Well, we didn't look on it as charity. It was just people getting together to help out.

"We don't have people like that in the movement anymore," Maureen said scornfully. "Now it's just a bunch of thugs. Joe gave a lot."

That was true. Few republican prisoners spent as much time behind bars as Joe Doherty did. When Doherty was released from Northern Ireland's Maze prison in October 1998, half his years had been spent incarcerated. In the New Lodge area of north Belfast, where he grew up, Doherty's life is the stuff of republican legend.

In 1980, Doherty was arrested and charged with murder. His IRA squad had been captured after a gun battle with a British army unit left one soldier, Captain Westmacott, dead.

Doherty was convicted and sentenced to life in prison in June 1981. He heard the verdict from a safe house in west Belfast because days earlier—in an audacious daylight breakout—Doherty and seven IRA comrades had escaped from Crumlin Road Prison where they were being held.

After a few months of hiding in the Irish Republic, Doherty escaped to New York, where the FBI eventually recaptured him. His battle against extradition from the United States won widespread media coverage, galvanized Irish America, and went all the way to the Supreme Court before Doherty was forced to return to Northern Ireland.

Joe Doherty is a venerated hero, but out of touch with the current scene. A whole generation has passed since Doherty went on the run. The current republican motivations, tactics, and even the cease-fires would have been inconceivable when he first became involved. I wanted to know what a respected republican thought about the current movement. Not least, I wanted to know what he thought about the ugly business of punishment beatings. After all, a comrade from this new generation—Eddie Copeland—had reputedly ordered the killing of his cousin's boyfriend, Andrew Kearney.

Now, in his late forties, Doherty has resumed the normal life he abandoned as a young man. The fighting is over; he is rebuilding his community. I met him at the Ashton Center—a co-op office building in the New Lodge—where he works with a youth scheme and prisoner resettlement program.

The decades spent behind bars had not taken much off his appearance; Doherty seemed fit and healthy. And despite his status in the community, Doherty is a singularly unpretentious man. Until recently, there was a mural portrait of Doherty on the side of a prominent wall around the corner from his office. It was completed while Doherty was fighting extradition from America. He appreciated the sentiment, but one of the first things Doherty did upon his release was arrange for its replacement.

"I was getting tired of looking at it," Doherty said with a laugh. "I came back and was getting some abuse about it."

He designed a replacement—two panels chronicling the challenges young people in the area have faced over the generations. The first, in black and white, looks at the nineteenth century through child labor and disease. The second depicts modern problems like drug abuse and truancy.

"It's a kind of social comment," Doherty said. "It's political, but it's not sectarian. This mural could go up on the Shankill Road; it could go up in London or New York."

When Joe Doherty was fifteen years old, he installed a sink. It was part of a vocational course, and he remembers fitting the pipes and basin, connecting the nozzles, checking for leaks, and when it was done, sitting back in satisfaction. He felt proud, like he had accomplished something. Before joining the IRA, Joe Doherty was going to be a plumber.

It was a modest dream, the kind shared by many young men in Catholic north Belfast, but when the Troubles started, particularly when the British soldiers arrived, the dreams were dashed.

Doherty did not grow up in a staunch republican family. He grew up surrounded by British music, television, and culture. He was not particularly politically minded as a youth, and it was only when his neighbors started coming back from the civil rights marches of the early seventies bloodied and bruised, and when Doherty himself was systematically harassed by the security forces, that he developed a political understanding of the situation.

"I came to a decision," Doherty said. "It was not as if I hated anybody. I had no real grand plan that I was going to create a thirty-two-county democratic state, nationalize the banks, and create a republic. It was in response to the violence on the street. . . . I had no intentions of going to war. That is why I always say, 'It was not me who went to war. The war came to me.'"

Doherty has given hundreds of interviews. In Belfast, as it was in America, Doherty's long and colorful IRA involvement draws the media. Later that day he was doing an interview with a Finnish television crew. As we chatted over the next hour, I could hear Doherty slip into one of his well-worn speeches about the peace process: where it was going; where it would end. The war is over, Doherty said, and it's time to put violence away for good. The British will have to leave. The republican cause is being fulfilled. But if the need for violence is through, I asked, why are paramilitaries still carrying out punishment attacks?

With that, Doherty suddenly became flustered. "Could you repeat the question?" he asked.

"When will they end?" I asked again. He fumbled for a minute and then retreated into a canned republican answer.

"You have to live in the real world," he started, unconvincingly. "We don't have a policing service. There are no police in this community. They drive around in their Land Rovers. They are hemmed into their barracks. There is no communication. They don't represent our community. They are not accountable to our community. . . . The change that Sinn Fein is pushing for is the total disbandment of the RUC. . . ."

All right, but does that justify the IRA beating, maiming, and even killing people? "The police can't deal with it, and I don't believe . . ." Doherty struggled, then caught himself. "I'm not saying that the IRA is ever involved in punishment beatings. I don't know, and I can't speak for the IRA. You have to go to the republican movement."

But Doherty killed for the IRA; when he was jailed, the IRA freed him. Through his battle against extradition, Doherty became a republican folk hero. When he was shipped back to Northern Ireland, he served another seven years on the IRA prison wing. Through it all, Doherty remained loyal to the cause he joined as a teenager. If Joe Doherty could not speak for the IRA, who could?

The IRA is a cloak-and-dagger world that, if Sinn Fein's explanations were taken at face value, barely even exists. Some self-confessed republicans can explain the philosophy of the movement and justify years of violence. Asked awkward questions about IRA atrocities, they dodge, defer, and equivocate. "I don't speak for the IRA—you'll have to ask them about it."

Of course Doherty could speak for the IRA. He was no longer active, but he still had some moral authority. Doherty had dedicated his life to republican goals and, like a dwindling number of activists, had watched the movement develop from its infancy. At almost every important step, Doherty was there. Now the movement is changing and Doherty is still there, proud of his involvement.

As Doherty tried, uncomfortably, to explain IRA punishments, something he said earlier in the interview came back to me. I had asked him about the prison break and how they did it. All the prisoners must have wanted out. So how did they decide who got to go? Did they draw straws? Was it just an opportunity and his gang took it? What?

Doherty seemed impatient with my naïveté. Had I not been paying attention? It was not his choice. He had no say in the matter. He was a soldier, and he was being held prisoner. Someone on the outside wanted Joe Doherty out of jail, and so he was ordered to escape. It was no accident; it was a command. He was just doing what he was told.

I was beginning to understand Doherty's commitment. When he joined the IRA, Doherty made a pledge with one hand on a gun and the other on the Irish flag. He swore his obedience and loyalty above all else. Nothing would shake that commitment, and nothing would make him betray that trust. He was only one person in an organization where the parts are inconsequential. His duty, as always, was to the movement. There was nothing else.

Doherty knows people who have been victims of IRA punishments. I could understand why he did not want to talk about it. He did not want to defend punishments; he was opposed to them. But he would not criticize the IRA, so he buffered his comments.

"We have a criminal element within our community," Doherty said. "There is a lot of drugs and a lot of antisocial behavior. People want that to be tackled. I am against punishment beatings; that is why I am actually a member of a restorative justice group. The idea of restorative justice is supported by the movement, and that is a nonpolitical, nonviolent approach to social problems within the community.

"I am trained up in that as a mediator in relation to youth. And that is an alternative to the statutory bodies. . . . In the existing system, the victim and the perpetrator never get to meet. You bring them through the statutory system and they cannot deal with it. You put them in

prison or fine them, and that's it. We believe restorative justice is a positive alternative—it certainly is an alternative to punishment beatings."

When we finished our meeting, Doherty invited me to the opening
of a new restorative justice center in the area. I went, and saw that he
was right. It was an alternative to paramilitary street justice; Sinn Fein
supported it and it was spreading, slowly. Doherty's involvement was
just his latest contribution to the republican movement. It is a different
movement from the one he joined, but it will always have his allegiance.

Across the road from the Ashton Centre stands Fianna House, the
apartment building where Andrew Kearney was killed. It is a cold, towering slum—a landmark for a blighted neighborhood. After the ribbon
cutting of the new restorative justice center, I walked over to the building, passed through the graffiti-scrawled entryway, pushed a steel but-
ton, and waited for the elevator. I heard it slowly creaking down the
shaft before the doors opened onto the small steel cubicle where Andrew Kearney bled to death. I stood there for a moment. I wondered if
the same acrid smell of piss was there on the night he died. It probably
was. The thought sickened me a bit.

I took the elevator to the twelfth floor, imagining with dread what
those moments might have been like: the yelling, the gunfire, the smell
of cordite. Then the panic and desperation. I stood out on the landing,
scorched in places by mischievous children playing with fire, and gazed
out on the city. It looked peaceful. I did not want to turn back around
and face the dingy hallway—when I did, I decided to take the stairs.

For the first twelve months after Andrew's murder, Maureen's campaign ran on her own adrenaline and indignation; it was sheer will that
pushed her. By spring, though, the fickle media—which, early on, had
paid such attention to the story of a mother's crusade for justice—lost
interest. There was no more demand for interviews or meetings with
politicians. Maureen was suddenly left with a dwindling campaign and
her grief, both of which were taking their toll.

Her crusade had put paramilitary punishments under a spotlight.
Beatings, particularly from the IRA, were curtailed because of Maureen's

efforts. Some people surely owe her a debt. Maureen took some satisfaction knowing that she might have saved someone's life, but she always secretly hoped her campaign could, somehow, bring Andrew back. When she slowed down enough to realize that Andrew was gone, there was no hiding her disappointment.

On the first anniversary of Andrew's murder, Maureen felt she was slowly dying. Never in good health, a chronic heart condition was tightening its grip. She had been hospitalized several times in the previous year, but doctors never reached a proper diagnosis.

I last spoke to Maureen a few weeks before the first anniversary of Andrew's murder. His former football team had organized a memorial reception. It would be informal, just some friends having a drink, but I would be quite welcome to come along, Maureen said.

I sensed a little plea in her invitation. For some people, Andrew Kearney was fading into memory, but Maureen was not ready to let go. Time was passing, and though I would never meet her son, the reception would prove that he had been loved. Guests would be telling their favorite stories about Andrew; there would be laughter and fond memories. If I were there, someone else would have an understanding of what Andrew had meant to the world. If I could meet his friends and measure their loss, I could see how much Andrew was missed. Maureen would have liked that.

I promised to try to make it to the reception, though in the end I missed it and felt mildly ashamed when I phoned Maureen the next day to apologize. I felt worse when I heard her voice. It was lovely to have all of Andrew's friends together, Maureen said, sounding disappointed that she had to explain it to me. She had noticed my absence, and though she reassured me it was all right, I sensed it left her slightly bruised. That guilt lingered with me through early August amid news of Maureen's death. Maureen's sister Faye blamed it on a broken heart. Mary, Maureen's youngest daughter, said that the people who killed Andrew might as well have put a gun to her mother's head because though she kept living, her life had ended on that night.

Maureen's wake was held at the family home. Her open casket sat in the living room, under the front window. Mass cards collected around her legs. Lying there, Maureen's stature was diminished. She did not look like the woman who had stood so tall and defiant.

Tommy, Maureen's husband, was gentle in his grief. Andrew's death had made Maureen want to fight. It stirred something in her that she barely knew existed, but Tommy had accepted his son's death with resignation. He had made his own peace after that loss, and he showed the same composure after Maureen's death.

For Andrew's girlfriend, Lisa, Maureen's death opened new wounds. It was like Andrew's murder was happening all over again, she told me. Lisa never went back to her old apartment after Andrew's murder. Instead, she moved into a house not far from Maureen. With little family of her own in Belfast, Lisa had found a surrogate mother in Maureen. Were it not for Maureen, Lisa said she might not have made it through the ordeal. She was feeling more alone than ever.

The family assembled in the house to greet a steady stream of mourners. Some were crying; others were chatting at ease. In the kitchen, dirty teacups were piled high while a pot of vegetable soup simmered on the stove. In the living room, friends were reminiscing about Maureen: what a quiet woman she had been before Andrew's death and how outspoken she had become. Maureen's daughters remembered the pen and paper set they gave her for Christmas, what with all the letters she had been writing.

Crowds of mourners packed the chapel the next day for Maureen's funeral. Friends and family were there with strangers—people who only knew Maureen by name, who had heard her story and joined the service.

Hearts etched by Maureen's kindness were mourning the loss of a companion. Those people had come to close the book on her memory. For others, like me, who only got to know Maureen after the tragic loss of her son, the feelings were a bit different.

The last year of Maureen Kearney's life had been a sad, strangely noble happening. It was a break from the rest of her life; it was a time of inwardness and intensity that she had never before known. Maureen had suffered profound loss and, somehow, found the strength to lead a campaign with poise and dignity. Her grace was so rare and good it made you ashamed.

I was there to say good-bye to a remarkable woman, a reminder of true humanity. Standing there at the graveside, I thought that an end to paramilitary punishments would be the greatest tribute to Maureen's life, but it was not to be.

About eight months after Maureen Kearney was buried, within a few days of meeting the Cairns family, I met Darren. He was twenty-two years old, a Protestant being forced to flee the country, and he agreed to meet me for a drink at Belfast's Hilton Hotel just a few hours before his flight. When I arrived, Darren (that is not his real name but the one we agreed to use) was already sitting at the bar smoking a cigarette and drinking a pint of Guinness with a one-way plane ticket in his lap and a gym bag at his feet.

It had started with a game of pool, Darren explained. He and a friend had been playing when they got into a fight and turned the cue sticks on one another. It ended without either of them being badly injured, and Darren thought the incident would be quickly forgotten. But Darren lived in a rough Protestant housing estate just outside of Belfast, and his friend's father was a top loyalist commander. The next day, the father went to Darren's home and told him to leave the country within twenty-four hours or be shot.

Darren refused, and so a few days later, while Darren was walking home one evening, the friend's father and three other men attacked him; beat him with baseball bats until they broke both his legs, an arm, and battered his head. They left him lying there just a few feet from his home. Darren could not open his eyes; they were swollen shut.

Darren spent three days in the hospital, and when he was sent home, a Molotov cocktail was thrown through his window. His parents started getting phone calls from undertakers wanting to know if they could bury their son because they had seen his obituary in the newspaper. Then the police came and confirmed that his name was on a death list and recommended that he leave the country. Three of Darren's friends had been in similar circumstances, and one of them had moved to Wales after he lost a leg in a punishment attack, so he knew the threats were serious.

Darren assessed his options with a fatalism that I was finding common. He had a choice of whether to stay or go. If he stayed, he might be killed, so really there was no choice at all.

He was flying to Manchester, England; a Christian charity group had agreed to put him up for a while. Darren had done some work as a mover, so he would probably find a job doing something like that. And he would stay in touch with his family; maybe they could come and visit before long.

"But I am not coming back," Darren said. "Or, I don't expect to ever come back. See, my attack was sanctioned. It came from the top. If it gets to the stage where, with the peace process, the paramilitaries cannot approve these attacks, maybe then I might be able to come back."

I kept thinking that little scrapes like the one Darren had were the sort of thing that a young man should have been able to walk away from with a few cuts and bruises and, maybe, a lesson about holding his temper. It was not the sort of thing that was supposed to ruin a life. But it had, and I wished Darren luck as we parted.

As my taxi pulled away from the hotel, it stopped at a set of traffic lights. Saint George's Market, full of open-air vendors, was in front of us, and Belfast's law courts were directly adjacent. Between the two, just across the street, a scraggly looking sheep dog was eyeing cars as they came around the corner. He was panting with his tongue hanging out, poised. "See that dog?" the driver asked, laughing. "That dog is there every day. I don't know who he belongs to, but he is always there. He goes for the flaps on the back of your car when you pass. What's he gonna do? He can't stop the cars. He just nips at them."

I laughed as well; the dog did look out of place. He had no business being in the middle of downtown Belfast traffic, and he did not have a chance at stopping a car. It was hopeless to try, but he kept at it. And he looked so earnest, so completely natural as he got ready to pounce. Chasing was just his instinct, I thought out loud. Maybe in another life he would have been chasing sheep, but since cars were the only thing around, he went after them instead. "You have to admire his determination," I told the taxi driver.

"Ya," he said. "And if he keeps it up, he's gonna get hit."

The Disappeared

O
utside its few cities, Northern Ireland is a rural country where the landscape yields to a beautiful monotony. Narrow roads wind for miles, broken by occasional villages like Killyleagh, just south of Belfast, where pubs are wrapped in pebble-dash stone and brick shops are built flush to the street. Through the Troubles, most small towns like Killyleagh were spared serious violence. Bombs and riots in other parts of the country rarely touched the pastoral village. Neighbors in Killyleagh get along; there are too few to quarrel.

Helen and Seamus McKendry like it that way. They moved to Killyleagh from west Belfast for some respite. When I first met the couple at their home, the crisis that drove them out of Belfast seemed a million miles away. The sun was shining. It was a mild spring day. The only traffic was an occasional passing tractor. The couple was doing some spring cleaning and discussing plans for their new house to be built on the corner of the property. When it was finished, the family would truly be settled. Then visiting the grave of Jean McConville, Helen's mother, would be the only reason for them to return to Belfast.

Jean McConville is one of Northern Ireland's "disappeared": people abducted and killed by paramilitaries, their bodies never recovered. In all, there were sixteen such cases; most of the victims were Catholics who had been murdered by the IRA for alleged treachery or informing. The IRA had denied involvement with the disappeared until the spring of 1999, days before I visited Seamus and Helen McKendry, when they admitted responsibility for nine of the cases and promised to reveal where the bodies were hidden.

That day, as we spoke in the front garden, Helen and Seamus Mc-Kendry were waiting for a call. An intermediary was to reach them with word about McConville's secret grave. "Every time the phone rings we jump up," Helen told me, "expecting that it is the phone call that is going to tell us: 'We have got your mother's body.'"

By the end of that day, no one had phoned. It was several more weeks before any of the families would receive word about the location of their loved ones' remains. During that time and through the official search, the Irish public was transfixed by the story. Like few events since the peace process began, the search for the disappeared forced people to reckon with thirty years of violence. McConville's story in particular reminded them that decency had been the first casualty of the Troubles.

In late summer, 1969, the McConvilles had to move. The Troubles had erupted, and mixed communities like the one the McConvilles lived in were dissolving into stark contrasts. Most people in Northern Ireland already lived among their own religion. The violence just erased the spaces in between.

Hundreds of families were forced out of their homes, either by intimidation or at the point of a gun, in what would become the greatest forced migration Europe had seen since World War II. Everyone was being labeled: Catholic or Protestant, Irish or British, us or them, right or wrong. There was no splitting hairs, and no staying neutral. When ten-foot walls of brick and razor wire were going to separate two communities, people wanted to know which side of the wall you came from. "Neither" wasn't an answer.

Many families fled to ghettos of their own religion, but things were more complicated for the McConvilles. Jean McConville was born Protestant but had converted to her husband Arthur's Catholic faith when the couple married, and their ten children were being raised Catholic as well. Instead of the family having two communities welcome them, they would be shunned by both.

The McConville family had been living in Protestant east Belfast. Few people knew their religion or cared until the violence broke out.

Then the neighbors wondered why the McConville kids did not attend the local state-run school with the rest of the children. One day, a neighbor followed them to Saint Matthew's Primary in the Short Strand, and late that night a gang of armed men arrived at the McConville house. One of the men came into the living room, walked over to Arthur McConville, laid a knife against the crucifix dangling from his neck, and said that if they were not out in an hour, they were dead.

After a year living in emergency accommodation, the McConvilles had to choose a side. They decided to leave their Protestant neighbors for Catholic west Belfast, where they thought they would be safe. They were given a house in the Divis Flats ghetto at the bottom of the Falls Road but found that community no more welcoming than the one they had left.

"If you were an outsider," Helen remembers, "they kept you an outsider."

Within a year, personal tragedy struck. Helen's three-year-old brother lost a kidney. Then, within four months of his diagnosis with lung cancer, Arthur McConville was dead. Helen's oldest brother was arrested and interred—imprisoned without charge—later that year for being Catholic and old enough to join the IRA. That pushed McConville over the edge. She was truly alone. The man she had been with since her teens was gone. Her relatives were across town, but might as well have been across the world. Her family was falling apart, and she could not stand it anymore. Jean McConville tried to kill herself three times before she was admitted to a psychiatric hospital for severe depression.

The world did not change much in the three months that McConville was away. The Troubles were still raging, and that year, 1972, would become the bloodiest single year of the conflict. Areas like the Divis Flats were caught right in the middle. There were skirmishes between the IRA and security forces nightly, so people in the area just learned to deal with it. IRA snipers occasionally secured the roof of the Royal Victoria Hospital adjacent to the Divis Flats. Each night, nurses and other live-in staff had to decide whether to get to bed after the shooting had stopped or turn in early and try to sleep through it.

Helen remembers her family would hit the floor whenever they heard gunfire. It became a routine, almost instinctive. One night, while they were ducking for cover, they heard some shooting directly in front of the house. Then there was a *thud*. Then the screaming started. "Oh, God! Help me! Someone help me!"

It was coming from the other side of their front door. They tried to ignore it, but Jean McConville could not take the ceaseless wailing. She told her children to be still while she opened the door onto a British soldier lying shot and seriously wounded on the front stoop.

The soldier was the enemy. McConville's neighbors had shot him. He was not supposed to be shown any mercy, but Jean McConville did not see a soldier; she saw a scared boy in agony. She got a pillow and cradled the young man's head, whispering prayers in his ear until his colleagues came and took him away. It was all over in a matter of minutes. When the soldier was gone, McConville's son rebuked her. That act of humanity was sure to annoy the IRA, he warned.

A few days later the rumors began to swirl and the intimidation started. Paint was poured over the McConvilles' door and windows. "Soldier Lover Beware" was daubed across the front of their house. McConville did not respond. She did not flee or protest, and within a few days the intimidation stopped. McConville hoped it was all over, but she should have known it would never completely end.

Life got back to normal for a time, but the community was too small to ever forget what had happened. McConville was suddenly very vulnerable. One word to the IRA that she was an informer and she would be questioned. Any accusation, just one, and she could have been exiled from the country. No one would have been there to defend her because if they spoke up in Jean McConville's defense, they were protecting the "Soldier Lover." Then they would be under suspicion too.

"You have to understand what it was like to live in Belfast in the early seventies," Helen said. "It could have been even a grudge, a personal grudge from a neighbor. It only had to be someone's word, because I have seen it myself, firsthand, where someone's word has been taken. . . . I mean, if you are a member of the IRA and you don't like someone . . . ," Helen's voice trailed away.

Jean McConville was already emotionally fragile after her stay in the mental hospital. The incident with the soldier only increased her anxiety. As one of the eldest children it was Helen's job to look after her mother. A weekly game of bingo was one of McConville's few joys, but as Christmas approached she wanted to save some money for presents and forgo bingo for a few weeks. But Helen dared not let her miss the game. It was a buoy that kept her mother from sinking back into depression, and Helen insisted she go with her friend.

Later one night, around the time McConville was due home from bingo, her friend dropped by the house. She wanted to know which one of the children had been hit by a car and how they were. Helen did not know what she was talking about. A woman had asked for Jean McConville by name at the bingo hall. Jean's friend told Helen that the woman had said that one of Jean's children had been knocked down and that she was going to take her to the hospital.

Helen knew her mother was in trouble. She went to the hospital, but her mother was not there. She started looking around west Belfast, fearing the worst. Around three that morning the army rang the house. Helen remembers a soldier telling her they found her mother "wandering the streets without her coat, very distressed."

Helen collected her mother from the army barracks. McConville was shaken but managed to tell Helen what had happened: The IRA had lifted her from the bingo hall, bundled her into a car, thrown a bag over her head, and taken her for interrogation. McConville did not know where she went: a house somewhere. She said she had been tied to a chair, beaten, and asked questions about "things she knew nothing about." McConville was terrified, but managed to escape when she was left alone for a while. That is when the army found her.

Helen begged her mother to stay at their grandmother's for a while until things blew over, but her mother refused. She had done nothing wrong, McConville insisted, and she was not going to run away or abandon her family. It's unlikely, if Jean McConville had been an informer, that she would have returned to her home after escaping from an interrogation. Yet that is exactly what she did, knowing, as she must have, that she was still in danger.

The next day around teatime, Helen was sent to the shop while her mother climbed into a hot bath to soothe the bruises from her beating. That is when eight men and four women wearing masks came for McConville. It was all over by the time Helen got back. She could tell something was wrong as she approached the house. The door had been forced open; the neighbors were gathered around whispering into their hands; her brothers and sisters were crying. The day was December 7, 1972, Helen remembers, "and that was the last we have ever seen or heard of my mother."

Jean McConville was likely killed soon after her abduction, but the ordeal was just beginning for her children. Three weeks after her disappearance a stranger came to the house with McConville's purse and the three rings that, until then, had never left her fingers. Helen asked what had happened to her mother, but the man left without a word of explanation. That began twenty years of silence and rumors about Jean McConville. "When the IRA did this we were ten kids left on our own," Helen told me. And since their father was an only child and their mother's family was so distant, "Who was going to ask questions?" she lamented.

Women caught dating soldiers were often shaved, tarred, and feathered. Children accused of "touting" to the police were often tied to a telephone pole with a scarlet letter hung around their neck. Some alleged informers were killed, but more often they were ordered to leave the country. It was unusual for someone to completely disappear.

The IRA claimed that everything they did, no matter how brutal, was done to advance the cause or protect local people. Jean McConville was a widow and mother of ten. What threat could she have possibly posed? How was the IRA going to justify her murder? But with no body, there was no murder, and the IRA did not have to explain themselves. They only had to wait and let the rumors churn.

Neighbors told the children that their mother had abandoned them. Some people said McConville had run off with a soldier. Others said she was living on the Shankill Road with a new, Protestant family.

McConville's youngest children believed these stories and came to hate her. Helen thought they were lies but no matter what, she hoped that at least her mother was still alive.

Helen and her brother tried to keep the family together, but they were too young. Their grandmother was not willing to take charge of ten children, and no other family was going to keep the kids, so the McConvilles were taken into state care and separated. They were no longer a family, just ten children in one system.

Helen spent about a year in the Nazareth Lodge Orphanage. In that time she often ran away, back to the old house where she hoped to find her mother alive and ready to take the family back. Even when she left the orphanage at sixteen, Helen expected to find her mother alive.

Eventually, when Helen came to accept her mother's death, what was still unknown gnawed at her: the trauma of McConville's abduction, her last living moments, who was responsible, where was her body? It all haunted Helen's life. McConville's last thoughts must have been for her children, Helen thought, and what would become of them if she were killed. Remembering her mother was not a diversion; it was a burden. There were responsibilities. Yes, Jean McConville was dead, but she was not at peace.

Helen knew there were people who could tell her what had happened to her mother. There was hope of ending the uncertainty. The truth was there; she just needed to find it.

Seamus McKendry met Helen when he was an apprentice carpenter at the Nazareth Lodge Orphanage. They met again when Helen left, and they were married at eighteen. Marrying Helen meant sharing her loss. Seamus knew that. He could not take away her burden, but he promised to help her carry it. That became the couple's unfinished business, and nothing could be done until it was resolved.

They could have escaped and started a new life. Seamus was offered a job and a house in Australia, but they could not leave Jean McConville's memory behind like that without giving her some peace. Helen and Seamus missed out on lots of opportunity in their life, but they knew from the start that they had a responsibility together.

Seamus was always looking for answers. If he was in a pub, his eyes scanned for people he knew to be involved with the IRA. He would pry furtively, so as not to draw attention to himself, listening for a rumor different from the ones he had already heard. Seamus did not search systematically: that would draw suspicion. He did not ask directly: there was no hiding behind blunt questions. Seamus would just talk and invent little stories to ingratiate himself. Oblique questions were woven into casual conversations, so if anyone accused him of nosing about what happened to Jean McConville, well, he had been misunderstood.

The McConvilles had bred pigeons. Maybe there was a republican at the pub who had an interest in pigeons too. Maybe after a few drinks Seamus would muse about the McConvilles. "That family down in Divis who used to raise pigeons," Seamus might innocently say. "I wonder what ever happened to them?"

Some people honestly did not know what Seamus was talking about. Others knew but chose to ignore him. Others knew and said, "Sure, she ran off with a British soldier." Others demanded, "What the hell are you asking about that for?" Then they understood and told him to "Stop asking so many fucking questions!"

West Belfast is a small community. People there are intuitively suspicious of strangers but trusting of locals. While Helen and her family were being thrown out of their east Belfast community, Seamus McKendry was growing up in Andersontown, west Belfast, where his family was known and liked. Seamus was raised on a republican ideology and in surroundings that nurtured it. He became involved in the republican movement and was even interred at the Long Kesh prison camp, the precursor to Maze prison, for a time. Seamus's family connections and republican involvement earned him a longer tether when it came to asking about Jean McConville, but he could push it too far.

There was one time, while Seamus was at his usual line of polite interrogation at the Bee-Hive bar on the Falls Road, that he must have been asking the wrong person the wrong thing. Seamus did not notice, but a crowd was beginning to gather around him as he spoke with one fellow at the bar. Luckily, a family friend was sitting nearby and must have seen what was happening, because he scribbled something on a bookie's docket, handed it over with a five-pound note, and asked,

"Young McKendry! Do us a favor will ye? Away now and do that wee bet." That was not unusual in a pub next to a bookie, but when Seamus got outside and opened the note, it read "Get the fuck out of here as quick as you can and don't come back!" He took to his heels.

Helen could not ask questions without being conspicuous, but she already had some answers. She knew one of the men who took her mother. She also knew some of the women who were involved. Many were living in the neighborhood. She even used to pass them in the street.

Still, there was nothing she could do. If Helen confronted them they would just deny their involvement. If she went to the police, she might end up like her mother. In the time that Jean McConville was unaccounted for, more than one of the women who abducted her raised families and buried their own mothers. Helen does not know how they could do that.

Helen and Seamus kept quiet for over twenty years, but by 1994 they could bear it no more. Helen's sister Anne had just died, and Helen began to fear that all of Jean McConville's children might pass away without giving their mother any peace. She was depressed and sick at the thought. There were rumors of a paramilitary cease-fire, and Helen felt it was time to go public. Maybe if they really raised a clatter in the press the IRA would respond.

Seamus showed a little more forbearance. He knew things would move faster with the IRA's cooperation. If the IRA knew where McConville was and what had happened, better to just ask. Rather than shame the IRA in the press, he decided to approach them himself, privately, and see what they could do. So he went to a contact, someone he knew, and asked if the IRA could do the courtesy of investigating McConville's disappearance. The contact said he would do what he could and for Seamus to check with him later.

"Well, what do you have for me?" Seamus asked after a few weeks. "Why? Who are you?" The contact feigned ignorance. Well, that was it. They had tried to get the IRA to cooperate, but it seemed that going public was the only option left.

The McKendrys had hoped the IRA cease-fire would change the mood, but many people resented their campaign. Criticizing the IRA was not tolerated in their Poleglass neighborhood—not even by people who had been so wronged. And in Helen and Seamus's calls for Jean McConville's remains there was an implicit criticism of the IRA.

When the new campaign on behalf of the disappeared began, the press told the story of Jean McConville's abduction as a tale of innocence swept away by ruthless terrorism. But many people thought that with the cease-fire those stories were best forgotten. The IRA was changing, they said. McConville was taken during dark days when many awful things happened on both sides. Helen and Seamus were seen as dragging things out.

When the campaign started, it was easier to be cynical about McConville than let it raise awkward questions. Many people scoffed at claims that she had been an innocent victim and clung to IRA accusations that she was an informer. It kept them from answering what they had done during those dark years and whether their hands were clean.

It was a long conflict, some said, many people had been killed and many had been jailed. But the dead were buried and the prisoners were being released. Where was Jean McConville? Helen did not know, but she was going to recover her mother's dignity.

"Seamus and I were classed as traitors," Helen said. "We were betraying the people who were supposed to be protecting us."

Few people understood what the McKendrys were fighting for. Most did not try because there was something more than tragic in the story of McConville's abduction. It was disturbing, too. A mother of ten had disappeared, and no one had raised a question. A woman was taken away and killed with her neighbors' connivance. There was something disquietingly familiar there. It was a reminder of all the simple acts of complicity it took to perpetrate the Troubles. McConville's decency and hardship illustrated that fact and shamed those who heard her story.

Jean McConville was dead, but her spirit endured. While few people had known her in life, Helen introduced her to the world. There was a justice there, a penultimate right over wrong. It was cleansing for

Helen, but with a touch of vengeance, a triumph over the shadows that had taken her mother's life and clouded her own. But most of all Helen's campaign was a catharsis that lifted unmerited guilt.

Some people understood that. Others thought that Helen and Seamus had to be stopped. Most of the abuse came from what Helen calls "armchair republicans": thugs who were useless to the struggle but who used it to stir up the community and inflate their own ego. They were the same sort of people who had poured paint on the McConvilles' house after the soldier was shot outside the door.

When Helen and Seamus went to the local bar, people turned their backs. Then their children were beaten. Their car was destroyed. Seamus was approached and told to keep his mouth closed or he would end up dead. "We were ostracized by the community," Seamus remembered. It was a time when the whole family lived on nerve's end, and it was also when they decided to leave for Killyleagh.

But McConville was not the only "disappeared" victim. There were at least fifteen other missing bodies; many were alleged army informers or criminals. Brian McKinney was one of them: abducted by the IRA after he robbed a local pub. There were many people involved in the robbery, but only McKinney, twenty, and John McClory, twenty-two, were taken for questioning by the IRA.

The IRA admitted right away that they had the men. A senior contact came to the McKinney house and told Brian's mother, Margaret, not to worry; the pair was being questioned but would be released. Mrs. McKinney was concerned but expected to see her son soon. The stolen money had been returned to the pub owner days earlier, and he seemed to accept an apology.

The first day of their abduction passed with no word. Then the same IRA contact visited the house again. "He's still being questioned," he said. Another day passed: no news. Then another. As the days wore on Margaret McKinney did worry. She wondered how her son was being treated. Was he scared? Had he been beaten? Still, the same contact would visit and reassure her, and there seemed no reason for him to lie.

The IRA had been known to interrogate people for days. Even a week was not unheard of. But after ten days, Margaret suspected something was wrong and she was getting impatient. The contact seemed agitated, too, and one day changed his story. Now the family was told the two men were being exiled from Northern Ireland and that McKinney should pack a bag for her son because he was leaving on the ferry. She did as she was told and phoned relatives in England to let them know to expect Brian in a few days. Then she waited again. There was still no word. He never arrived in England, and when Margaret McKinney spoke to the contact again he ignored her. The IRA did not have Brian McKinney, he said.

Margaret McKinney was fearful, but what could she do? If she went to the police and Brian was alive, he might be killed. If the police investigated and he was already dead, the IRA might never tell what had happened. So she waited. Weeks turned into months and years with no word. Margaret McKinney was heartbroken. She used to lie in her son's bed, wrapped in his jacket, hoping that he would someday return.

Margaret McKinney was ready to speak out around the time the McKendrys went public. Together they formed "Families of the Disappeared" to campaign for the return of all the bodies, and their effort soon started to gain momentum. Seamus stubbornly continued his crusade, questioning anyone he thought might have answers and telling the world about their efforts. The group wrote to President Clinton, Nelson Mandela, anyone they thought could help.

Everyone made some sacrifices through the campaign. Most of the expenses from "Families of the Disappeared" came from the families themselves. It meant the McKendry children went without certain things. Margaret McKinney and the others gave up much of their time, but their efforts eventually yielded results. In 1995, the Royal Ulster Constabulary's Serious Crime Unit began a fresh police investigation into the disappeared.

Detective Sergeant Terry Brown, a twenty-year veteran of the force, led the new investigation, but before he could begin, Brown had to update the existing reports that still classified people like McConville as missing persons.

When McConville had first been reported missing in 1972, there was very little the police could do. It was a year of such instability in

Northern Ireland. Even Detective Brown, who like all police tends to understate the security situation, admitted, "If it was not civil war, it was not far from it."

Bombings and murder drove hundreds of people from their homes either seeking safety or fleeing from paramilitaries. It was impossible to keep track of all the people on the move.

Jean McConville was gone—the police knew that for sure—but there was no evidence that a crime had been committed. There were no willing witnesses, there was no body, and police resources were already stretched to the limit investigating crimes that were confirmed.

The case was never closed, but it had never properly been opened, either. Police were still investigating in the way they were still investigating dozens of unsolved murders and disappearances: Any new information was followed up, but the matter was no longer given specific attention. With no leads and no one clamoring for action, the case gathered dust for nearly thirty years. The same was true for the other disappeared cases. When the new investigation started, Helen asked to see the original file on her mother's disappearance. Inside a folder were a few sentences written on a single piece of paper.

Detective Brown measures victories in solved cases and convictions, but after spending some time investigating the disappeared he "would have been happy just to have the families get the bodies back." Heading the new investigation was a thoroughly frustrating ordeal. There were no new clues and, with so much time having passed, finding new forensic evidence seemed hopeless. Leads were cold, and while some people were more willing to speak than they had been in the past, they were recalling events that occurred a generation ago.

After questioning some suspects, Brown made some arrests and he was certain some of the conspirators were in custody. But with no corroborating evidence, there was little the police could do. The suspects knew that and did not cooperate. They were eventually released, but pressure was beginning to build and more people were getting involved.

Monsignor Denis Faul was once regarded as an IRA sympathizer. In the seventies, he was an advocate for the IRA suspects who had been tortured by the security forces during interrogation. But Monsignor

Faul proved to be a defender of all victims, and when the IRA did wrong, he could turn just as easily on them.

Monsignor Faul helped convince Helen McKendry to go public with her story. He had offered advice and counsel to other families of the disappeared and through his contacts applied pressure on the IRA where he could. He was trusted, and in 1997 a former IRA activist contacted him with some information about Jean McConville. The man said that he had been part of the team that interrogated McConville and that she had been accidentally asphyxiated with a plastic bag during questioning. The IRA had not meant to kill her, he said, so they panicked about how to dispose of the body.

The man did not know exactly where McConville was buried, only that several people took her body away on foot and returned in five minutes. She had been held in a house on Beechfield Avenue, he said, a street just off the Falls Road. New homes were going up in the area at the time. Her body could have been dropped anywhere in the building site. "The trouble was there are ninety-one homes in the area," Monsignor Faul said. "Which one is it?" The informer would not give any more information and was not heard from again.

But there were other tips. Police spent days searching a stretch of sidewalk in west Belfast with an X-ray scanner looking for the remains of John McClory and Brian McKinney. The IRA had not intended to kill the pair, the police had been told. One of them was shot trying to escape and the other was killed to eliminate the only witness.

The sidewalk was waste ground at the time of their abduction and could have served as a shallow grave, but the search proved fruitless. It became clear that precise information was essential. Without an exact site, searches could go on indefinitely. It was not enough to say a certain field; police needed to know at which end of the field, near what tree, specifically where. Given good intelligence, there was nothing modern technology could not find. The British and Irish governments promised to unearth the bodies wherever they were located. If that meant pulling up building foundations, so be it. But first they needed proper information to go on.

The McKendrys felt more secure living in Killyleagh. The country village was miles from their west Belfast tormentors, and the daily harassment ended. But there was still no progress, and the couple was becoming more strident. The IRA was ignoring them, so they turned their attention to Sinn Fein. By that time Sinn Fein had abandoned some of its militancy to become a mainstream political party, but the McKendrys wanted the movement to account for its past.

"They gave us a meeting to shut us up," Helen said. It was one step closer to the IRA, and the McKendrys pressed on. "When we got a meeting with Sinn Fein we said, 'Why talk to you, when you are not IRA men?' " Helen said. "We want a meeting with the IRA."

Whether the IRA felt a genuine pang of conscience or were responding to political pressure is impossible to say, but in late October 1998, the McKendrys got a phone call asking if Helen would come to Belfast for a meeting with the IRA. "The meeting is for Seamus, not for me," Helen replied. No. They would not meet Seamus. Only Helen. Alone. Helen was terrified. She knew the IRA's patience was waning. If she met them she would be completely vulnerable, just like her mother. It was like daring fate.

"My mother always taught me to stand up for something I believe in," Helen reminded herself and agreed to go. "What else could they do to me, these people?"

Helen met a contact and was taken to a safe house in west Belfast. She sat across the table from an IRA unit assigned to investigate the disappeared. Few words were exchanged. Helen was shaking. "For the first time ever, they admitted to me that they had killed my mother," Helen claimed, "and they tried to apologize for it."

McConville should never have been killed, they said, not like the other thieves and traitors. So why was Helen getting involved with the other disappeared cases, they asked, ones that were not guiltless like her mother? It was a matter of principle, she insisted, and then she asked them to make a public statement. "Okay, they admitted to me that they killed my mother, why not go public with it and tell the public what they did?"

The IRA was not willing to do that. The matter was going to be resolved on their own terms and without losing face. The men said they were making all efforts to find the bodies and would release the information soon.

Eamon Molloy was nineteen in the spring of 1975 when he went into hiding. The IRA wanted him as a suspected informer, and the security forces were after him, too. The Irish Republic must have seemed like a safe place to drop out of sight, so he left his west Belfast home and fled there. A few months later Molloy's brother was shot dead by loyalist gunmen while sitting in his living room. It was a risky time to come home, Molloy's mother knew, but she was surprised not to see Eamon at his brother's funeral.

It was just too dangerous for him to stay in touch, Molloy's mother told herself. He had to keep out of sight. As long as he was safe, she said, that was all that mattered. And through all the years she heard nothing, when decades passed without a word, that is what Mrs. Molloy told herself: He was safe.

Father Pat McCafferty is the Molloy family parish priest at the Sacred Heart Church in north Belfast and has served as spiritual advisor to many families of the disappeared. Mrs. Molloy knew about Father McCafferty's work but never spoke to him about her son because the "disappeared" did not involve her. Eamon Molloy was not dead; he was alive and well but in hiding, away from Northern Ireland, she insisted.

"She had her fears," McCafferty said, "but she always thought that he was somewhere." It was only when Eamon Molloy's name was included on the IRA's list of the disappeared that his mother accepted that he was gone. "Animated suspension" is how Father McCafferty described her grief.

When I met Father McCafferty in late May 1999, he was not wearing his clerical collar. He was dressed casually in a shirt and trousers, with a wooden crucifix around his neck. Not even forty years old, his unceremonious nature seemed the perfect antidote to a Catholic Church seen by many as formal and detached. He was at ease, utterly lacking pretension, but manifestly spiritual. He also seemed relieved. The IRA had promised to reveal the exact locations of the bodies by the end of the week.

Father McCafferty, or Father Pat as he prefers, met Helen and Seamus McKendry while serving at the Church of the Nazarean in Poleglass. They were his parishioners; he was their priest, yet for years he knew nothing about Jean McConville's disappearance. The McKendrys never brought it up. It had been the family's private burden until the campaign went public. When it did, Seamus McKendry asked for Father Pat's help. Father Pat agreed and served a mostly pastoral role.

For the first time, someone was attending to the families' emotional distress. The loved ones of the disappeared had never said good-bye. They needed that. One of the first things Father Pat McCafferty did was arrange a memorial service. It was held in Saint Mary's church in central Belfast. The Bishop was there. The families lit candles for their loved ones and read the names aloud. It was recognition, the first, of what had happened.

"It was a very moving service because the families had never had the opportunity to formally grieve, and a religious service is a way, a very powerful way, for people to do that," Father Pat said. "The point of the service was that to God they are not disappeared. God knows where they are." It let the grieving begin, but Father Pat knew there needed to be more.

An Irish wake, Father Pat explained, is an unusual event. It combines celebration and mourning and smirks at the ephemeral nature of life. "It allows people to cry and to lament and also to remember and to talk and to celebrate the person and be happy with friends."

For three days, the deceased's house is thrown open and mourners stream through. The family does not lift a finger, for the guests are forever pouring the tea and looking after them. Instead, they sit and receive the line of well-wishers. There is drinking, joking, crying, and storytelling, while choking sobs echo with raucous laughter. It is a solemn occasion but not without levity.

The coffin lies in the house through the wake and is treated with great reverence. Mourners are not ashamed of its presence. It is a part of the vigil. When the funeral nears, pallbearers carry the casket from home, to the church, to the burial site. During the funeral service, holy water is sprinkled over the coffin as a reminder of baptism. Burning incense wafts around its frame.

Such ritual is part of any grief and healing, but it is also distinctively Irish. "It is important for people to see, and touch, and be there in the presence of the body," Father Pat explained. He is familiar with bereavement. He understands how to relieve its burden.

Other families had a grave to visit. It proved that someone had lived. It said when they had died. The headstone confirmed that they had been loved. It sounds silly and petty to say, but some families of the disappeared were jealous that others had a place to put their flowers. A funeral and burial would allow the survivors to move on. Until then, while the bodies were unaccounted for, they could not stop searching.

Two days after I met Father Pat McCafferty, the first body, that of Eamon Molloy, was found. The IRA had disinterred the remains, put them in a coffin, and left them in a cemetery just over the Irish border. A local priest had been led through the ancient headstones to where the casket was hidden beneath the drooping branches of a laurel tree. The IRA said the other bodies were buried at sites around the Irish Republic—not in Belfast like many families had expected. Police had hoped to recover all the remains within a few days, but it was nearly two weeks into a fruitless search for Jean McConville when I visited the excavation site.

According to Irish legend, a prosperous landowner named O'Hanlon willed his fortune be split between his two surviving sons, but Conn, the eldest, hoarded the riches and left his younger brother, Lorcan, with a barren plot in the Cooley Mountains of County Louth. Destitute, Lorcan sought his fortune in Spain, where he met a beautiful noblewoman named Cauthleen. To win her hand, Lorcan boasted of his holdings in Ireland, but when Cauthleen reached his desolate mountain home, she dropped dead with despair. "The Long Woman's Grave" is said to lie somewhere in the Cooley Mountains. At their foot, near the coastal town of Carlingford, police were searching for Jean McConville.

Seamus and I had last spoken on the first day of the dig. It was a Saturday evening, and the family had been summoned to a seaside parking lot near Ballagan Point, a few miles south of Carlingford. Dusk was falling, and the sun was setting over the Cooley Mountains. His voice was unsteady and lacked its usual assurance. "We were told we would find her five feet underground," he said. "It should not be long now." It would be a matter of hours, he thought. By the end of the weekend for sure.

Days earlier, one of the men who had allegedly helped kidnap and bury Jean McConville pinpointed the spot with an intermediary. He walked to the edge of the parking lot, stood between two spaces, and marked an *X* in the asphalt. That was it, he said; that was where he had buried McConville. An X-ray scanner later picked up a "void" in the earth, indicating an oversized object, possibly human remains.

Police cut a few square yards of asphalt over the "void" and began to dig gingerly, careful not to upset the remains with McConville's children crowding around the hole. Everyone stood by expectantly, but their initial hope evaporated when, after digging several feet, the team found the boulder causing the "void." They were disappointed but continued the next day. Using the boulder as their marker, they slowly and deliberately pulled in the earth around it, tearing up more asphalt and disturbing the nearby dune. A few animal remains were found. More boulders and some household appliances were dug up, but nothing human.

As the days wore on, the family began to feel foolish for their initial confidence. It had been almost thirty years since McConville's abduction, they reminded themselves. She was probably buried at night by men who were scared, unfamiliar with the area, and had no plans to ever return. Even if they remembered exactly where they buried the body, it may have shifted through topographical changes. The parking lot being excavated was only seven years old, so pinpointing a spot was meaningless. The entire area was probably unrecognizable.

The McKendrys had fought so hard to get this far that they naïvely hoped fate would do the rest. As the dig continued, the emotional intensity gave way to tedium. Manual digging was no longer feasible, so cranes were used to reach the bedrock six feet down. Three men sifted through every bucket-load of earth in the ever-increasing hole. It was the size of an Olympic swimming pool the day I arrived. The first boulder, still sitting at the bottom of the site, punctuated the desperation.

Helen looked sanguine despite her exhaustion. The coastal sun and breeze had colored her face. Her thick blond hair unfolded to her shoulders. Expecting to find her haggard, I was struck by her poise. But she could not mask her anxiety, and the long wait was taking an emotional toll. An occasional smoker, she was going through several packs a day.

Seamus was back to his cheerful self, but he seemed strained. Helen was becoming depressed, he thought, and not getting enough rest. She had rarely seen her siblings before this ordeal, but they were all there at the dig site and petty differences were beginning to resurface. A British television crew was filming a documentary, and she was not always happy about that, either.

Standing next to a mound of excavated earth, Helen, Seamus, and I spoke about the last few days. "Local people have been brilliant," they agreed. "Really, they have been very supportive." Each day strangers arrived with kind words for the family or to sign a book of remembrance. In the evenings, a nearby priest often held a short service. Their concern was poignant, but hope was fading. Even the police, who began with undaunted determination, had started to examine their efforts more critically.

The Carlingford dig was based on a lead. If the lead was worthless, they may as well quit. Helen knew that, too. Her feelings were manifest. I did not need to probe her wounds to see that she was frustrated and disappointed. Words were needless, and they had all been spent. The only question was what Helen would do if the body were not found. I could not bring myself to ask. "I am convinced we are at the right spot," she said.

Seamus and I left Helen and strolled along the beach. The digging team was having their lunch, so the machinery was quiet but the tons of earth it had extracted formed an impressive mound next to the parking lot. The soil, sifted to the grain, was fine powder. "We have hardly left here since the digging started," Seamus said sullenly. A local man had opened his house for the family to stay as long as they needed, but Seamus was "trying to convince Helen to come home for a while," he said. Their kids were on their own at the house.

It was difficult to pry Helen away from the site. Even when they went into town for lunch she would want to hurry back, saying, "I don't like to be away for too long." Until her mother was found, Helen's time was not her own. It was as if she were attending to a sick relative. There was little she could do to help, but she felt guilty being away.

As we walked around the scene, Seamus and I stepped over the cluttered debris that had been pulled out of the hole: a rusty wheel rim, a washing machine, twisted bits of metal. Seamus pointed towards the dunes on the other side of the hole. "The other day," he said, "when the lads were on their lunch, I was over there reading when I thought I saw something in the hole." It was a glint of white; Seamus's heart skipped a beat. He dropped his book, scampered down to the spot, fell to his knees, and started brushing away the dirt. It was a bone. "They all came in after me." Seamus laughed. "I think they would have been embarrassed if I ended up finding the body." When they dug away the area they found another animal carcass. "That is the way it has been the last few days," Seamus said.

At five other sites across the country, other families were going through the same thing. They stayed in touch and prayed for one another. No other bodies had been found, but the McKendrys were told their search was the most promising. The beach was relatively easy to excavate, and the information had been fairly specific while other digs were more desperate. One was in the middle of a forest; another was at a bog where pumps had to draw thousands of gallons of water just to clear the area. No. If there was to be success, police were confident it would come at Carlingford.

Seamus gathered some stones and erected a small altar around a ceramic Sacred Heart of Jesus figurine, candle, and small bottle of holy water to lift Helen's spirits. The IRA had not deliberately misled them, he said. Even looking at the circumstances cynically, it was in the IRA's interests for a discovery to come as soon as possible. As the digs went on, the media had vengefully turned on the IRA for failing to end the families' ordeal. Seamus was not sympathetic, but he understood how they might have honestly, if mistakenly, thought their information was good enough. "If you and I came out here one night and sat out in those dunes," he said, "and then came back two days later, there is no way we would find where we sat." They just needed more time.

"The [Irish Police] have promised that they will dig up the rest of the parking lot," Seamus said. "That should bring us to the end of June." After that, there were no promises. Seamus and Helen used to think that time was on their side. That once it started, there was only one possible ending: that the body would be found. Now they were forced to consider what they would do if the police stopped searching. They had contemplated continuing the search themselves—raising the money on their own to keep digging. "We have looked into it," Seamus said, "getting the money together." It sounded rash, but the family was convinced they were at the right spot. McConville might be found with the next shovelful, or she might be fifty yards away. They would only know how close they had come once she was found.

On the first full day of searching, police cordoned off the site in a chain-link fence wrapped in a blue tarp for privacy. Crime tape was hung around the perimeter. It was a police investigation, after all, but it gave the scene a morbid sense of gloom. The resting place of Jean McConville was transformed from a placid stretch of beach into a sterile mine where police worked diligently but with indifference. When Helen's sister Mary wove a rose stem through the chinks in the fence, there was a small reminder of why everyone had gathered. In the next few days, more flowers were added to the single red bud, and the impersonal partition was transformed into a touching tribute. Hypercium polyps were wound with baby's breath. White September was tied with coarse twine. Carnation sprays were twisted through the fence. Bunches of orange gerbera were tucked into the gaps like sunbursts. "To Jean," read the message folded among a batch of red carnations, "whose only crime was kindness."

"Jean. So sorry we stood idly by," signed a family in Derry. Helen hoped the flowers might survive until the funeral, but as new bouquets arrived the verdant petals of the old began to wilt. The condolence messages became rain-smudged and runny. The tattered bouquets were a mildly depressing reminder of how long the search had been going on.

Finally, ten weeks into their search, police found a body. It was not Jean McConville, but John McClory, buried with Brian McKinney in a peat bog in County Monaghan. At the time, some of the searches had already been halted. Police were just days away from abandoning their hunt for the two men when the discovery was made. The McKendrys were initially elevated by the news; it proved that the IRA had given accurate information. The search at Carlingford went on for another few days, but it, too, was eventually abandoned. There was simply not enough information to justify a protracted dig. Police promised to return if there was any fresh information. Of the sixteen disappeared cases, only three bodies were ever recovered.

On December 7, 1999, the twenty-seventh anniversary of Jean McConville's disappearance, her children returned to Carlingford. The diggers and bulldozers were no longer there, and the massive hole had been refilled. As she had done every week since the dig was halted, Helen McKendry attended to the flowers left at the scene and said a prayer. She did not know whether the dig would ever resume, but that desolate stretch of beach was where her long journey ended.

Freedom Corner

⊓   ⊓

There was a loyalist mural at the end of my street that local people called "Freedom Corner." It stretched the length of four apartment blocks, about a hundred yards, and marked the edge of UFF-controlled territory. Across the street was the Avenue One Bar, the UFF's local hostelry. Adjacent to that was the grandly named Post-Conflict Resettlement Office, the UFF's local aid and advice center for former prisoners. Frankie Gallagher, a man whose ruddy nose resembled a strawberry and who wore his graying hair in a bouffant, worked there.

One afternoon, I dropped by Gallagher's office. It was cramped and drafty, with damp crawling up the walls. The Post-Conflict Resettlement Office was nearly broke, Gallagher said. Loyalist groups had always struggled for money, but Gallagher was expecting a change of fortune.

Some distinguished foundations were taking an interest in Northern Ireland, and scholars from around the world were being dispatched to study life in the province, find out how people here were going about reconciliation, and then teach them how to do it right. Some of the new ideas must have caught on because, before long, community workers who had never finished school were talking about "redemptive processes" and "transforming conflict." When the foundations looked for worthy projects to fund, anything that brought Protestants and Catholics together or gave former prisoners something new and productive to do with their time found favor. Frankie Gallagher told me that his group had just come into a cash windfall under those parameters and some of his members were going on a retreat, a "self-actualization session," he called it, to discuss what was to be done with the money.

I joined about twenty former UFF prisoners, prisoners' wives, and their children for a weekend at the Corrymeela ecumenical center. Situated on the edge of Northern Ireland's rugged Antrim coast, Corrymeela is tucked away in one of the most isolated and inhospitable corners of the province, but during the Troubles it was one of the few places where Protestants and Catholics could meet one another in safety. Children from rival urban ghettos, families, even members of warring paramilitary groups went there to talk about their differences and shared experiences, work through their prejudices, and even make friends. Anyone who saw an emotional exchange at Corrymeela or the ambitious plans for peace that were mapped out on napkins over a communal dinner could be excused for thinking that progress was being made. It seemed that if everyone could go there, the Troubles would be over for sure. But breakthroughs at Corrymeela were often short-lived, because everyone eventually packed their bags and went home to where the lessons they learned would only alienate them from their own community.

Frankie Gallagher was turning the pages of a flip chart and giving a lecture about conflict resolution. Phrases like "ideological perspective," "conforming history," and "restorative justice" seemed to fit uncomfortably in Gallagher's mouth, while my heavily tattooed neighbors fumigated the room with cigarette smoke and sipped Pernod or whatever other alcohol they had snuck into the compound. Jaci, whom I recognized as the clerk in the liquor store back in Belfast, heckled Frankie while the rest of the women sniggered. A rotund American caretaker occasionally entered the room with a smile, cleared the brimming ashtrays, and politely tried to ignore the blue language and booze.

Later, when Gallagher finished his lecture, the men crowded around the floor plans of the new, centrally heated Post-Conflict Resettlement Office to be built with a generous foreign grant. It was around that time that I noticed Jim Neill. He was sitting in the corner of the room, his young son was playing at his feet, and he had a vague look on his face like he was thinking about nothing, nothing at all.

Ten years earlier, Jim Neill had killed a Catholic. He was a man of rather faint conviction himself, but he had gotten involved with Johnny Adair's gang and had shot a Catholic father who was standing on the doorstep of his own home. Jim went to prison and had just recently been released. He was not really sorry for what he had done, Jim said, because there was no point living with regret. And he could not say that he was resentful about how his life had turned out since it was just about all that he had expected from his life and no worse than many other people that he knew. But then Jim told me something that must have come from a place deep inside himself because he said it with fervor, and he did not impress me as a man capable of mustering false emotion. He said he could live with the things that he had done, but it did not make sense that his son should have to go through it, too. That was why Jim was on the retreat; he did not want his son to ever go to jail.

Bloody Sunday

❐   ❐

n the corner of the Bloody Sunday Centre, a television plays a constant loop of black-and-white news film. There are scenes of protesters walking en masse. Banners rise and unfurl. Young people, the elderly, mothers pushing buggies, and men in suits stroll in a jovial mood. They are bundled for the cold, but the sun is steadily shining. In fleeting glimpses, the camera scans some of the marchers who, minutes later, will be dead. Their faces beam momentarily and then pass out of sight.

All is peaceful, and then the marchers hit a wall of army and police. The crowd pulsates. The security forces are fixed. The film lingers on that eerie moment of tension and inevitability. Then, suddenly, young men emerge from the crowd, their faces covered, hurling stones over the barricade. Army and police hold the line, wait for the attack to subside, and then let loose a volley of tear gas and rubber bullets. Water cannons are turned on the crowd. Suddenly people are vomiting and choking in the haze.

All at once, armored cars batter through the line and skid down the street. Protesters flee. Troops debark. Soldiers take aim and fire at some unseen target. The streets empty. Women are yelling; gunfire crackles. A priest attends to a wounded boy, blood streaming from his face. An ambulance screeches to a halt. Medics urgently dash around the scene. Lifeless bodies are carried away like rag dolls. Fatigued soldiers march civilians away at gunpoint. Then there is calm. People wander around, dazed. A stray dog licks a blood-soaked banner crumpled in a heap. Suddenly, the film snaps and sputters off.

I saw that film on my first trip to Derry in the autumn of 1999. At the time, everything I knew about Bloody Sunday could have been summed up in about three sentences. Soldiers of the British army's parachute regiment shot and killed thirteen Catholics on the streets of Derry on Sunday, January 30, 1972. Fourteen more people were wounded. It was a seminal event of the conflict, an opening volley of a war that would go on for another quarter century.

I had picked up that much through casual conversations and what passed for general knowledge. The details, though, were just as disputed as they had been when that grainy footage was filmed and the British army had to explain how a peaceful civil rights march had turned into a scene of carnage. None of the immediate answers were very good, so the British government hastily convened an official inquiry. Ostensibly, the aim was to find out what had really happened on Bloody Sunday, but in authorizing the inquiry, Ted Heath, then British prime minister, reminded his staff that they "were in Northern Ireland fighting not only a military war but a propaganda war."

Two days after Bloody Sunday, Lord Widgery, the British lord chief justice, was appointed to head the official inquiry into the shooting. When some observers in Derry learned that Widgery was a landed English gentleman and former British army officer, they suspected that the inquiry would be a whitewash. When they saw the perfunctory way in which Widgery proceeded, all doubt was removed.

Hearings were held in the modestly appointed Coleraine County Hall, about thirty miles from Derry, and after 114 witnesses had given their testimony over seventeen days, Widgery produced his findings. In a thirty-nine-page-long report, Widgery, almost without exception, exonerated the British army and supported their claims that soldiers had fired at IRA gunmen and bombers. More than that, Widgery suggested that the protesters had brought the violence on themselves by providing cover for the IRA.

Derry's Catholic community never expected Lord Widgery to

condemn the army's action. Still, many found Widgery's methods and conclusions bewildering. Why had hundreds of witness statements—many from priests, doctors, and even former British soldiers—been ignored? How could Widgery conclude that the army came under sustained IRA fire when not one soldier was wounded, and no illegal guns were recovered? Five of the victims were shot in the back. One man was shot while crawling on his hands and knees to safety. Did that square with army claims that the victims were IRA gunmen? But no answers were forthcoming. The Widgery Report was the final word on Bloody Sunday, and it hung over the Catholics of Derry like a badge of ignominy.

"The British were the first to tell the story and, as you know, the first story is the one people believe," John Kelly, whose brother Michael was killed on Bloody Sunday, explained. "Because of Widgery, our people were known all over the world as gunmen and bombers. People say that we should just forget about it, but we can't. This event was so much a part of people's lives. Not just for the people who were killed and their families, but for the people wounded and the witnesses. They all were affected by the event. They all have questions that they want answered. We want to get on with our lives as best we can, but the point is that we cannot get on with our lives until we know the truth."

And that is what drew me to Derry in 1999. On the twenty-sixth anniversary of Bloody Sunday the British prime minister, Tony Blair, had announced a tribunal that would establish the truth about what happened on that day, and he named a new British magistrate, Lord Saville, to oversee the proceedings.

The place to start was where the last inquiry left off, so all the old Widgery papers needed to be collected, sifted through, and studied. Relevant parties needed to find counsel and prepare their cases. Relevant witnesses needed to be contacted. If the inquiry was to be done right—and it had to be done right—then it was going to take time. Lord Saville had spent two years preparing the new tribunal by the time I arrived in Derry and he had been accommodating, exceptionally accommodating, from the outset. All evidence, no matter how small, and all leads, no matter how cumbersome, were being pursued. He imparted no time limit for reaching conclusions, and apparently he had no budget constraint.

Before the inquiry even opened, over twelve million dollars had been spent; over 70,000 pages of documentary evidence, thirty-six hours of videotape, thirteen hours of audiotape, over 5,000 photographs, and other exhibits had been compiled, tagged, and organized. Stenographers, reportedly using technology that was developed during the O. J. Simpson trial, were posting hearing transcripts to an official Web page. Because some key buildings had been demolished since Bloody Sunday, a computer-generated simulation was devised to recreate the scene. A battery of forensic experts had been commissioned, and the witness testimony alone—which may surpass one thousand—was expected to take months.

The survivors and relatives of those killed on Bloody Sunday helped uncover much of the new evidence and they were the driving force behind the fresh inquiry. The Bloody Sunday Centre—the large, formerly disused office building set just inside the ancient walls that surrounded Derry's city center—served as their headquarters. The ground floor was maintained for the public. On the second floor, the families' legal teams worked on their cases. On that first visit I saw attorneys frantically scuttling up and down the stairs, across the cobblestones of Shipsquay Street, through the granite portal leading to Guildhall Square, and up the stairs of the Guildhall.

If the Bloody Sunday march had passed peacefully, it would have ended at the foot of Derry's venerable Guildhall. Situated between the river Foyle and the city's defensive ramparts, the Guildhall was conceived as a Victorian commemoration of the seventeenth-century London artisans, apprentices, and guilds that saw the city reborn. It was a rebirth of industry, but also of controversy—not only because the new Protestant city fathers pushed the native Irish Catholics into the rural hinterland, but also because they rechristened the town "Londonderry."

The IRA nearly leveled that perceived monument of oppression when, as their bombing campaign intensified in the months after Bloody Sunday, they detonated two five-hundred-pound bombs in the Guildhall. But while the explosions cast a five and a half ton marble statue of Queen Victoria through the vestibule's stained glass windows and all but destroyed the Guildhall's ground floor, the grand hall on the second floor was largely unscathed.

At the head of the grand hall, Lord Saville sat at an elevated desk between the two other jurists—one Canadian, one New Zealander—who made up the rest of the tribunal.

It was a remarkable setting. The wall behind the men was braced by hundreds of stained glass windows. Over three thousand leaden and wooden organ pipes rose in tiers against the wall to their left. The ceiling fixtures were carved from California redwood, and the side paneling was solid oak. White-haired and wizened all, the three men who would oversee one of the most complicated proceedings in British legal history looked like suitable additional fixtures to such a classical room.

Against that backdrop, the whirring clutter of computers and television screens, the coiling microphone cables and piles of legal briefs that covered the main floor offered a marked contrast. That is where the lawyers worked, and there were well over a dozen of them—counsel for the victims' families in general and individually, the military, soldiers who had fired live rounds, those who had not, the media, the police, and finally, representatives for the inquiry itself. Some of Britain's greatest legal minds were working on the case, and a cordon of clerks and researchers were on hand to assist. The seating arrangement was so complex that a chart was devised to help people tell who was who.

Saville had given plenty of time for attorneys to prepare their cases, but he was clearly growing impatient. Evidence was still being gathered; fundamental procedural matters were yet unresolved. Saville had reluctantly postponed the official opening of the inquiry until the spring, but this was the last week to resolve any outstanding issues. Because there was so much business, proceedings stretched from morning till dusk. Attorneys blustered for hours in what, for those unfamiliar with legal theatrics, was often a baffling display.

"That is your first point," Lord Saville told Edwin Glasgow, a solicitor acting for the soldiers. "The second point is if it is too early to decide, nevertheless the soldiers must remain anonymous. Otherwise we preempt the decision."

"No, the first point is the submission has to be made because it follows," Glasgow replied. "The second is a timing point. If it does have to be reconsidered on its merits, it is too early to do it until one has seen the prima facie of these evidence is of the role played by individuals or of individuals."

Along a lone bench in the back of the hall, the survivors and families of those killed were seated. They watched as the personal pain and anguish of Bloody Sunday was bound in legal jargon and questions of jurisprudence. They did not fully grasp every legal maneuver, many admitted, but this was where their long fight for truth had brought them. This was the beginning of the end of their ordeal.

Getting to the truth was surely a noble aim, I thought, sitting in the public gallery later that day, but I also had misgivings. Would anyone actually recognize the truth if they saw it—particularly when so many people claimed to already know what they would find? Depending on whom I spoke to, the victims of Bloody Sunday were either IRA gunmen or innocent civilians. Opinions were split, not surprisingly, roughly along religious and political lines. It was a situation that I found so commonplace I wondered if truth itself had a denomination.

Or did the truth still even exist? Whatever could be known about Bloody Sunday had already been trod upon by the original Widgery investigation and then buried under more than a quarter century of time. Any knowledge to be sifted from so many disputed facts, past distortions, and foggy memories would surely be incomplete. In the end, truth or not, the new inquiry would only end up with a fresh narrative of events. How was that an improvement?

And, of course, the truth is nothing if it is not put to use. The first thing that the survivors and relatives of those killed wanted from the new inquiry was exoneration. Any evidence that would discredit military and political leaders of the time would also be welcomed, and for some families, it was hoped that Saville's conclusions would lead to murder charges against some of the soldiers. Not surprisingly, members of the political and military establishment were hoping for something closer to the status quo—conclusions that would put the Bloody Sunday matter to rest while leaving them relatively unscathed.

But despite these complications, Saville was almost universally acknowledged as working in good faith. In that regard, the inquiry would
become one of the early gifts of the peace process: a clear-minded reckoning of deeply controversial events.

The inquiry was not self-serving revisionism. The British government's willingness to convene a new inquiry was a preface to an
apology to the victims. As the Saville inquiry took shape, it was becoming clear that one of the simplest truths would also be one of the most
potent: that Bloody Sunday involved many ordinary people caught in
extraordinary circumstances. Ordinary people are flawed; they can be
well-meaning, but also naïve. Ordinary people make decisions out of
frustration, fear, hope, and despair or take action without knowing exactly where that action will lead. And once history and providence have
conspired, they often watch with indifference as other ordinary people
are helplessly carried away.

Newly uncovered documents and other evidence to emerge from
the Saville inquiry have helped expose the heroes and villains of
Bloody Sunday, but so has it revealed a cruel symmetry to the lives that
were once lived in desperate antagonism. Mixed in with stone-throwing
youths and callow British soldiers, political and military strategists, civil
rights organizers, and paramilitary groups were people of good intention who made bad judgments and opportunists who exploited the
situation to their own advantage. Many people, most people really, tried
but failed to stay out of the way.

Bloody Sunday did not begin when the first shots were fired. The
roots of that day were set deep in the history of Northern Ireland—and
its legacy would last for a generation. Father Edward Daly, a priest who
gave last rites to several of the dead on Bloody Sunday, became an em-
blematic symbol of the Troubles when, with a blood-soaked handker-
chief, he beseeched soldiers to clear the way for bodies being carried to
an ambulance. Time and again on prison visits in the years that followed, Father Daly heard prisoners say that, but for what they witnessed or heard about Bloody Sunday, they would not have gotten
involved in the conflict.

In that way Bloody Sunday stands with South Africa's Sharpeville,

India's Amritsar, and the Boston Massacre in America—state atrocities that radicalized a mass movement.

But before Bloody Sunday was a tragedy of historic proportions, it was a personal tragedy. For Helen, Maura, and Leo Young, Bloody Sunday is not the day that the British army shot twenty-seven people on the streets of Derry; it is the day that their brother John was killed. Private 027 (so designated by the Saville Inquiry) watched his colleagues carry out the carnage. This is a tale of how such lives collide. John Young's story comes from his siblings. Private 027's account comes from his official submission to the Saville Inquiry. The rest of the details have been largely sifted from the wealth of Saville's recently uncovered evidence.

Derry, Northern Ireland's second largest city, is tucked away in the corner of the province, seventy miles northwest of Belfast, over the Sperrin Mountains and across the Bann River—the customary demarcation that officially puts it outside Belfast's influence. The first known settlement in the area was a monastery founded by Saint Columba in the fifth century, which he called *Doire*—Irish for "oak grove." That, Catholics claim, is the historic birth of the distinctively Irish city of Derry. Geographically, since the city center lies on the west bank of the Foyle River, the natural border with the Irish county of Donegal, and demographically, since Catholics have traditionally outnumbered Protestants, that claim is strong.

Protestants trace the city's founding to the artisans who arrived in the early seventeenth century, built mighty walls around a colonial outpost, and called the place Londonderry. The city prospered as a hub for Protestant plantation farmers and merchants before it was tempered by the historic siege of 1689. Catholic King James II had been dethroned by Protestant King William of Orange in Britain's Glorious Revolution, and had plans to capture the city as a step to regaining his crown. But when a group of Londonderry's young apprentice boys saw soldiers approaching the city, they shut the gates. Over seven thousand Protestants took refuge inside Londonderry's walls. When after thirteen weeks of sustained artillery bombardment, starvation, and disease the city was relieved two thousand survivors emerged. Londonderry became the Maiden City in Protestant folklore—a symbol of their defiance and sacrifice. The siege was over; the siege mentality persisted.

Protestant control of the city has always been precarious, while Catholic designs on it remain unfulfilled. It says something about the ambiguous nature of the city that even its name is undecided—Catholics unanimously call the city Derry; Protestants generally refer to it as Londonderry. They do not so much share a city as occupy a place with an uncertain, almost schizophrenic identity. Precariously straddling the Foyle River, a nameless town with an impossibly complicated history, Derry/Londonderry suppressed its natural impulse for violence, mostly through political gerrymandering and discrimination that disempowered Catholics.

Past the narrow, marshy, flood-prone valley to the west of Derry's walls, up the steeply rising hills where King James launched his siege of the city, stretches an area that has traditionally been Derry's largest Catholic ghetto: The valley is known as the Bogside and the hills are called the Creggan. Thomas and Lily Young raised five of their children—Patrick, Eilish, Helen, Leo, and Maura—in that area from the early 1930s. The young family and their neighbors were poor but shared an acute sense of communal solidarity. They could not rely on the state, so they relied on each other. Without a house of their own, the Young family did what was customary and moved among the already overcrowded homes of friends and family. Sometimes they all stayed in the same house; sometimes they had to separate. But wherever they stayed, it was only as living room tenants because that was where they would wake, dress, eat, socialize, and sleep. Conditions were often so cramped that they could stoke the fire without getting out of bed.

The Young family began the slow ascent out of poverty when they moved into a tin hut in Springtown Camp—a compound left behind by American soldiers after World War II. There was no electricity; gas lanterns were used for light. Still, it was the first place of their own. By 1959, when the family was allotted a three-bedroom house at 120 Westway perched on a hillcrest in the Creggan, four of the Young children—

Eilish, Patrick, Helen, and Leo—had moved out to start families of their own. Only Maura, the youngest girl, and John, the new baby brother just five years old, were left in the house. When they moved in, Maura remembers, John gleefully ran up and down the stairs switching the electric lights on and off in amazement. He had been born on the wooden floor of the Springtown hut, but he would never have to endure the privation his siblings had known.

A stocky boy, exceptionally tall, broad shouldered, and in robust health, John Young cut an imposing figure from an early age. He always seemed a bit older than his contemporaries and someone who, at first glance, would have appeared to be an able athlete. But John Young was somewhat ungainly with his size and not inclined to sports. In fact, he was more of a sensitive boy with a wistful, slightly detached nature that he wore awkwardly as a child but that he grew into as an adolescent, around the time that he grew into his looks—an open, handsome face and thick, dark hair.

In the neighborhood, John had many friends; at school, he was known as a bright student. Family life was settled, and as the youngest child, he got plenty of attention. Had John Young not been living in a Catholic ghetto, he might have taken more interest in his education. Instead, he quit school at fifteen and started working at John Temple's, a men's clothier in Derry's city center, first as a stock boy but later as a sales clerk where he would fit customers for their tailored shirts and suits.

John's older brother Leo delivered coal in the area; Maura was a seamstress in a garment factory. John was good at his job and glad to be working in a more salubrious setting than his siblings. He was never pretentious about it—friends and family would have cut him down to size if he had been—but John was a conscientious observer of men's fashion. Maura remembers him appraising the style sense of celebrities of the time. "He'd look at somebody on television and say, 'I like that revere, but maybe not out as far as that.' Or he'd say that somebody's jacket would be better with a vent so many inches up the back."

The best thing about working was what it let John do in his free time. Living at home meant no rent, no bills, and few responsibilities.

John was free to enjoy his adolescence and indulge his whims, which, at that age, were girls and rock and roll. "He had his own room, with a record player and stacks of records," says Maura. "After work, he would go in there and just listen to the Beatles for ages."

At that same time John's sister, Helen, shared a two-bedroom house with her husband, their five children, and another couple. There was an outside toilet and no running water. When Helen went to the Derry Corporation to request a larger house she was told there was nothing available—maybe she'd have a chance if she tried again in seven years. At the same time, a newlywed Protestant friend with no children applied for housing and was granted a three-bedroom house. And that sort of thing happened all the time.

Catholics outnumbered Protestants in Derry by two to one, yet Protestants controlled the city council, which favored Protestants in public housing. Since only property owners could vote, Catholics were disenfranchised. The same corrupt system operated to maintain Protestant control of Stormont, Northern Ireland's parliament.

Religion and politics held no interest for John Young—not when he had so many other diversions. But Helen knew the hardships that their parents had gone through to raise a family; she was determined not to endure the same herself. Catholic discontent, that kinetic energy, had been building for generations. The inevitable backlash started in Derry and was patterned after the civil rights movement among American blacks that was going on at the same time. Students, liberals, and Catholics of all classes marched and sang "We Shall Overcome."

"Now I was at most of the main marches," Helen remembered. "I was not an active member of the civil rights movement, but if I heard of a march, I went to it. For me, it was about 'one man, one vote' and better housing conditions. I had five daughters at the time, and I wanted—when they got married—that they could put their name down on the list and get a house. I was very determined about that."

Northern Ireland had never seen anything like the Catholic civil rights marches, which is partly why so many people found them unsettling. The campaign began peacefully, steadfastly so, but that did not last long. Neither the politicians who ruled the province nor the Protestant-dominated security forces that maintained order understood the sort of change that was afoot, but they were afraid and tried to stop it. Many civil rights marches were banned.

In January 1969, in a march that was inspired by the American civil rights walk from Montgomery to Selma, Alabama, Catholic civil rights activists walked from Belfast to Derry. At Burntollet Bridge on the outskirts of Derry, a Protestant gang ambushed the marchers, attacking them with wooden planks, cudgels, iron bars, rocks—anything that they could get their hands on. The few police who were there to escort the march might have recognized some off-duty colleagues among the attackers. Thirteen people were hospitalized—an improbably modest casualty toll compared to what would come, but notable for its time.

The Burntollet attack sparked off the first widespread rioting. Derry was the crucible, but the unrest spread to Belfast and across the province. For the first time in a long time, the British government in London began to scrutinize events in Northern Ireland. The Protestant regime at Stormont had resisted pressure for election reform but, under orders from London, they began to relent, as Catholics dismissed the proposed measures as too meager, while Protestants saw them as too ambitious. In the meantime, the political and security situation was quickly unraveling. One more tug and the province would come undone.

Thousand of Protestants from around Northern Ireland arrived in Derry on August 12 for an annual commemoration of the lifting of the 1689 siege of Londonderry. They marched around the city's ancient walls in a coat-trailing exercise that had been long sanctioned by time and tradition. But times had changed. When the march skirted the Bogside, it touched off a riot that continued unabated for forty-eight hours. Over one thousand police operating with armored cars and water cannons tried to subdue the crowd but—choking on their own tear gas and staggering from a barrage of rioters' stones—the police relented.

Two days later, James Callaghan, the British home secretary, ordered a company of the Prince of Wales Own Regiment to Derry; a day later, troops were on the streets of Belfast, too. It was the first time that the British army had been sent to deal with unrest in Northern Ireland—one of many precedents that were dramatically set, only to quickly fade into insignificance as violence escalated. At the time, there were about two thousand British troops in Northern Ireland. By 1971, that number would increase to seven thousand; a year later, it hit nine thousand. The British army was in Northern Ireland to stay, and they quickly took over the police's security role.

No one knew it yet, but the Troubles had started. John Young, a precocious adolescent in 1969, kept a meticulous diary of his adventures for that year in a small, red leather school calendar embossed in gold lettering "St. Mary's Girls School," which he had pinched from his sister Maura. It is the sort of handy notebook that fit neatly in John's back pocket, which, because of the personal stories it held, is exactly where it stayed.

The diary charts the flourish and demise of romance, carefree nights on the town, and friendships made, broken, and mended again. One Thursday, John walked Kay home. He decided to give her up over the weekend, and by Monday she was with Liam. John's nights out would typically begin or end at the Stardust, a dance hall in the Bogside. That much is clear from the diary, though there's no explanation for the eight girls listed in the back binding or what merited the series of checks next to their names. Years after John's death, Maura discovered that "nothing unusual," a common passage, was a footnote for another, more personal diary that was never found.

Of all the things that John Young chronicles in his diary, the omissions are notable. John dances at the Stardust while civil rights activists march the streets of Derry. He dreams of the Beatles and police ransack a house down the street. When John escorted a girlfriend home, he must have seen some of his neighbors erecting makeshift barricades to repel the police, but he did not put a word of it in his journal. In a year of infinite freedom, the vagaries of life can go unnoticed or are easily ignored. Nothing could penetrate John Young's world of innocence and exuberance—not even the soldiers on the streets, who were at first welcomed by Northern Ireland Catholics.

"Wee women and girls would bring tea out to the soldiers at their checkpoints," Maura remembered. "Things seemed to quiet down for a while." The army presence did curb the unrest for a time, but in the absence of political reform, soldiers were soon seen as an agent of the status quo. Goodwill evaporated, resentment grew, and Catholics became impatient. Civil rights activists found that their campaign had inadvertently awoken a more powerful force. A dormant republican spirit, a yearning for a united Ireland that had been lying just beneath the surface, emerged with a vengeance.

"Our campaign was absolutely not a question of nationalism," says Eamonn McCann, an early leader of the civil rights movement. "The key to our strategy was really mass action. We were trying to get social change by getting people out onto the streets, but we vastly underestimated the capacity of the state for savagery and oppression. We also underestimated the burden of history."

Before the civil rights campaign started, the IRA had been a spent force without resources or a rally cry. But as the unrest intensified, many young Catholics were growing angry, disillusioned, and eager to lash out. The IRA's simple message—that the British were to blame and needed to be forced out of Ireland—began to resonate. Many young men felt compelled to join.

But even the IRA could not decide exactly what to do next. The traditional wing of the IRA, known as the Official IRA, saw the conflict in Northern Ireland as a class struggle against British colonialism. In rhetoric at least, they wanted to emancipate all workers, Protestants and Catholics, from the chains of oppression. Official IRA activists split their time between weapons training and lectures in revolutionary theory. In one episode, an official IRA unit in Derry raided a shoe shop and "liberated" one thousand pairs of shoes for distribution to the poor.

But most young men had no time for such high-minded abstraction; they wanted to know how to hurt the British, and they wanted the weapons to do it right. The Provisional IRA, a more militant force, became Northern Ireland's first guerrilla army. They aimed to make Northern Ireland ungovernable. In Derry, the IRA launched attacks against the security forces. At the height of their bombing campaign, Eamonn McCann describes, Derry looked as if it had been bombed from the air.

Catholic opinion in Derry was divided. On the one hand were the civil rights campaigners, trying to change the state from within. On the other hand was the IRA, trying to drive the British out.

Whenever possible, civil rights campaigners tried to remain utterly untainted by the IRA. Their quarrel was with the government and the politicians, not the soldiers on the street. But each army transgression seemed to push people to the extremes. In early July 1971, the British army shot and killed two unarmed rioters, Seamus Cusack and Desmond Beattie, in the Bogside. They were the first two civilians to die at the hands of the army in Derry. "As often predicted, there has been a tragic inevitability about the way things have gone," Brigadier Alan Cowan, head of British forces in Derry, noted at the time. "Oversimplifying, we handed the IRA on a plate on 7 and 8 of July what had been denied them for eighteen months, i.e. we were sucked in, used our weapons for the first time in Derry and turned the population against us and towards the IRA.... We have in effect broken rule one in the internal security book; instead of having a friendly population, or at least one which practices benevolent neutrality, we now face an entirely hostile community."

Militancy was in the ascendancy. In 1970, there were 213 shootings in Northern Ireland and 153 explosions. A year later, the totals were 1,765 and 1,022, respectively. The IRA began to organize and recruit more openly, so the Stormont government responded with a policy of internment of anyone suspected of being a member of the IRA. The idea was to apprehend leading IRA figures and hold them until the crisis had passed, but the operation was plagued by poor intelligence. On August 9, 1971, in predawn raids across the province, the police and army set out to capture over 400 IRA activists. Only 342 were actually arrested, and over 100 of them were released two days later. The rest were held in the prison ship *Maidstone* in Belfast Lough and the Long Kesh prison camp outside Belfast.

"They were held at 'Her Majesty's Pleasure,'" Helen Young described. "Which meant they might never get out. If they were charged with having arms, or even being a member of the IRA, they had a release date. If not, they were there to whatever the hell time. That was the thing about internment: next it could be your brother, husband, or father. My husband worked for a well-known republican who was interned, so there was a good chance, by association, that he would be interned as well."

As a security and political exercise, internment was a disaster. In the six months after internment was introduced, there was a threefold increase in explosions, a sixfold increase in shootings, and an over eightfold increase in civilian deaths. The Catholic community was united in outrage. The IRA used internment as an excuse to step up their attacks, and the civil rights leaders had a new cause to champion.

In the Bogside and the Creggan, local people cooperated in a defensive campaign to keep the security forces out of their area. The entire community was sealed off with roadblocks and makeshift barricades so that there was no way for the security forces to get in or out. "I remember helping to set up the barricades. They were called 'no-go' areas," John Kelly remembered. "The security forces were not welcome in the Creggan and the Bogside, so we had to guard ourselves. Everybody was part and parcel of what was going on. You felt you had to take part."

When complacent Catholics lived in the two dreariest, most neglected slums in Northern Ireland, no one paid attention. But when those residents commandeered their neighborhood and kept the security forces out, the province's rulers were suddenly troubled. "Free Derry," as the Bogside and the Creggan came to be known, was an icon of Catholic resistance. For many Protestants, this was an uncomfortable twist on their celebrated siege of 1689.

The Bogside and the Creggan residents had won—for a time. The security forces gave up trying to control the area and just tried to contain the disorder. The unrest eventually settled down to a predictable routine with gangs of young rioters standing sentry guard. William Street—the narrow road connecting the Bogside and the center of Derry—is where rioters and security forces would engage in what Maura Young described as an almost farcical standoff: "On a normal Saturday afternoon around two o'clock, the riot started. At around six o'clock it finished. Everyone went home to go to the pictures or to go and get their tea. It was a strange situation: 'We'll throw stones at you; you fire a couple rubber bullets at us; then we all disperse.'"

Rioting was simply a part of life. For adolescent boys and young men in particular, it was a chance for bravado and heroics. There was camaraderie and daring in finding out who could throw a stone the farthest or who could outrun a baton charge. Riots were not something to be avoided; they were a novel game to be played with gusto. It was the nearest thing to a community pastime.

Through it all, John Young kept to his routine. In the morning, his father would wake him. After breakfast, he would walk past the IRA gunmen that patrolled the neighborhood, across the barricades, past British soldiers, up the hill and through the gates of Derry city center to John Temple's clothier. If the shop had not been bombed, John worked. At the end of the day he walked past armored cars, across the barricades again, past the rioters to home. John Young's siblings were civil rights activists; his friends were joining the IRA, but he was not interested. Occasionally, because John was impressionable and it looked like fun, he threw some stones at the army and police. More often, he just stood by and watched.

But then a soldier shot Annette McGavigan, a fourteen-year-old girl from the Bogside, in the head after a riot one evening in September. John Young happened to be walking home from work at the time, past the spot where the dead girl lay with an ice pop in her hand. "He came in from his work that night with tears blinding him," Maura remembered. "He was as quiet as Saint Jude for ages after that. 'It's gonna get bad now,' he told me, 'if they're shooting weans in the street.'"

Reality had abruptly intruded on John Young's life, and it snapped him out of his daze. He had been picked for a managerial course in England at work and he intended to take it, John confided to his sister. He would be eighteen in May, and when that came he was going to settle in England and start a life of his own. John Young was getting out.

Private 027, a radio operator with the antitank platoon of the British army's First Parachute Regiment, arrived in Belfast a few weeks after the introduction of internment. He was nineteen years old; he had only been in the army for a year. Suddenly Private 027 was on active service in the most dangerous corner of British dominion. It was not a far-flung spot on the globe but an unsettled state just across the Irish Sea, geographically near, yet foreign and distant.

Like most of his young colleagues, Private 027 was crafty, confident, resourceful, and hungry for action. In a sense, he was a typical British squaddy, but as a member of the Parachute Regiment, one of the toughest units of the British army, he was exceptional. The Parachute Regiment was conceived during World War II as an elite, advance force that could be dropped behind enemy lines. Its members are generally physically fit, mentally strong, courageous, exceedingly disciplined in obeying orders, and exceedingly ferocious in carrying them out. In short, as Private 027 said, the Parachute Regiment is "the Rottweiler of the British army."

Still, for a young man from England, arriving in Northern Ireland was "an eye-opener; an unreal situation." News reports over the previous years had shaped Private 027's opinion and understanding of the conflict—if those words can be used to describe his loose grasp of events. From there, as a new recruit, he took his cue from the older, more experienced soldiers who had been hardened, even brutalized, by the intensity of serving in the province.

Foot patrols were a surreal experience; nothing like the straightforward military training soldiers had received. Private 027, dressed in fatigues, radio equipment strapped to his back, standard-issue British army SLR (self-loading rifle) in hand, and wearing the distinctive red beret of the Parachute Regiment, would work the urban streets with several other colleagues, sight pedestrians down the length of a rifle barrel, scan the alleys and passageways for gunmen while crouched behind a garden wall or jogging across junctions that flowed with everyday civilian traffic. As he did, hostile neighbors would taunt and provoke him; children would tease and chase. But Private 027 had to remain alert because a sniper could emerge from any window; any of the parked cars he passed could contain a bomb. The enemy was everywhere and nowhere, so Private 027, like every soldier in Northern

Ireland, became vigilant to the point of paranoia. Were those schoolkids leading him into an ambush? Was that fourteen-year-old girl transporting a rifle in her baggy trousers?

And yet, despite the dangers, there was a strange satisfaction, even enjoyment, in being deployed. The biggest frustration for the soldiers was that their foe was ephemeral and infrequently chose direct confrontation. Private 027 and his colleagues were sure that if the IRA ever dared engage the soldiers in a conventional way, the rebels would be outmatched. But the IRA rarely came out into the open, and the soldiers were contemptuous of that.

The pressures to get results and to stay alive were intense. And they never let up. Soldiers had virtually no social life. An off-duty squaddy was just as attractive a target for the IRA as a soldier in uniform—even more so for his vulnerability. When they were not on the streets, Private 027 and the other soldiers of his regiment were confined to Holywood Barracks on the outskirts of Belfast. It was a stifling, macho environment where soldiers asserted themselves by swapping stories of harrowing exploits on the streets. "Trust was at a premium," Private 027 said. "The only people we ended up trusting were our mates. Our lives centered around our section, which was our home and family, the only known quantity."

Soldiers understood each other's frustrations and the occasional outbursts. When soldiers vented their feelings with wanton violence, they were excused. A rifle butt might find a civilian's head. During a search, a television or stereo might be gratuitously destroyed. There were also more serious infractions; people were badly beaten, maimed, and killed. Soldiers had names for it: "going ape" and "beasting."

"Personally, I do not consider myself an aggressive or violent person; however, I did things that I was ashamed of in Belfast," Private 027 said. He occasionally hit civilians; that was the extent of it for him, while some of his colleagues relished the chance to lash out. "A soldier with a weapon in the streets had power. He could stop a bus and search everyone on that bus when he felt like it, whether or not it was necessary. Some people developed an inflated sense of their own importance."

Victimizing civilians was not a tendency unique to the Parachute

Regiment; any soldier might do it if given the opportunity, but the practice seemed more prevalent among the paratroopers. Beyond routine patrolling duties, the Parachute Regiment served as Northern Ireland's main reserve unit that could respond, within a moment's notice, to any serious incident. They were regularly called in to quell riots or sweep through a suspected sniper's nest. "Our ethos was to get stuck in, direct and fast," Private 027 remembered. "It was not uncommon to see a small number of paras going headlong into a crowd of hundreds. Due to crowd dynamics, if you could turn a few people at the front, you could control the rest. We always tried to impose authority in a more direct way than other units."

In the first three days after internment was introduced, twenty people were killed. Almost half of those deaths, including a priest who was administering last rites, were attributed to the paratroopers. The Parachute Regiment had inarguably earned their reputation for zealousness, but their methods were not always called for or welcome. "The paratroopers undid in ten minutes the community relations which it had taken us four weeks to build up." Those were the words of a British officer in Belfast as reported in the British newspaper, the *Guardian*, four days before Bloody Sunday.

"I have seen them arrive on the scene, thump up a few people who might be doing nothing more than shouting and jeering, and roar off again," another officer reportedly said. He acknowledged that the paratroopers were effective soldiers but said that "wading into people as if this were jungle warfare simply isn't on in Belfast." The story claimed that many units in Northern Ireland had specifically requested that the paratroopers be kept *out* of their areas.

The Parachute Regiment's reputation, according to Private 027, "put a certain onus of responsibility on those in authority. As a unit, it was one of a range of tools available to those in authority to choose from. If misapplied or directed either by senior commanders or politicians, then that is where the responsibility must lie."

Harry Tuzo was the general officer commanding Northern Ireland at the time of Bloody Sunday—the man with operational control over the military in the province. Tuzo was reasonably dovish, that is to say that he was a canny officer with the experience to recognize that short-term victories could lead to long-term failure. Tuzo had opposed internment. He did not object on moral or humanitarian grounds but because, after a detached assessment of the benefits and drawbacks of the policy, he simply determined that the disadvantages of internment outweighed the advantages. It would hand the IRA a propaganda victory without delivering much assistance to the military. When Northern Ireland's Protestant rulers pushed ahead with internment despite his objections, Tuzo carried out the policy as competently and dispassionately as he could. That was his job: to consult political leaders about the military situation, give them the best information and advice that he could, and then enforce the decisions that they made. Tuzo's sharp tactical mind and delicate political sense dovetailed nicely in that role.

But General Tuzo had many disparate responsibilities, so he left many tasks to General Robert Ford, commander of land forces, a trusted advisor. General Ford's rank did not fit neatly into traditional military hierarchy. He had a role created by the unique circumstances in Northern Ireland. He served as a troubleshooter and enforcer who would travel the province as the eyes and ears of the senior command, briefing lower-ranking officers and meeting occasionally with civilian and political leaders. General Ford was the most senior-ranking officer to have regular contact with combat soldiers across the province. He floated easily among the ranks and was regarded as someone who had a sense of the mood on the ground.

Ford proved to be a clever planner and quick study. Within a few days of having arrived in the province, he was preparing the operational orders for internment and overseeing arrests, but his skills as a diplomat were wanting. General Ford was known to be forceful and direct, but he lacked General Tuzo's sensitive political judgment. It was expected that the commander of land forces would help mend relationships with the police, but Ford was never able to do this. Instead, he exuded a confidence that the army could handle whatever was in store if they were only allowed to get on with it. Ford believed that the army was operating with one arm tied behind its back; with just a little more latitude, they could put the province in order. In that sense, Ford aligned himself with many Protestant rulers at Stormont who often pushed the army to take a harder line.

General Ford knew of the Parachute Regiment's reputation for brutality, but he had his own opinions. Ford had seen the paratroopers at work in Belfast and was impressed that one platoon of First Parachute Regiment could achieve more than an entire company of another battalion. "I can remember after internment being caught in a street in cross fire," Ford has recollected in a statement to the Saville inquiry. "There I was with my little tactical group, and we were absolutely stuck. I thought, 'My God, this is going to take two companies to sort this out.' They would have to go right through all the houses and get the terrorists. Not a bit of it. 'Round the corner came a platoon of First Para, who tumbled out of their vehicles and went down the street and everything stopped. Everyone disappeared. The terrorists were frightened of First Para."

The British military had developed sophisticated counterinsurgency tactics by the time unrest broke out in Northern Ireland. After all, they had had generations of practice administering a colonial empire that stretched from central Africa to the Far East. The military shorthand for the subject was "internal security," something of a preoccupation among senior commanders. Their tactics began with a cold appraisal of the enemy and a reminder that, no matter what the specific conditions might be, every counterinsurgency campaign was a battle for hearts and minds. The trick was to subdue the rebel faction and mollify everyone else.

Before Brigadier Frank Kitson became the head of the Thirty-ninth Brigade in Belfast, he drew on his years of service in Kenya, Cyprus, Malaysia, and Oman and wrote a paper on internal security called "Low Level Operations." Some native movements should be ignored, Kitson allowed, but others should be infiltrated and sabotaged by the military. The choice of tactics should be unencumbered by conventional morality, he believed. It was simple a question of what worked best.

The most vexing internal security matter at the time was the situation in Londonderry. Casualties were generally lower there than they were in Belfast, which was encouraging, but to have the Creggan and the Bogside sealed off like some sort of rogue state was intolerable. The temerity of the residents, their open defiance to the security forces, was an embarrassment and undermined the army's claims that they had the province under control. What should be done? The answer was debated among military planners from Northern Ireland right to the highest ranks of the British Ministry of Defense. There was no immediate consensus, and so the response was somewhat indecisive. The army had gone in hard to enforce internment, which only seemed to incite more violence. Then the opposite tack was taken: The army stayed out of the neighborhoods. But that only allowed the residents to fortify their positions. Almost weekly, General Tuzo faced hard questions from Stormont officials about why the army was still allowing the "no-go" areas in Londonderry. Tuzo expected Ford to come up with the solution.

On December 14, General Ford wrote a report suggesting future military policy in Londonderry. "At present, neither the RUC nor the military have control of the Bogside and Creggan areas," Ford noted, and he outlined three possible courses of action for future military policy: (1) maintain the policy of containment; (2) launch occasional operations into the Creggan and the Bogside; (3) completely subdue the neighborhood.

"The best that can be said of course one is that it does not stir the pot unduly in Creggan and the Bogside," Ford noted with some disdain, "but it must be recognized that the price to be paid is the fact that a community of some 33,000 citizens of the UK will be allowed to remain in a state of anarchy and revolt."

Ford reluctantly recommended option one, contain the Bogside and the Creggan, but he concluded, "Although course three is the correct military solution to the problem of restoring law and order in Londonderry, the political drawbacks are so serious that it should not be implemented in the present circumstances. . . . The risk of casualties is high, and apart from gunmen or bombers, so-called unarmed rioters, possibly teenagers, are certain to be shot in the initial phases. Much will be made of the invasion of Derry and the slaughter of the innocent."

Three weeks later, Ford went to Londonderry to assess the containment effort for himself. He was not pleased with what he found. Both

Brigadier MacLellan, the new army commander in Londonderry, and Frank Lagan, a chief superintendent of police, briefed Ford. Relations between Ford and MacLellan, fellow countrymen and officers in the same army, were generally good. But Ford regarded Lagan, a local officer with a reputation of being overly sympathetic with the Catholic population in Londonderry, with some suspicion.

"I was disturbed by the attitude of both the Brigade Commander and the Battalion Commander, and also, of course, by Chief Superintendent Lagan," Ford wrote in a three-page-long, personal memo to General Tuzo after his visit to Londonderry. "All admitted that 'The Front' [of rioters] was gradually moving Northwards and, in their view, not only would Great James Street go up in time but also Clarendon Street unless there was a change in policy. This admission meant that this major shopping center would, in their opinion, become extinct during the next few months. . . ."

Between the introduction of internment and Bloody Sunday, there were over 2,200 claims for damages among properties in Londonderry, which were expected to exceed £4 million. Continuing with his memo, Ford noted that the Strand Market Traders, a group of reactionary Protestant businessmen in Londonderry, wanted the army to sweep through the Creggan and the Bogside and stop the IRA bombing attacks. Now Ford dropped the moderate pretense that he displayed in earlier memos and began to accuse the general Catholic population of conniving with the terrorists. He was now of the opinion that the situation was urgent and called for extraordinary action.

> In the last two weeks there has been the usual daily yobbo activity in the William Street area and this has been combined with bombers making sorties into the Great James Street and the Waterloo Place area. . . . In addition the vast majority of the people in the shopping area not only give no help to our patrols but, if they saw a youth with a very small bag which might contain a bomb, they would be likely to shield the youths [sic] movement from the view of our patrols.
>
> However, the Londonderry situation is further complicated by one additional ingredient. This is the Derry Young Hooligans (DYH). Gangs

of tough teen-aged youths, permanently unemployed, have developed sophisticated tactics of brick and stone throwing, destruction, and arson.
Under cover of snipers in nearby buildings, they operate just beyond the
hard core areas and extend the radius of anarchy by degrees into additional streets and areas. . .

The weapons at our disposal—CS gas and baton rounds—are inef-
fective. . . . As I understand it, the commander of a body of troops called
out to restore law and order has a duty to use minimum force but he also
has a duty to restore law and order. We have fulfilled the first duty but are
failing in the second. I am coming to the conclusion that the minimum
force necessary to achieve the restoration of law and order is to shoot se-
lected ring leaders of the DYH, after clear warnings have been issued. . . .

Such a move would be reverting to "the methods of [internal secu-
rity] found successful on many occasions overseas," Ford pointed out,
and the time had come to get tough.

As Ford was giving this assessment, three weeks before Bloody
Sunday, civil rights organizers in Derry were preparing a peaceful anti-
internment rally for January 30. It was to be a massive event, the biggest
demonstration yet, and a reminder that despite the escalating IRA violence, there was a nonviolent way for Catholics to express their frustration. But the government had banned all marches; the civil rights
activists would be breaking the law if they proceeded, and senior security force command had to decide how they would respond. Chief Superintendent Lagan suggested that the march be allowed to go ahead in
the interests of avoiding a major confrontation, but General Ford rejected the idea. Instead, he dispatched a special intelligence unit to Londonderry to give an assessment on the possible IRA threat during the
march. He put the province reserve, the First Battalion of the King's
Own Border Regiment, on notice and he told Brigadier Kitson in
Belfast that the First Parachute Regiment would be required for an operation in Londonderry.

One week before Bloody Sunday, C Company of the First Parachute Regiment was unexpectedly called to Londonderry to patrol a
small anti-internment protest. The *Maidstone* prison ship had become

overcrowded, and fifty internees were transferred to a new holding center near Magilligan beach thirty miles north of Londonderry. Approximately four thousand civil rights activists marched down Magilligan beach towards the internment compound, where they hit a cordon of barbed wire and the paratroopers.

Instead of turning around, the marchers linked arms and waded out into the sea and past the barrier, part of the ritualistic cat-and-mouse game often played with the security forces, but this time the paratroopers began beating the crowd. "I remember thinking that a civil disruption situation seemed an odd use of soldiers who had the reputation of being the toughest troops and were usually used in a front-line war situation," Dan McGuinness, one of the protesters, noted. Nigel Wade, editor of the *Chicago Sun-Times*, was covering the march for the *Daily Telegraph*, a British newspaper. "I recall seeing paratroopers firing baton rounds into the chests of marchers at very short distance and that the regiment's NCOs had to use riot sticks to control their own soldiers. On one occasion I saw an NCO beat one of his own men so hard with his riot stick in an attempt to get him to disengage the marchers that the stick broke."

At dusk, the marchers, beaten and bloodied, withdrew from the beach. As they trudged home, the paratroopers taunted them with the promise, "See you next week."

The army's plan to control the civil rights march of January 30 was called "Operation Forecast." "We expect a hooligan element to accompany the marches and anticipate an intensification of the normal level of hooliganism and rioting during and after the march," the operational brief stated. "Almost certainly snipers, petrol bombers, and nail bombers will support the rioters." Soldiers were to refrain from firing tear gas and use rubber bullets with restraint since the army initially intended to "deal with any illegal marches in as low a key as possible." But once the rioters and marchers had separated, an arrest force was to be "launched in a scoop-up operation to arrest as many hooligans and rioters as possible."

At General Ford's insistence, the First Parachute Regiment was to lead the "scoop-up" and arrest operation. This went against standing operational procedures for internal security duties in Northern Ireland that suggested, "It is generally better to use reinforcing troops to man a baseline and use those soldiers with local knowledge of the area to carry out flanking movements."

Troops with a local knowledge of Londonderry were available and some senior officers disagreed with the decision to use the paratroopers in the "scoop-up." "First Para did not know the area and had not operated in the Bogside before," noted the commanding officer of Royal Anglicans, the longest-serving commanding officer in Londonderry at the time. "Also, everyone was aware that the paras had a reputation for tough action, and the citizens and hooligans of Londonderry would be greatly surprised if rougher Belfast procedures were carried out on them. I just wondered who had thought out this deployment: It reflected a change of policy and emphasis on future operations in Londonderry."

Generations ago, when industries like linen dominated Derry, Sunday was the one day out of seven when the factories were closed. Families would gather for morning worship, a roast dinner, and then often sit in repose. Even now, Sundays are a day to relax, joke, chat, maybe take a walk or a drive. The march on Bloody Sunday was planned with that in mind, a family outing where everyone was welcome.

"That was the difference about the Bloody Sunday march—it was the first one held on a Sunday," Maura Young remembered. "Before that, protest rallies were held on a Saturday. It made perfect sense because almost everyone was free on Sunday. But if it had been held on the Saturday, half the people who were killed would not have been there."

That afternoon, Patrick, Leo, Helen, Maura, and John Young gathered at their parents' house in the Creggan, which was near the starting point for the march. A peaceful protest was planned, but there was always a danger of violence breaking out. The march had been banned, which signaled trouble, but the Young family had seen the notice in the local *Derry Journal* that Friday titled "Organizers Want Big Derry Rally Incident-Free" that went on to say "violence can only set back the civil rights cause" and predicted that Sunday would be a " 'make or break' day for the cause of civil rights and the release of internees." There was likely to be some rioting, but a full-fledged gun battle during a crowded protest was not the kind of engagement the IRA favored; there were rumors that they had agreed to stay away.

The Young children knew the march was serious, but they were also looking forward to meeting up with friends from the neighborhood. Helen's husband, Jim, would be driving the flatbed truck at the front of the march, and that was where John intended to be. He was dressed smartly in a black-and-white checked shirt, trousers, a blue zip-up jacket, suede shoes, and a hat. His friends would tease him later— "We're going to a march, not a dance"—but they secretly agreed that John was wise to look sharp since there would be plenty of young girls along the way. Maura and John left the house together, their mother chasing them to the door. "Have you got your rosary beads with you?" she called after them. John turned to Maura in mock disgust, they laughed and kept walking down the road.

That morning, Private 027 sat in the rear door of an armored car and took in the clean, cool air as the convoy of troops headed over the snow-capped Sperrin Mountains, past Lough Neagh and across the Bann River. He looked out on the line of gray vehicles behind him. It was an impressive sight, and he was somewhat proud to be a part of it. Four companies of his battalion were going to Londonderry that day. He had never seen anything like it; something big was happening.

The previous night, Private 027 and about seven other soldiers in his section were briefed about the operation. It was a casual meeting; they mostly talked about Londonderry's notorious reputation, how IRA bombs had pulverized the city center, how the Creggan and the Bogside were "no-go" areas completely overrun by the IRA. Other army units in Derry hadn't been able to get control; maybe they were too timid or afraid of the repercussions, but the paratroopers would get results. They would be going into the IRA's lair—finally! It was exciting. This might be their chance to get some kills. Wasn't that why they were being sent to Londonderry? To get some kills? That phrase was heard again and again, "get some kills." The soldier next to Private 027, a Lance Corporal, heard it, nodded, and repeated it. "Get some kills." It was as if he had made up his mind.

"The mood was great," Helen remembered. "It was a dry, crisp day. It was cold, but you could walk around and not feel it. As you went along, all the doors in the neighborhood were open. The old people would be standing there saying, 'I wish we could go with you.' It was like a carnival. If you saw people you knew, you might stand for a minute yarnin' and chatting."

The march twisted through the Creggan and the Bogside. While they were in their own areas, marchers felt completely safe. As they moved along, the sight of paratroopers, identifiable by their distinctive berets and wearing flak jackets under their fatigues, unnerved some people. They knew security would be tight, but there seemed to be an unusual number of soldiers stationed like fixtures at major intersections. Snipers could be seen on rooftops.

When the marchers reached William Street and the expected security cordon, rioting broke out as if scripted. But it was a pretty perfunctory effort compared to the intensity of past clashes.

"John was always working on a Saturday, so he would miss the riots," Maura remembered. "His mates would tell him how much fun there was throwing stones down on William Street, but he could never make it himself."

But John was rioting that day. There are photos and film footage of him shifting restlessly among the crowd and occasionally throwing stones at the security barricade. He looks bored. John's friends say that he wandered off when the army turned on the water cannons, which does not surprise Maura. This was a young man with three suits and over two dozen shirts in his wardrobe. "Well, he was very vain. There was no way that he was getting his hair wet or his clothes wet," Maura surmised.

Stewards pled with the rioters to disperse. Many complied and moved down Rossville Street, away from the barricade and towards Free Derry Corner in the middle of the Bogside, where civil rights leaders were preparing to address the crowd from a makeshift podium fastened to the truck John Young had been following.

Meanwhile, the other end of the march was backing up. Leo and Patrick Young were stuck in the crowd a few hundred yards before the barricade. They could hear rubber bullets being fired and smell the tear gas. They wanted nothing to do with it, but Leo knew that John was probably in the thick of things. If he was, John was in trouble. He was just too naïve and inexperienced to get himself out.

"See, I knew this whole area back to front because that is where I spent my days delivering coal," Leo said. "So I said to Patrick, 'Go back up and stay up at the chapel and I will cut around here to find out where our John is.' I was hoping to find signs of him near the lorry at Free Derry Corner."

Troops of the Royal Green Jackets were manning the barricade at William Street; behind them were the paratroopers. Private 027 could hear the clatter of the march, its swell and ebb. Tear gas was beginning to waft past. The soldiers had been sitting in their vehicles for hours with the tension and expectation building. Someone passed around dumdum bullets, standard issue ammunition that had been altered with a deep groove carved into the tip to cause maximum damage. Were those bullets going to be fired? Private 027 did not know; there was no time to think about it. When were they going in?

Brigadier MacLellan was in his headquarters with Chief Superintendent Lagan, monitoring the march through radio contact with his troops and a helicopter flying over the Bogside. Both men were still harboring misgivings about the whole arrest operation. They knew that General Ford wanted to teach the hooligans a lesson, but he did not seem to understand the subtleties at work in Londonderry. A little restraint was only prudent. But that day, General Ford was on the ground with the paratroopers. It was almost unheard-of for such a senior officer to be so near an area of confrontation and it made MacLellan uncomfortable.

Just before four o'clock, two hours after the march started, a senior officer radioed Brigadier MacLellan to say that the paratroopers were ready. "The paras want to go in," MacLellan told Lagan. "For heaven's sake!" Lagan replied. "Hold them until we're satisfied that the marchers and rioters are well dispersed." MacLellan told the soldiers to hold their position. Moments later, General Ford got on the line directly over a secure radio and said it was time to "get a move on and send in the paras." MacLellan gave the order.

The paratroopers revved their engines, the Royal Green Jackets peeled back their barricade, and the vehicles sped past, tear gas swirling in the wake. Adrenaline was pumping. The paratroopers had been confined in their vehicles for so long that they had no idea where they were when their armored vehicles came screeching to a halt.

Two buildings dominated that area of the Bogside. On one side of Rossville Street were the nine-story Rossville Flats. Directly opposite was Glenfada Park, a low apartment building encircling a parking lot. A long rubble barricade stretched across the road between the two buildings. Private 027 and the rest of his unit leapt out of their vehicles, crouching as they ran across the streets strewn with stones and bottles, and found cover behind a low stone wall facing the rubble barricade.

When the Lance Corporal who the night before had spoken of "getting some kills" reached the pavement by the end of the wall, Private 027 said "he went down into a kneeling position beside it, raised his rifle to his shoulder, and without pause or hesitation, commenced firing towards the center of the crowd [on the barricade]."

Living in the Bogside, local people developed sensitive hearing. They could distinguish the sounds of conflict and immediately knew the difference between the dull thud of a rubber bullet and the sharp clap of a live round.

"I was standing at the podium when the shooting started," Helen Young remembered. "Eamonn McCann was standing next to me, and he said 'Jesus, they're firing live rounds.' He pushed me and another girl on the back so we fell over. We could not believe it. We just crawled along a wall away from the shooting and looked for somewhere to hide."

Private 027 described a moment when the crowd seemed momentarily suspended, bewildered by what was happening as if they could not believe their ears. He just stood by the Lance Corporal who was firing and "within seconds, other soldiers came on the scene, some kneeling and some standing, joining in the firing. I could see strikes on the barricade," he said. "Two people towards the center of the barricade, who had just been facing us, fell within a few seconds of each other on the opening burst of firing.

"I stood at the wall and put my rifle to my shoulder. I looked through my sights, scanning across the crowd. . . . I did not see anyone with a weapon or see or hear any explosive devices. I was looking across the crowd with some concentration, aware of the firing immediately around me. I lowered my weapon and looked at the guys firing and tried to locate what they were firing at. I still failed to see what I could identify as a target, and it caused me some confusion. I have a clear memory of consciously thinking, 'What are they firing at?' and feeling some inadequacy."

Michael Kelly, John's brother, was shot in the back while standing on the rubble barricade. A minute later, Michael McDaid, dressed in his Sunday jacket and tie, was shot as he turned to see where Kelly had fallen. John Nash was shot there as well; his father was shot when he ran out to help him.

John Young was kneeling for cover behind a low wall near the rubble barricade, just watching his neighbors drop one after the other. He must have heard one of them yelling for help because he got up, dashed towards the barricade, and was shot through the head.

After a few minutes, Private 027 heard the commanding officer shouting "Cease fire! Cease fire!" across the radio, and he passed on the order. The soldiers stopped shooting, but then the Lance Corporal and another soldier with whom he formed "a duo and always acted together as a pair" leapt over the wall. Private 027 viewed them running towards an entry into Glenfada Park, and saw them continue shooting with the same intensity and abandon as before.

A hundred yards away from where John Young lay dead, Leo was looking for him. "To be honest, I did not consciously hear the shooting. When I seen people coming running—young people, women and all, terrified looking—I knew there was shooting. That is when I came across Joe Friel. As he was coming out of Glenfada Park, I was coming in. He came running and fell. I thought he just stumbled, but it was not a natural fall. He run a good distance after he was shot and fell out the wee alleyway. I run up and turned him over and his shirt was all blood. These other boys came, and we carried him into a house.

"It really does not dawn on you how serious it is. Nobody had ever seen anybody getting shot before, so it was completely new. But Friel was not dead. I was thinking, 'How could somebody be shot and not be dead?' But Jesus, he was shot all right. Everyone was panicking, shouting at people, 'They're still shooting! They're still shooting!' People were coming flying in every door they seen that was open. When I walked to the door and looked across into Abbey Park—somebody said there were two bodies lying over there.

"There must have been about thirty people just standing and looking out the door. I was thinking, 'Jesus, a body.' I took off. I run along a wee alleyway, between two houses. I was concentrating on the body. The closer I run, the more I could see it. Just as I came into an opening, I looked out of the corner of my eye and I saw a soldier standing with his rifle raised. It was in a little gap; the houses were offset. As soon as I passed, I saw him start and heard the *whack*. I fell forward and heard the bullet hit the ground behind me, but after I run on another five yards, I could not see him at all."

The young man that Leo Young had gone to assist was Gerard Donaghy. He was seventeen years old, the same age as John Young, but in many ways Donaghy was a more typical example of a Catholic Derry youth. He was a member of the Fianna, the youth wing of the IRA. Five weeks earlier, Donaghy had been released after serving a six-month sentence for stone throwing.

For the previous seven years, since his parents died, Gerard Donaghy had been living with his older sister Mary. On the day of the march, Gerard Donaghy was wearing a denim jacket, a blue shirt, a blue sweater, and a pair of tight Wrangler jeans that he had asked Mary to buy for him while he was in prison. The pants were so tight that Gerard could hardly fit spare change in the pockets.

"I turned the young lad over, and he let out a sorta squeal or moan," Young said. "But he was so heavy. He was just deadweight; he wasn't moving. I could hardly move him even though I had good arms from hauling coal. I tried to drag him behind a wee wall, and took him by the shoulders and cuff of his coat. He was really moaning then, so I let him go. I just lay him down, down on his stomach. By then, two other people came, and I caught his arms and two boys caught his legs, and we carried him into a house. We went into the kitchen and left him down. We realized then that he had been shot.

"There must have been forty people in the house. People were saying, 'Who is he?' I never left him, but stood over him. There were two wee pockets in the top of his coat, and I put my hands in there to see if he was carrying something that might have his name on it but there was nothing. A doctor came in by then, and he was down on the ground, looking at him. He said, 'It's bad.' He said it a couple of times. 'This is bad. This is bad.' He didn't say he was dead, but that he was bad."

Leo Young and another man, Raymond Rogan, brought Gerard Donaghy out the back of the house and into a car to drive him to the hospital.

"He was lying with his knees up. There was a lot of blood, and his guts were hanging out of his stomach and everything in my lap. I was rubbing his hand. He was white. His face was white. He didn't speak. His eyes was rolling in his head. I was saying to Rogan, 'Push on! Let's go here!'

"They were bringing Joe Friel in the car in front. When we reached an army checkpoint, the soldiers were hyper. They were very aggressive. One pulled me out of the car. The minute I got out, I pushed him away. Then your man came back at me and put the rifle across me and pushed me toward the car. I was trying to get him to help the young fella. I said, 'This young fella's dying.' He just said, 'Let him die.' He threw me against the wall and said, 'Turn your head away from that wall and I will blow your head off.' Then they took Gerard Donaghy away."

Back in the Bogside, the shooting over, Private 027 walked around Glenfada Park in a daze. There were wounded and dead bodies in the parking lot and along the sidewalk. Other soldiers, ones who had not been part of the shooting, were just coming into the area. The look on their faces said, 'Something big went down here,' but they did not speak. Some of the soldiers seemed disappointed that they had missed some action and compensated by roughly searching civilians before marching them out of the area at rifle point. Medics attended to the wounded.

The medics had no idea what Private 027 had just seen. They just got on with their tasks. It was as if the shooting had been a private affair, none of their business. No one was asking questions. "Something shocking and appalling had occurred out of sight, and I thought it would go unrecognized and would remain some sort of secret. I think I was just human for a short time, rather than a soldier. Some instinct in me prompted me to act, and I grabbed a press man nearby, indicating for him to come with me saying, 'You've got to see this.' It has since dawned on me how illogical that was. There was probably nothing to see by then as the bodies had been taken away. A plain-clothed man then turned to me and asked what I was doing. It was like a douche of cold water." Private 027 did not answer but walked away to join his group.

Later, sitting back in their armored car waiting to pull out, the mood among the paratroopers as Private 027 recalled it, was "not so much euphoria as a release of tension. There was almost a silence and a sort of feeling of 'Bloody hell, what happened there?' " Already they knew there would be some explaining to do. The soldiers started to think of ways to corroborate one another's stories. They tried to agree on the details—how they had engaged in fire, what their targets had been. Everything had to sound justifiable. There would be an ammunition check to see how many shots each soldier had fired, but many soldiers kept a personal supply of rounds from the shooting range, so they could lie about that. But would the rifles be tested for forensics? Just as the armored car was about to pull away with the soldiers busy making their plans, a civilian casually jumped into the back of the vehicle. "You will need some good PR after this," he said, and then he jumped out again.

■   ■

John had missed his dinner that day, which was not unusual in it-self. He played in a band; Sundays were often spent practicing. That must be where he was, Maura thought, as she sat with her parents in their house. Maura had left the march before the shooting started and expected that everyone would be drifting back soon. Just then, Helen appeared in hysterics. Soldiers had gone on a rampage, she said, and people were lying dead all over the Bogside. She had managed to crawl to safety and find a lift back home.

At first, no one believed her. It made no sense. "And what would they have been shooting at?" her father asked, incredulously. Rubber bullets, maybe, but not live rounds.

Helen was overwrought, her family decided, as she left them and returned to her own home. But as they were watching television in the living room, the news told how two people had been shot dead dur-ing riots in Derry. More were wounded. Maura and her parents were dumbfounded.

Back then, in working-class areas like the Creggan, few homes were fitted with a telephone. People relied on pay phones, which were often available at the local shop. Calls were not spontaneous; they had to be planned. Every week, on Sunday evening, John's girlfriend in En-gland would ring him. That was their routine. But when Maura Young went down to the shop after Helen had left, the shopkeeper said that John had missed his call.

"Well," Maura said, "he must have been up playing with his band."

She noticed the shopkeeper's odd look. "There have been a lot of people wounded," the woman said, and went on with a touch of con-cern, "Would you not be better phoning Altnagelvin Hospital just to make sure he is not there?"

Maura got impatient and told the woman to go ahead and phone herself if she wanted to. So she did. "Maura," the shopkeeper said after putting down the phone, "I think you had better go over to Altnagelvin."

Maura went home and told her parents. They were uneasy but thought that John had been arrested or, at worst, wounded. Her father started to put on his coat, but the anxiety nearly brought on an asthmatic fit, so Maura said she would go on her own. Since they had no car, Maura got a neighbor, Mr. Ward, to take her.

"We went down to Altnagelvin, and the halls were full of people who had been shot. It was like a butcher's shop. These nurses—you know the way nurses are always in their whites?—they never have blood on them; but these women were covered in blood. There was a young fella lying there—I'll never forget—with a hole in his eye.

"So we stood there and some priest came over, asking if he could help. His face, his hands were covered in blood. There was blood on the white cuff of his shirt. I'll never forget that, because he lifted his hands and he had a list. That is when I got scared. I thought, 'Oh my God, there's a list.' Well, he looked down this list and asked how old John was. I told him that John was seventeen. The priest said, 'Well, we have a boy. But he is not seventeen.' I told him that John looked about twenty-three. The priest just nodded. He asked Mr. Ward to come with him. I was left standing there. I did not fall down, but my knees must have given way because the next thing I was on the ground."

That afternoon, a neighbor came around and asked Mary Donaghy if she was alone. She was. The neighbor said that Gerard had been shot, but not to worry because he had only been hit in the leg. When Mary's husband went to the hospital, Gerard was not there. It was Mary's cousin who had been shot in the leg; her brother was unaccounted for. Around nine o'clock, five hours after Leo Young had been stopped while bringing Gerard Donaghy to the hospital, the army delivered his dead body to the morgue. Four nail bombs were clumsily protruding from his pockets.

News of the day spread quickly through Derry's small and insular Catholic community. That night, priests roamed through the streets like grim harbingers, telling families whether their loved ones were among the arrested, wounded, or dead.

By the time Maura returned from the hospital, word of John's death had already arrived. The house was packed with neighbors wandering in a daze. Her parents were sitting there, crying for John and wondering what had happened to Leo. There were rumors that some of the

wounded had been brought across the border to the town of Let-
terkenny. Others said bodies were still lying where they fell in the Bogside. Eventually a priest arrived with news that the army had Leo.

"They kept me for two days," Leo told me. "They took me away
down to Ballykelly interrogation center on Sunday, and I never got out
until Tuesday morning. They took all my clothes off to be tested. They
left me standing with my underwear in the corner. I stood there for
about half an hour before they brought my clothes back. They took the
dirt from under my nails. They swabbed my hands. They had me in a
cell on my own and made me stand against the wall all night. No food.
They would question me every two hours. They were asking what had
been going on in the town and did we see any gunmen and did we
know any gunmen.

"They tried to tell me then: 'Did you know that you were almost
sitting on a bomb?' I said, 'How do you work that out?' They said, 'The
young fella you were with had nail bombs on him.' I told them it was
impossible. A doctor examined him when I brought him into the house.
I had searched his pocket, top pocket. All the people in the house never
saw anything. I had him on my knee. I told them it was lies because he
couldn't have; he definitely couldn't have.

"They tried to get me to say. . . . Obviously, they wanted me to say,
'Oh, aye, there were four nail bombs on him and I still got into the car
with him.' I would be a fool. They would say I was an accessory. They
could say a whole lot of things. They were trying to cover their actions.
Somebody planted them on him to make it look justified. You can't
shoot and kill thirteen people and not find nothing.

"On Tuesday, they came to let me go. There was a car that come for
me to bring me up to Derry, up to the barracks again. They sat me there
for half an hour or more and just as I was coming out this detective
came up to me with a clipboard and he said, 'Young.' I said, 'That's me.'
'Leo.' 'Yes.' 'Two brothers?' I said, 'Yes.' He said, 'Well, you have only
one now.'

"I didn't know what he was talking about right away. He just said I
could go. I walked out the door and I walked over to the corner of William Street; I was making my way home then. People were looking at

me—ones that I knew. You could sense then that something had happened. I did not know that thirteen people had been killed; I hadn't a notion. I walked on and somebody pulled up in the car and said, 'Leo, are you going home?' I said, 'I am going home, but I would rather walk. I'm not feeling the best.' He looked as if he wanted to tell me something, but he never spoke.

"See, my mother's house had a big, long walkway over to it. You could park the car away from the houses. I was walking across there, and Patrick came running out to me, and I knew by the look on his face."

Helen Young remembers when a local priest, Father Rooney, came to the house the day after the shooting with her asthmatic father sitting in the living room next to her frail, helpless old mother. The cardinal would be arriving specially to say the funeral mass, Father Rooney said, which would be an honor. "And he wants to know, can you forgive the soldier who shot John?"

"My mother never even batted an eye," Helen remembered. "She just looked up and said, 'Yes, I can, because he is some mother's son.' "

"I could never understand that," Helen said, perplexed. "John was her last son. I was in the next room when she was giving birth to him. He was the most chubby, beautiful baby—he was huge, ten pounds eleven. And my mother forgave the soldiers who shot him?"

One funeral was held for all the dead at Saint Mary's chapel in the Creggan, thirteen coffins in a row. Three weeks later the Widgery inquiry started. It was held in the town of Coleraine, because holding it in the place where the deaths had occurred was considered too dangerous. Few of the wounded or families of the dead cooperated. A British government that sent soldiers to kill was not going to turn around and say that it had been murder, the families were sure. But some witnesses and the wounded did testify.

Joe Friel, who survived his injuries, had just been released from the hospital when he went to the Widgery inquiry to defend himself against charges of being an IRA gunman.

"The soldier who took me to the barracks had said that I turned around and admitted that I was carrying a gun. One sentence quoted by the policeman who interviewed me in the hospital was that 'Mr. Friel is a quiet-spoken, intelligent young man who was obviously involved with civil disorder in this city.' That is the sentence. 'This is the young man who admitted to a soldier that he was carrying a gun, but because of his injury and that he was in the hospital, I did not press him on the matter.'

"But I have never been pressed on that matter. I have never been questioned about carrying a gun, ever. The more you look—they were trying to frame me. They were just trying to frame me. If you read the soldiers' story about Glenfada Park, they said they were hit with nail bombs, petrol bombs, there was a full-scale riot. But we have photographic evidence. If you look, there are bodies lying around, but there is not one stone, not one bit of broken glass, nothing. My impression of Widgery was that he was sleeping, well the nearest thing to sleeping, when I was giving my evidence. He hardly opened his mouth."

To Leo Young, "Widgery was an arrogant, cheeky bastard. He did not want to know nothing. He only wanted to get the whole thing through. He did not want to know, but I had to get my thoughts across because they were trying to say that the young fella had bombs. I knew that he did not have nail bombs on him. There was no way. But they dismissed me as insignificant. 'Do you mean to say that a soldier fired on you from twenty or thirty yards and did not hit you?' one solicitor asked me. I felt like saying, 'You sound disappointed.'"

Private 027 arrived at the Widgery Tribunal via helicopter from Belfast. He could see that the details of what happened were being systematically fabricated; soldiers were openly discussing their testimony together in the corridors. Eventually he was called into a bare room to talk to a lawyer. The lawyer sat Private 027 down and began taking his statement about what happened on the day. Private 027 had planned to tell the truth, or as much of the truth that he could tell without implicating his colleagues. But when he described indiscriminate shooting towards the barricade, the lawyer stood up from his chair and looked down at the private with surprise. "We can't have that, can we, Private?" he asked. "That makes it sound as if shots were fired into the crowd."

■   ■

It was the spring of 2000, and dusk was falling. The hushed crowd at Free Derry Corner shuffled in the cold. It was the eve of the inquiry, and along the streets and alleyways aging locals, young families, witnesses, and survivors gathered. On a curbside, a father knelt next to his young son, solemnly tracing the landscape with his finger. "That is where the people marched from, son," he said softly, recalling the day. "They came along that road. There were thousands of people—even wee ones like you—marching for their rights." The boy's eyes were transfixed by his father's expressive face.

"I'm not the best at these things," Maura Young told me through an anxious smile. She was on her own. Her brothers and sisters, like many other witnesses and survivors, found these commemorations too painful, though the night was unusually full of relief, even cheer. The campaigning was over. The truth would be out. Beneath the somber mood was a sense of fulfillment. But before the end of the road, thousands gathered to march Bloody Sunday in reverse: from the streets consecrated with blood to the steps of the Guildhall.

Bearing torches, survivors and family members congregated on Rossville Street. Among the crowds that fell in behind, candles sporadically appeared. Past the streets where Catholics were once packed into overcrowded homes, past the murals and cenotaph in memory of the dead, past the former scenes of riot and violence, they marched. Bright flames answered the darkness. It was simple and dignified.

"You know, this is the spot." Mickey Bradley turned to me as we headed down William Street. "This is where we were when the rioting started."

Then, stopping to lift his walking stick, he pointed down an adjacent alley. "Down that is where I ran to, and along that road is where the soldiers came." He paused there a moment, stared intently down the alley, turned again, and walked away. The march was over in twenty minutes; in that time, someone pointed out, thirteen dead bodies were lying in the Bogside.

The march went on until the Guildhall Square was filled with light.

Even above, along the ancient walls of the city, flames flickered. Children carrying photos of those killed were hoisted onto a flatbed truck, where they stood and faced the crowd in silence. Eamonn McCann had been interrupted from speaking twenty-eight years earlier, but he gave his finest oration this night.

"We have spent years giving witness to the truth, and now we come to demand the truth. We demand to know what happened, but we want to know more—we want to know why it happened.

"There is a trail of the truth, and no matter where it leads, to the military or the politicians, let us seek it out. Everything is in place at last in this building behind me to do that, so we will watch, and the world will watch closely, as the inquiry proceeds. And when the truth comes out, at long last, we can find what we need to ease our pain and put Bloody Sunday behind us."

The Last Rebels

◻   ◻

Looking in the rearview mirror, Joe O'Connor could see his assassins closing in. Two men were in a slowly approaching car, the same car that had tracked Joe earlier in the day. Another two men were walking alongside looking clownish in their raincoats, fake beards, and wigs. O'Connor had no doubt what was happening—he had been expecting this—but the timing seemed so wrong.

"Oh no, Friday the thirteenth," O'Connor absently had told Nicola, his wife, on that morning in October 2000. It was a rare event for Joe O'Connor to be waking up in his own bed. Lately he had been spending most of his time with friends and comrades away from home because he knew that the IRA was after him, that they were determined, and that they were getting close.

On a stormy morning two weeks earlier, Nicola heard a car pull up outside the house and she thought that Joe had returned. Looking through the upstairs bedroom window, she could see that the driver had turned off the headlights but the engine was still running. Through flashes of lightning, Nicola saw the driver take a pistol from his raincoat, put it in his lap, and load. She was terrified, so she gathered the children in the bedroom and waited for the front door to come off its hinges. But the men seemed unsure about the address and drove off after a few minutes.

"Are you staying for a while?" a barman asked Joe a week later when he was out for a drink at a local pub. He was, but what a strange question. Joe got uneasy and left just minutes before two masked gunmen came in after him.

Joe O'Connor was desperate; it had all come apart so quickly. The first seven years of Joe and Nicola's marriage had been happy. They started their family at eighteen—young but that is what they wanted. Joe was industrious; he got their house into shape and worked hard at his jobs. At twenty-five, Joe got enough money together to open his own pool hall and made it a success. But then, in the spring of 1999, Joe O'Connor joined the Real IRA—a dissident IRA faction that is opposed to the peace process and committed to war against the British. Within a year, the police recovered some weapons from the pool hall. The IRA issued a death threat against Joe O'Connor, and then kidnapped and interrogated his uncle Anthony. Joe started wearing a bulletproof vest.

"From there, Joe's life and our marriage just went straight down the tubes." Nicola remembered constant arguing and fighting. "After I found out he was involved, I was trying to make him see sense. I was telling him, 'Joe, you've got more than most your age. You have a wife, kids, a business.' He would not listen."

But Joe knew that Nicola was right; he had been neglecting his family, and he wanted to make amends. So that morning, Joe got his two eldest boys dressed and walked them over to Vere Foster Primary School. Then he went down to the corner shop and brought home some eggs, bread, and bacon to make Nicola breakfast in bed.

While the frying pan crackled, Joe had one eye on his favorite film, *Braveheart,* and the other eye on his young son, Eamonn. That evening he was going to take the boys to Funderland, an amusement park. Nothing, not the summons that arrived through the mail that morning or the police who came to ask him questions an hour later, was going to deny Joe that modest moment of domestic contentment. All Joe needed was a little bit of money. Since he had stopped working and the pool hall had been shut down, Joe was broke. But he would go down to the Social Security office and ask for a "crisis loan" so he could take his kids out.

Just before one in the afternoon, Joe and Nicola bundled Eamonn into the stroller and headed over to Ballymurphy, a nearby Catholic housing district. Through the Troubles, Ballymurphy maintained a reputation as an IRA heartland and one of the most neglected ghettos in Belfast. But Joseph and Nicola did not need a reminder of that as they walked through the streets strewn with empty wrappers, where stray dogs barked and nipped at their feet, and where placards hanging from every lamppost and the graffiti dabbed on every wall exalted the IRA.

The couple split up at Whitecliff Gardens—Nicola took Eamonn to see her sister, and Joe went another block to Whitecliff Parade, where his family lived. Joe dropped in to see his mother, but his sister said that she was not well, so he went across the street to ask his uncle Anthony for a lift to the Social Security office. Joe told Anthony what he had not told Nicola, that he felt sure they had been followed on their way into Ballymurphy. Anthony asked if Joe wanted to stay in the house for a while, but he said no, he just wanted to get out of there.

The two men got into Anthony's white Peugeot parked out in the street. Joe strapped on his seat belt and rolled down the passenger side window—a ritual that he followed whenever he got into a car. When the two men saw what was coming from behind, Anthony scrambled out onto the sidewalk, but Joe's door was pinned shut by the approaching car. Two gunmen then ran up to Joe's window, jammed their feet against the car door, and started firing. The first shot hit Joe's hand as he tried to unfasten his seat belt. Then seven shots came from an automatic pistol, five to the head and two to the face.

When Nicola arrived at the scene, the street was choked with neighbors and bystanders. "They've shot him! They've shot him! He's dead!" Joe's sister Margaret was shouting. It was true, but Nicola could not believe that the body sitting in the car with a towel over its face was the husband she had left only five minutes earlier.

In the wake of Joseph O'Connor's killing, "Who was responsible?" was a natural first question. The answer was the worst-kept secret in Belfast. Neighbors who witnessed the shooting recognized the fleeing gunman as local IRA activists, and ballistics showed that the weapons used were part of a recent IRA arms consignment from Florida. Sinn Fein leaders, in words that echoed past responses to IRA violence, called O'Connor's murder 'tragic,' but refused to condemn the killers.

"In light of the speculation and allegations surrounding the killing of Joseph O'Connor the IRA wishes to state that it was not involved in his death," read an IRA statement released on the eve of O'Connor's funeral. "Malicious accusations suggesting IRA involvement are designed to heighten tension and promote the agenda of those opposed to the current IRA strategy." The statement concluded with "condolences to the O'Connor family," displaying mind-boggling temerity, that proved the IRA's supreme confidence that they were getting away with it.

If, as local people might say, "even the dogs in the street" knew that the IRA had killed Joseph O'Connor, the next question was: Why? Not that the IRA had ever needed much of a reason. Even while they ostensibly observed a cease-fire, the IRA had occasionally killed people for drug dealing and informing. There were some feeble rumors that Joseph O'Connor had been killed for this kind of reason, perhaps because of the cigarette bootlegging operation he ran or because through his own bravado, O'Connor had fallen foul of some IRA members. But that simply was not plausible. Whatever might be said about the IRA, they are extraordinarily disciplined—even more so while observing a cease-fire. That means that the IRA leadership must have sanctioned Joseph O'Connor's murder, and they did so for the only reason that mattered: Joseph O'Connor was fighting a battle that they had abandoned.

"He told me bits about why he joined the Real IRA," Nicola remembered of her husband. "His reason was that everyone seemed to be losing their sense. No one seemed to know what they were fighting for. The Provos [Provisional IRA] were not fighting for the things Irish men died for, and the British seemed to be running the place. Joe's attitude was that he was going to change Ireland. He was going to make such a big change; he was going to change it all."

Joe O'Connor had been the Belfast commander of the Real IRA, and his funeral included a final act of defiance. The coffin was draped in an Irish flag with a pair of black gloves and a beret lying on top. As it was carried out of his mother's front door, down a set of stairs and onto the street, the pallbearers paused for a moment. Despite a heavy security presence, six men and two women in paramilitary dress, their faces covered, emerged to salute while one of the men produced a handgun and fired a three-shot volley over the coffin.

In its traditional republican pageantry, Joseph O'Connor's funeral made a mockery of his killers. It was the same sort of tribute that IRA activists had been given in death, but there would be no more IRA funerals because the IRA had made peace. Now Real IRA soldiers were fighting and dying. Now they deserved such honor. As the funeral procession passed the end of Whitecliff Gardens the graffiti scrawled on the end of a gable wall proclaimed "The Real IRA Fight On."

When the IRA called a cease-fire on August 31, 1994, the working-class Catholic heartland of west Belfast—a community from which the IRA has drawn a large measure of morale and untold recruits—erupted in celebration. A cavalcade of cars, horns blaring and Irish flags waving from the windows, drove up and down the Falls Road. Judging by the mood, one could be excused for thinking that the IRA had finally driven the British out of Ireland when they had, in fact, simply called a halt to their violent campaign.

In a unique, almost paradoxical way, the IRA cease-fire was a victory. After all, violence had been a tactic. It had served its purpose, and the tactics were changing. From now on, republicans would advance their cause through negotiations and politics. That was the new line coming from Sinn Fein and the IRA, which masked a less satisfying conclusion: The cease-fire represented a comprehensive and arbitrary about-face.

It was a measure of the implicit trust the grassroots republican movement had stored in its leadership that, while some people found the cease-fire unexpected and even disquieting, most activists remained loyal. For many, it was a loyalty bordering on the devotional, a confidence that the republican struggle was unfolding at an almost preordained pace and direction. It was a faith that remained largely unshaken when, eighteen months after the IRA cease-fire was called, it ended with a massive car bombing in London's Docklands. But that resumption of violence was short-lived, and a further, indefinite cease-fire was called in July 1997, paving the way for inclusive political discussions and the Good Friday Agreement.

Through it all Sinn Fein and the IRA maintained the broad support of the republican movement, but a growing number of activists were becoming dissatisfied. They were not about to watch the republican leadership turn generations of Irish history on its head with an elaborate flourish as if they were fastening a bow. And that, some argued, is exactly what they were attempting. Dissident republicans did not accept the notion that cease-fires and politics were just two effective new devices in the same old cause. For them, republicanism was a revolution fought by men and women with passions and ideals. Those ideals remained the same, and they were to be pursued by time-honored republican methods: political sabotage and revolutionary violence.

Not long after the first IRA cease-fire, the first rogue republican element appeared. The Continuity IRA—a small, poorly armed force—began to launch sporadic attacks against the Northern Ireland security forces and commercial targets. The strikes were generally pretty desultory events prone to mishap. The group's bombs would fail to detonate, security forces raided their arms dumps, and abortive gun attacks were thwarted. A few Continuity IRA bombings, however, were notably successful in destroying property, although without fatalities.

The Real IRA, of which Joe O'Connor was to become a leader, was the more reactionary dissident republican faction. The group emerged with a vengeance immediately after the Good Friday Agreement with a mortar attack on a rural police station and a massive car bomb that devastated the town of Banbridge.

On August 15, 1998, the Real IRA planted another car bomb, this time in the provincial town of Omagh. It was a sunny Saturday; the streets were full of shoppers. The Real IRA telephoned a warning, which was customary, but there was some confusion about the position of the device, and crowds of people were inadvertently corralled towards the car bomb. Twenty-eight people were killed and over three hundred more were wounded in the worst single bombing atrocity in Northern Ireland's history. A few days later, the Real IRA officially called a halt to their campaign, but they began to secretly reorganize within months. Through most of 2000, the group maintained a steady pace of low-level attacks in Northern Ireland and Britain.

"In our eyes there is little difference between the Continuity IRA and the Real IRA," a British Army spokesman told me. "Personalities who do work for one group do work for the other. They share weaponry and probably share the same bomb makers. There are very few people involved, maybe a few hundred strong supporters and half that who are prepared to launch an operation."

The security forces in Northern Ireland measure a terrorist threat on two scales: capability for violence and violent intent. A group with an abundance of both is dangerous. Through the Troubles, the IRA's intent remained steady, fierce. Their capability was always high, too. While observing a cease-fire, the IRA has no intention of using its capability for violence. The dissident republican elements find themselves in the opposition condition. They have the will, but not the ability to launch a widespread campaign.

The danger is that the dissident republican elements could over-come their shortcomings—heavy infiltration by the security forces and even the IRA, and a lack of recruits, cash, and weapons—and become a formidable threat to peace. Their best chance is to provoke a backlash from the security forces and the paramilitary groups now observing a cease-fire, draw them into open confrontation, and hope that confronta-tion spreads. No one knows how many disaffected IRA members have crossed over to the dissident groups, but many have, bringing invalu-able know-how and even some weapons along with them. Can the dis-sident groups wreck the peace process? It seems unlikely, but that's a secondary question.

It is an uncomfortable truth that the dissident republicans are ideal-ists. One can say that because idealism is not always romantic or noble. Nor does it have to be moral. In fact, idealism allows people to behave immorally in pursuing the cause. Anything is justified in reaching the ultimate goal. Individual activists may get involved for any number of reasons—revenge, hatred, fear—but it is the idealism of the struggle, the sanctity of the ultimate goal, that holds the movement together. It seemed to me that the real question was not whether the dissident republicans could win, but why do they fight? If their idealism is widespread enough, if it can motivate enough people, if it can endure, it may fail in the short term but eventually meet the time and circumstances when it can thrive.

Ruarí ÓBrádaigh served as president of Sinn Fein during the early years of the Troubles. The movement was unsure of itself then and ÓBrádaigh, a fastidious and venerable republican, helped inspire confidence. But as the Troubles continued and there was no end in sight, tensions began to develop between ÓBrádaigh, an unbending idealist, and a crop of young pragmatists like Gerry Adams and Martin McGuinness. Adams and McGuinness were pushing a modernizing agenda; they saw ÓBrádaigh as ideological and out of touch. By 1986, it became clear that Sinn Fein was guiding the movement from armed conflict towards politics—ÓBrádaigh led a walkout of the party conference that year and formed Republican Sinn Fein in his own puritanical image. When the IRA called their first cease-fire, ÓBrádaigh invited disgruntled IRA and Sinn Fein supporters to join Republican Sinn Fein. A battle for the heart and soul of the republican movement has raged ever since.

I started looking for answers to my questions at Republican Sinn Fein's austere headquarters along Belfast's Falls Road. "One thing I want to make clear—Republican Sinn Fein is often labeled the dissidents," Michael ÓDuibhir, a young, stout, bearded activist told me. "But in my mind, the dissidents are the ones who break from tradition. We are the ones who are faithful to the Irish republican ideal."

On the night before the Republican Sinn Fein offices in Belfast were due to open, someone tried to have them bombed, hoax-bombed, or both. No one knows for sure. According to an IRA statement published in the *Republican News*, a suspicious figure at the back door of the office set down a package and then fled. An IRA activist who had seen this went to investigate, found that the package contained a bomb, and defused it. Later, the IRA released a photograph of what they claimed to have found: a box containing lumps of some gray substance with colored wires connecting it to a timer.

If the IRA ever had a problem with one of their own bombs they would, at most, notify the security forces. The clear-up operation would cause a welcome disruption to normal life with the outside chance that a British Army bomb disposal team would be wiped out in the process. If the IRA found a bomb planted by another group, the same held true. The thinking was brutal yet logical: Why endanger your own activists in doing something that your enemy would willingly do for you?

No one could remember the last time that the IRA had ever defused a bomb. The popular consensus was that the incident had been a message from the IRA to Republican Sinn Fein, a reminder of who was in charge. The IRA did not need to drive Republican Sinn Fein out of the area—but they always *could* drive them out, and now Michael ÓDuibhir and his comrades knew it.

ÓDuibhir was genuinely aggrieved by the "bomb attack." It was positively undemocratic, he said, and just demonstrated how low Sinn Fein and the IRA would stoop to stifle dissent. But didn't Republican Sinn Fein support the Continuity IRA and their use of violence? ÓDuibhir said, "No."

But in a small anteroom to the office, just past the steel door and security cameras, there sat an old woman selling republican literature and memorabilia from a plain wooden desk. Above her head and along the walls, there were poster tributes to the Continuity IRA. On the desk, a Republican Sinn Fein newsletter congratulated the Continuity IRA for a successful mortar attack. Next to the papers was a collection box for republican prisoners. "Continuity IRA prisoners?" I asked. The old woman smiled at me.

"Well," ÓDuibhir said, "we certainly have sympathy for the people who are taking up arms against the British. All I can say to them is 'good luck.'" ÓDuibhir could call Sinn Fein and the IRA undemocratic because "democracy" for him meant to keep fighting until there was a united Ireland. He could insist that Republican Sinn Fein did not support violence because he meant there was nothing *wrong* with Republican Sinn Fein supporting violence. Language, no less than a bomb or a bullet, is a useful weapon in the struggle. Republicanism has always been adept at using words to shape ideas. The whole movement is founded on history, myth, and myth masquerading as history, that can change, almost imperceptibly, to meet the practical needs of the present.

On Easter Monday, 1916, Patrick Pearse, a young Irish rebel, stood on the steps of Dublin's General Post Office and declared that Ireland was free. His small band of revolutionary soldiers had stormed the post office around noon that day, and hundreds of others had captured other key positions around the city in what, Pearse and his comrades hoped, was the small insurrection that would spark a widespread revolt against British rule in Ireland. Within five days, the uprising was crushed; hundreds of rebels were arrested and sixteen of them were executed, among them Patrick Pearse, who before he died predicted, "We shall be remembered by posterity and blessed by unborn generations."

It was a foolhardy revolt that Pearse himself expected would fail, but in time, the Easter Rising changed from an ignominious failure into a glorious defeat. Irish resentment against British rule had been simmering for generations, but until the Easter Rising, the widespread mood had been for a greater degree of autonomy, not complete independence. The execution of Patrick Pearse and his comrades radicalized the Irish population. From that moment, Britain began to slowly but inexorably lose control.

A disparate group of political interests united as Sinn Fein, Irish for "Ourselves Alone," to campaign for an Irish Republic. In time, an equally disparate group of Irish militias joined the fight under the banner of the Irish Republican Army. It was a fragile alliance sealed by an abiding reverence for the martyred heroes of the Easter Rising and a resolute commitment to their unfulfilled ambition. On January 21, 1919, Sinn Fein inaugurated Dail Eireann, the first Irish parliament. In a declaration of independence issued on that date, Dail Eireann was described as an embodiment of the Irish Republic "proclaimed in Dublin on Easter Monday, 1916, by the Irish Republican Army on behalf of the Irish people."

But the IRA was needed to turn those words into something more lasting than Patrick Pearse's bold proclamation from the steps of

Dublin's General Post Office. After a three-year guerrilla campaign against British forces in Ireland, a treaty was signed whereby all but six northern Irish counties with a Protestant majority—present-day Northern Ireland—would become a free state. The debate over whether to accept the treaty shattered the republican coalition. In the eyes of some, the treaty represented a partial, unsatisfactory victory. In the eyes of others, the treaty was a greater step towards an independent Ireland than they had ever dared expect.

The Dail narrowly voted to accept the treaty, but a group of hard-line republicans vowed to fight on. Irish civil war erupted; the militants were routed. Still, a small faction of determined republicans survived. By 1922, most Irish people got on with the business of building a new, if incomplete nation while a rump of committed republican activists—defeated in the debating chamber and on the battlefield—continued to fight.

That began a long stretch within Irish republicanism—years of failed border attacks, persecution, martyrdom, and disillusionment—when the small band of committed activists had nothing to show for their determination but a few rebel songs and their principles.

They claimed that the peace treaty that created Northern Ireland had been illegal, that the Irish Republic was conceived the moment Patrick Pearse uttered his proclamation—if not in fact, then in the hearts of the Irish people. It was a far-fetched assertion, based on an almost theological faith in the sanctity of the Easter Rising and Patrick Pearse's blood sacrifice. Still, it was a compelling argument: If someone believed it, they had to act. That was the history that justified the myth that perpetuated the republican cause.

There was a single thread of republican history that, since the IRA had called a cease-fire, was now in the hands of Republican Sinn Fein and the dissident republicans—the last rebels to continue the struggle. But was there anything more than that? If the peace process was a betrayal of republican principles, what was the alternative?

ÓDuibhir's eyes lit up. He pulled a brochure from his desk—part of the mounds of elaborate policy documents that probably no one, save ÓDuibhir and a few of the party faithful, has ever read—and turned it towards me convincingly, as if proffering a prospectus on a real estate venture.

"Éire Nua," New Ireland, was Republican Sinn Fein's plan to get rid of the Irish border and redistrict the island according to Ireland's four ancient provinces: Ulster, Leinster, Munster, and Connacht. If seventh-century Irish chieftains ever used such a system, they were the last, which is just what appealed to Republican Sinn Fein. Éire Nua promised to erase the country's history as a colony of England once and for all. The rest of the brochure included maps with mind-bending detail of how such a cumbersome new political system could work. "Irish people have demonstrated a native talent for formulating unusually effective policies for government," the brochure encouraged, but it all seemed a bit far-fetched to me. It was only a plan, ÓDuibhir said. There were others. Republican Sinn Fein would consider alternatives when they took power in Ireland.

ÓDuibhir's optimism was completely disengaged from political realities. He was one of several people I would meet in the Republican Sinn Fein office who seemed to be looking for an identity rather than a cause, a place where he could indulge his intellect, work through these issues like a puzzle, socialize with like-minded people, and then leave it behind. He did not have the passion or intensity to put himself at risk or sacrifice anything. He was not part of a dynamic struggle. If this was all that dissident republican factions could muster, intellectual rebels with no taste for the fight, the peace process was secure. I wanted to meet the other people, the ones who were willing to gamble their comfort and security for the cause. I wanted to meet the people willing to fight.

Josephine Hayden was found in possession of a shotgun and a revolver in 1996, convicted, and sentenced to six years in prison. When sentences were read against Hayden and her five male Continuity IRA codefendants in a Dublin courtroom, they all gave clenched-fist salutes to supporters who were shouting "Up the Republic" from the gallery. The men were to serve their time in the "special category" wing of Port-laoise Prison outside Dublin. But Josephine Hayden was the only female political prisoner in the Irish Republic and there were no special facilities for her, so she was held at Limerick Prison.

There is no direct service from Belfast to Limerick, so I had to go through Dublin. A modern train, the *Enterprise*, shuttles passengers between the two capitals in less than two hours.

During the week, young professionals and business commuters fill the carriages. For most of them, Irish politics is a bore if not an embarrassment. They are more concerned with skyrocketing property prices than the struggle for Irish unity. Along the route, through bustling towns like Dundalk and Drogheda, I looked out on an Ireland of affluence and culture. But transferring in Dublin and heading west, the scene changed drastically.

I boarded a rickety train at Dublin's Heuston Station that gasped and chugged down the line. Young commuters packed this train as well, but they were sifted out at the stations serving Dublin's sprawling suburbs. At each stop, more suits and ties got off and very few got on. Eventually, the train nearly empty, suburban sprawl gave way to farmland, and rural Ireland opened up like a new frontier. In Limerick, where the Shannon River does not flow but churn and where the skies, too, seem to swirl like a basin of dirty laundry water, the wind was blowing cold. Gray-haired men wearing tweed coats were cycling along the street. Old women hobbled along, packages tucked under their arms. I saw the traditional images of Ireland in Limerick, yet Dublin's prosperity seemed to be quietly encroaching. Limerick shops were filled with the latest fashions, and new construction was going up among dilapidated buildings.

I walked to Limerick Prison located, surprisingly, just a few hundred yards from the center of town. Built in 1821, the oldest prison in Ireland, it had once fallen into disuse before it was recommissioned to meet the demand of a growing prison population. Even the prison governor had once described the conditions in the women's wing as "the worst we have." The cells did not have toilets; prisoners had to "slop out" each morning. Barbed wire and modern security cameras were incongruously draped over its ancient walls.

Prison visitors are vetted at a small shed just outside the main entrance, and I walked in with some trepidation. I had tried to go through official channels to arrange the interview, but the Irish Prison Service would not authorize my visit. The department head based in Dublin simply did not want journalists talking to Josephine Hayden, so I lied and told the guard on duty that I was a friend.

The fact that I had never visited Hayden before and that I had forgotten my passport might have concerned the guard, had he not taken an interest in my being an American and started talking about his annual family Christmas visit to New York. "And the changes in that city! Well, I never used to take the subway, but I would now. No problem," he told me.

I waited a while with the other visitors—a few young wives and children—until I was beckoned to a small room where I was searched and then handed over to another guard who escorted me into the courtyard of the prison. Walking through the stone portal and past the sentry stations, the prison had a romantic, Dickensian feel that I realized was probably lost on the prisoners held behind the walls. The guard carried his keys on a huge ring and led me through a series of gates and doors with a clank and a thud.

The room provided for prison visits was bare but for a few chairs and a Formica table divided in half by a short wooden partition. As I took a seat on one side of the table, the guard leaned in towards me. "We are watching you now," he said, pointing to a small camera mounted into the opposite wall. With that, it began to hum and swivel. "Just so as you know."

A minute later, I heard a key turn in the only other door in the room. Josephine Hayden, dressed in a white sweatshirt, entered with an impish smile. I recognized her from literature I had seen in the Republican Sinn Fein offices. She was fifty-seven years old but looked younger, with a short, modern haircut and deep blue eyes. We greeted each other like old friends for the guard's benefit, though we had never met and I was not even sure she had been expecting me. I took a seat while Josephine Hayden stood, leaning conspiratorially across the wooden partition.

Josephine Hayden was allowed two personal visits per week, and this was one of them. I had scheduled it with Roisin Hayden, Josephine's daughter, days earlier so that we did not overlap. If I was not going to see her mother, then someone else might be able to use the time. Besides the guards and other inmates, I was probably the only person Josephine Hayden would see that week, which may explain why she seemed warm to me so quickly. More than anything, she wanted a good chat.

There were usually twelve women held in her wing—mostly young girls serving time for drug offenses or petty crime. As the oldest and longest-serving female inmate, Josephine Hayden was a matriarchal figure.

"I have never seen the things these girls have seen. Most of them have been abused as kids, then turned to prostitution or other crime. You hear people say, 'Well, not everyone who is abused turns to crime.' But that is easy for someone to say who was never abused. I don't think it's any wonder they turned out like they have. And since there is no re-habilitation in here, you can bet most of them will be back through these doors.

"But that is the problem with this country now. The greed is unbelievable. My daughter says I won't recognize Dublin when I get out of here. A few people are becoming prosperous, and more and more of them are poor and desperate. I don't know how young people afford to live when the property prices are so high. I really don't. But sure, it all traces back to greed. The drug problem and everything else can be traced down to greed."

Josephine pushed a few stray hairs away from her face. She was becoming animated. Republicans like her wanted more than the British out of Ireland. They were also socialists—passionate and hopelessly principled socialists who promoted a radical redistribution of wealth torn right from the pages of Marx. It was the sort of policy that might have stirred the Irish masses a century ago, when many were indebted to British landlords or languishing in the soulless factories of Dublin and Belfast. But now, Ireland is prosperous and content. But Josephine Hayden was right about greed; the sprawl I passed through around Dublin was the work of exploitative developers and planners on the take, but no one seemed to care. Still, Josephine Hayden was convinced that, in time, people would see that she was right.

"It's like what people said about the Soviet Union. 'When it falls and capitalism takes over, everything will improve.' But it has not improved. Things there are now worse than they ever were. See? That is what republicans are trying to show people here in Ireland. We are trying to show them that life here is not as good as they think. There are a lot of problems. There is corruption and greed and, of course, we still have the British here in our country. These are all the real problems that have to be dealt with.

"But Gerry Adams and Provisional Sinn Fein have turned their backs on the movement. They are part of the problem, and so they are getting all the attention. They are no longer the revolutionaries. They are part of the status quo. They go around with their big cars and living in their nice houses—see, it all goes back to greed? They sold out. It's as simple as that. That is why I got involved with the Republican Sinn Fein; we are still fighting for the important issues. Some people may say that these issues don't matter to people anymore, but they do. As long as there is injustice and inequality, there will always be republicans."

This is what I had come to hear about—I wanted to know what the republican movement looked like from the inside. Volunteering at Belfast's Republican Sinn Fein offices was one thing. It was another thing to serve a lonely prison sentence for the cause. Josephine Hayden was in her fifties, had served four years, and had suffered a heart attack in Limerick Prison by the time we met. Sixteen hours of her day were spent in a cell; she was allowed short recreation in a yard the size of a tennis court. Once a month, she was taken to see her partner, Michael Hegarty, serving ten years in Portlaoise Prison on an explosives conviction. She was not some young, impetuous activist but a mother doing hard time for a cause that, even in the most optimistic circumstances, would not achieve its goal until she was in the grave.

I looked over my shoulder at the guard sitting in the doorway. He had once been listening to our conversation but was now engrossed in his newspaper. Then I leaned over the partition and asked Josephine Hayden if she thought all the violence, bloodshed, and heartache was worth it.

"I am not sorry for what I did, if that is what you mean. I am just sorry that I was caught. I knew what I was getting involved with when I joined the movement. I knew there would be risks. Don't get me wrong—I wish I was not in here—but I'm not sorry for what I did. That was part of the risk. I took that risk, and I am paying the consequences.

"But even right now, I could turn my back on the movement and get out of here sooner. That is what two of the others who were arrested did. Did you know that? Four of us remained silent during our trial—we refused to recognize the court. But two of them pled guilty. They got shorter sentences for playing by the rules. The two of them are out of prison already. They turned their backs on the movement; but that was their decision. Does that affect my morale? No, my morale is good. I'm not sorry that they left the movement. It was their decision. But I could never do that. I could never go against my principles like that. I know I am right, so I cannot just say 'I was wrong' to get out of prison."

"But where does the struggle go from here?" I asked. "Republican Sinn Fein has no political representatives. Its support is pretty small compared to Sinn Fein. Prisoners like you have been denied political status. You can't get weapons or support from countries like Libya anymore. The security forces are crawling all over you. I mean, where will the movement be in another five years?"

She did not know. "There are more people than you think who are willing to keep fighting. They know that the British presence in this country is one of our biggest problems. I mean, we are not done yet. There are people who will keep fighting until the British are driven out. Those people have my full support. They will always have my full support. But where will we be in five years? I can't say. I think we can build up the support that the Provos [Provisional IRA] once had. We need to be better communicators and we need to attract young people, but our message is still right. When I get out, I am going to get back involved with the movement. As long as they keep to their principles, they will have my support."

I was a little taken aback by Josephine Hayden's blind and unshakable confidence. Clearly, she was committed, but her commitment had clouded her judgment. There was no way Republican Sinn Fein could muster the same support that early republicans had once enjoyed. Irish Catholics in the North were generally content—Hayden would say "complacent"—with their lives. The republican cause simply did not move people the way it once had. When people like Josephine Hayden were gone, I knew that there would not be many willing to fill her shoes.

About an hour into the interview, the young guard who had been sitting outside the door reading his newspaper began pacing around the hallway. Ten minutes later, he walked brusquely into the room and tossed a folded piece of paper across the table. It was my visitor pass and, I guessed, my signal to leave. Josephine Hayden eyed the paper, and then the guard. She must have recognized the sign, because her mood suddenly changed. She stood straight up and began mouthing off to the guard. "I always get the whole visit! I never have my visits cut short," she impudently told him. "I always get my whole visit! Call the governor! Ask him if I don't get the whole visit! Go on and ask him now, because I am not leaving!"

She sat down in her chair and folded her arms. "I'm just doing what I was told," the guard said, exasperated. "Now this fella was only supposed to be here for a half hour and it is nearly an hour now. I was told he has to go. I'm just doing what I'm told."

"I'm not leaving. So, what are you going to do?" Hayden taunted. "Are you going to force me out of here?" Then, pointing at me. "Are you going to manhandle him, too?"

The guard seemed confused. "What do you mean 'too'? What do you mean by that? What are you talking about?"

"You're going to have to drag me out of here. You're just going to have to, because I'm not leaving. I'm not done talking yet. I'm staying here until I'm done talking." It suddenly became clear that Josephine Hayden wanted to be dragged out of the room. She hoped that the guards would soon rush in, subdue her, and force her to leave while I watched on. She would have liked that, for someone in the press to see her being physically attacked. It would have good publicity for the cause.

But the guard just looked befuddled and a bit helpless, as if trying to order his mother around. I did not want to get caught in the middle of anything. "Ah, Josephine," I said meekly. "I think I had better go."

"No, no. They cannot make you leave," she said. "You stay here. Let's keep talking."

I got up, and she relented. Then, as I was leaving, Josephine Hayden walked over to me, shook my hand, and clasped my wrist with the other. "Now you have a story to write about," she said.

As I walked down the streets of Limerick, a bit dazed, I saw a tattered republican poster peeling off a telephone pole. It had gone up a few weeks earlier to publicize a commemoration of Patrick Pearse's Easter Rising. "The Easter Lily is a National Emblem. The Easter Lily represents North and South united in an expression of appreciation of the principles for which the men of Easter week gave up their lives. The Easter Lily is the emblem of the hope and confidence in the ultimate realization of every Irishman's dream—Ireland free and united from the center to the sea!"

Just above it, a fresh poster had gone up to promote a new nightclub.

In early January 1990, the IRA summoned one of their intelligence officers, Sandy Lynch, to Belfast. Lynch made his way from his country home in Magherafelt to a safe house in north Belfast, where he abandoned his car and drove with a comrade on what he thought was a reconnaissance mission.

But when the pair arrived at a house in Andersontown, west Belfast, Lynch was taken to an upstairs bedroom, partly stripped, bound, blindfolded, and gagged with cotton wool by an IRA interrogation man. The game was up. Lynch was an informer and the IRA knew it.

Since his early teens, when Alexander "Sandy" Lynch first got involved with paramilitaries, he had been taught to hate and fear informers. They were the traitors that existed somewhere on the margins of the struggle. Erstwhile comrades were always trying to root out these invisible foes while the informer's new allies in the security forces pushed them further in their betrayal.

Sandy Lynch knew all the perils, but when the Royal Ulster Constabulary's intelligence-gathering unit, Special Branch, approached him to become an informer while he was serving a twelve-year prison sentence for possession of explosives, he agreed. That life of estrangement and danger oddly suited Sandy Lynch. His republican involvement to that point seems to have been incidental. It was excitement and danger that he craved.

But in 1985, just two years after his release from prison, Sandy Lynch was caught in the informer's paradox. In order to protect Lynch's identity, only a few Special Branch officers knew of his collaboration. To the rest of the security forces, Lynch was just another known republican suspect. So when police raided a republican arms dump and found Sandy Lynch there, he was arrested and sentenced to four years in prison. Lynch's information had led to his own arrest, but no one could know that or he was dead for sure. That was the life of an informer.

When Lynch was again released in 1988, Special Branch ordered him to infiltrate the IRA. He set up a taxi company in the Ardoyne area of Belfast as cover, made his IRA contacts, and with his past experience, rose swiftly to work with an IRA intelligence unit. Lynch had access to high-grade IRA information as he helped plan paramilitary attacks and, ironically, sniff out suspected informers. All the while, Lynch passed information on to the security forces. Many ambitious IRA operations, including an assassination attempt on a local MP, were thwarted thanks to Sandy Lynch. He was, in the words of security sources, the best IRA spy Special Branch had ever recruited. Lynch's handlers began to jokingly refer to him as agent 007.

Lynch got the danger he was looking for, but as he sat gagged and bound to a chair in a west Belfast safe house with Libyan-trained IRA interrogators beating him, he must have regretted ever getting involved. Four IRA men questioned Lynch for two days. They wanted to know every detail of what he had ever done or said. They swore that they would break him.

"I was told to come clean and tell them everything and that they would do their best for me," Lynch would later say. But if he did not cooperate, Lynch's interrogators told him, he would be killed—taken to a cow shed in south Armagh where no one could hear his screams. When his wife found his body, she would not be able to recognize him because his face would be blown off.

Lynch was given a pen and paper to write his confession, and then he was forced to read it on tape. Sometimes stoic, sometimes sobbing, Lynch detailed the operations he had helped sabotage and the amounts of money he had earned for his betrayal.

Despite his interrogators' reassurances, Lynch knew what was coming next. A year earlier, Joseph Fenton, another informer, had been found shot three times in the face down an alley just a hundred yards from where Lynch was being questioned. After his death, Fenton's father heard his son's ten-minute confession tape at Connolly House, the Sinn Fein headquarters.

Lynch was probably only a few hours away from Fenton's fate when police and army raided the house on January 8, 1990. They found Lynch disheveled and disoriented. His confession tape was salvaged from the bathroom. And while the security forces flooded through the front of the house making arrests, Danny Morrison, the Sinn Fein publicity director who had arrived just minutes earlier, absconded out the back door.

A soldier spotted Morrison and ordered him to halt. Morrison ignored the order, calmly turned around, walked into the neighboring house, poured himself a glass of water, and started casually chatting with the family gathered in the living room. When security forces followed Morrison into the house, he asked them what the fuss was all about—he had just stopped by for a visit. If Morrison had only been able to name anyone in the room when asked, he might have gotten away with it. Instead, he faltered and was charged with kidnapping, conspiracy to murder, and IRA membership. Sandy Lynch and his wife were taken into protective custody and flown to safety in England.

Over the previous eighteen years, Danny Morrison had earned a reputation as being shrewd, direct, and infuriatingly self-assured in justifying a remorseless IRA campaign. Since he started editing *Republican News*, at twenty-two, Morrison had walked a thin line in the struggle, speaking for the men in the shadows of violence and excusing their bloody deeds while always remaining one step removed from their dealings.

"If that bomb had killed the British cabinet, examine then what would have happened," Morrison coolly mused to a British paper in the aftermath of the 1984 Brighton bombing, an attack on a British Conservation Party conference that nearly killed Prime Minister Margaret Thatcher. "There would have been a rethink within British political circles, and it probably would have led to British withdrawal in a much shorter period."

That was Morrison's inimitably direct style, and the rest of his media image—the clever wit, the wiry beard, the piercing eyes—was just as distinctive. He was the public face of a clandestine movement and effective because he never crossed into the world of violence—until the Sandy Lynch affair.

Days after Danny Morrison and the four IRA members who had been interrogating Sandy Lynch were arrested, Sinn Fein tried to get them back. A press conference was arranged with Sandy Lynch's father, William, saying the whole army raid had been a misunderstanding. The police had been putting Sandy under pressure to turn informer, he said. Sandy had resisted and gone to the house to clear the air with the IRA. He had not been kidnapped. The police were blowing the whole situation out of proportion just so they could make a few arrests.

The press conference was a clear message to Lynch: Retract any statements you have given to the police and the whole matter will be forgotten about. It was a final appeal, and backed up by the IRA's sense of black honor that, even though they tried to kill him just days earlier, they would keep their word and leave Lynch alone if he did retract. The same technique had been used effectively in the past. But Sandy Lynch was gone. Neither his former comrades nor his family could bring him back.

Months later, at his trial, Danny Morrison admitted that, yes, he had been in the house with Lynch, but only to escort him to a prearranged press conference. "The IRA will let you think you are going to a press conference," Lynch replied. "But the only place you are going from an IRA interrogation is to the grave."

The judge, too, wondered why, if Sandy Lynch was going to a press conference, the confession tape was made. He could not convict Danny Morrison and his co-accused on the charges of conspiracy to murder or IRA membership, but they were found guilty of kidnapping. Danny Morrison spent the next four years in the Maze prison.

As I sat at the dining room table of Morrison's spacious west Belfast home, where a cat was perched placidly on a window ledge overlooking a manicured garden, I thought that the Troubles must surely be over. Not least because Morrison used those words himself: "the Troubles." Twenty years ago that was the word for the middle classes, the people who followed the IRA's war for Irish liberation with indifference, tut-tutting the television news reports of the latest bombing or shooting. Republicans rarely used that word; it diminished their struggle. But Morrison used it, now, and as he pottered around the kitchen, tinkered with the coffeemaker, and produced a tray of biscuits before sitting down to chat, I knew I was not going to meet Danny Morrison the rebel. No longer the urgent man with the overgrown beard, Morrison was clean-shaven and cordial. He poured my coffee.

I had arranged to meet Morrison because, I thought, if anyone could defend accusations that Sinn Fein and the IRA had gone soft he could. But in such salubrious surroundings, when years ago Morrison had been living in a squalid apartment according to the republican and socialist principles he espoused, I supposed that I would be disappointed.

Morrison was living comfortably, which was not a crime, but the battle for Irish unity had not yet been won. Josephine Hayden was languishing in a Limerick prison because she would not renounce her principles. She was a republican sworn to fight British rule with every thought and deed until her dying breath. Danny Morrison had once made that vow, but he was no longer fighting. Now he is a writer. He has three novels to his credit and is no longer formally associated with Sinn Fein. I found that surprising because Danny Morrison had been involved in the earliest reemergence of republicanism and, more than most, he had led by word and deed.

"When I was very young, I was always interested in reading. I used to go to the library for my mother and used to get her books and then also do my own reading," Morrison remembered. "By then, the Troubles had broken out and I was torn between the politics of the street and college. I got emotionally and politically involved, and in July 1975, I became the editor of the *Republican News*."

In that time, Morrison became a skilled wordsmith and communicator and helped the paper develop from a one-dimensional propaganda sheet into a more sophisticated journal of republican thought. Make no mistake, the *Republican News* gave the IRA and Sinn Fein unfailing support while it stifled any dissenting views, but it advanced republican thought to something more than simple jingoism. The *Republican News* was the direct channel between the leadership of the movement and the broader base, which was largely drawn from Catholics living in urban ghettos and the border hinterland. It digested news events, spread socialist thinking, and cultivated enthusiasm for the struggle.

"The paper was run on a shoestring," Morrison said of the early days with the *Republican News*. "There was little generation of material. There were no reporters. As IRA prisoners were released, and people came with ideas, we started to get the staff together and generate stories. We learned on the hoof, but the British were always trying to shut us down. We were regularly raided and charged with IRA membership. Shots were fired at the office; we had a hand grenade thrown at us. Once, a car bomb was parked near the door and a distribution manager was shot outside the office. There were attempted murders against me."

Morrison ran through the hazards and hardships of that time as if he were reciting a grocery list—emotionless and thorough, so as not to forget anything. At the time, in the heat of the struggle, all those experiences must have woven quite a tapestry. It was exciting, Morrison admitted, but it was also exhausting and often tragic.

On the first day of March 1981, Bobby Sands, the twenty-six-year-old IRA commander in the Maze prison who was serving a fourteen-year sentence for firearms offenses, began a hunger strike "unto death" for political prisoner status. Republicans had once held that special designation and its associated privileges in the Maze—prisoners did not have to work, could wear their own clothes, and were given extra personal visits—but they had lost them five years earlier in a tightening prison regime. Almost immediately, prisoners began a nonconformity campaign to get their special status back. First there had been a blanket protest, where prisoners draped themselves in bedsheets rather than wear prison uniforms, but it had failed. Next was the dirty protest. Prisoners refused to wash or shave and smeared their excreta on the walls of their cell; that too failed. The hunger strike was seen as the ultimate protest. It had a long history in the republican struggle, and it was what had won the original "special category" status at the beginning of the Troubles.

During the hunger strike, Danny Morrison served as Bobby Sands's official spokesman outside the prison. His job was to muster public sympathy for Sands's protest and convert it into widespread indignation against the intransigence of the British state. Morrison succeeded beyond his wildest ambitions. For the first time, republicans showed that they were willing to endure suffering for their cause rather than simply inflict suffering in its name. And there was something about Sands's protest, the quiet martyrdom and penance of it, the determination in the face of overwhelming force, that broadly resonated with Irish Catholics.

As Sands's protest continued, his health deteriorated and his popular stature grew. Danny Morrison printed Sands's messages from prison, which had been excruciatingly written out on toilet paper and furtively sneaked out of his cell, in the *Republican News*. Sands's philosophical reflections on the republican struggle and his own mortality were received like messages from a prophet, while Margaret Thatcher's bluster against the hunger strike—"We are not prepared to consider special category status. . . . Crime is crime is crime; it is not political."—galvanized Catholic resentment. Often taking a cue from the church hierarchy, even moderate Catholics felt justified in their growing antipathy towards the British.

Republicans saw a chance to channel that resentment when, on the fourth day of Bobby Sands's hunger strike, Frank Maguire, a nationalist MP from the rural constituency of Fermanagh–South Tyrone, died. After other Nationalist candidates agreed not to fight the seat, Bobby Sands stood as his successor in what was broadly seen as a referendum on the hunger strike. On his fortieth day without food and having lost nearly thirty pounds, Bobby Sands became an honorable member of the British House of Commons.

Sands's political campaign and hunger strike had sparked wild media interest at home and abroad while uniting the Catholic community like nothing since the civil rights struggle at the beginning of the Troubles. It was speculated that, with Sands now a member of Parliament, the British would have to relent in order to end the hunger strike. But they did not. Bobby Sands died after sixty-six days without food, and nine more republican hunger strikers died after him before the protests were called off. In the aftermath of the hunger strike, the British government granted most of the prisoners' demands and then passed a law prohibiting prisoners from standing for Parliament.

The hunger strike had been an unmitigated disaster for the British and an unexpected boon for republicans. Conventional thinking had been upset; republicans could win elections even while the IRA continued their campaign of violence. The political landscape of Northern Ireland had shifted, and Morrison, the inveterate strategist, saw an opportunity. He wanted to harness the precedent of Sands's election and the widespread indignation over the hunger strikes. He wanted to politicize Sinn Fein and begin an earnest campaign for elected office. To do anything less would be to squander invaluable political capital. Many republicans agreed. Particularly among the younger generation, there had been a slowly building sense that the armed struggle was insufficient. If republicanism was truly a popular movement, it had to mobilize more than a few hundred IRA activists. The only thing that stood in the way was the Sinn Fein constitution, which specifically forbade its members from holding elected office.

The Irish nation is one and indivisible. Until that truth is observed in practice, republicans will abstain from politics. That was the immutable doctrine of republicanism that was set in the very foundations of the struggle and Patrick Pearse's Easter Rising. After Bobby Sands's election, that policy suddenly appeared antiquated and utterly encumbering. Danny Morrison and his allies planned to challenge the abstentionist policy at the Sinn Fein *ard fheis*, the party's annual conference, on October 31, 1981. Their opponents were among the old guard, people like Ruarí ÓBrádaigh, who thought politics would dilute the armed struggle. In one of the seminal speeches of the modern republican movement, a precursor to the events that would force Ruarí ÓBrádaigh to form Republican Sinn Fein five years later, Danny Morrison answered those misgivings with a flattering nod to the hard-liners and a spark of realism: "Who among us believes that we can win the war through armed struggle alone? But will anyone object if with a ballot box in this hand and an Armalite [rifle] in the other, we take power in Ireland?

"We knew that if we missed that chance, we would never see another circumstance when we could get involved in electoral politics," Morrison remembers. "All the senior republicans were told to get up there and talk and try to persuade people. When I used that expression about the 'Armalite and the ballot box' I was, in a way, playing to the gallery. I wanted to reassure people who had reservations that the armed struggle was not going to be interfered with and could continue but that we had to open another frontier and that was politics. In the end we won, arguably leading to where we are today."

Morrison said these words—"where we are today"—with a sense of satisfaction. He had helped bring the republican movement to a point where widespread violence was a thing of the past, yet that was not the destination he had originally charted. A united Ireland, no matter the costs or consequences, had been the goal. How many times had Morrison uttered those words over the years that he worked with Sinn Fein? But Morrison was not going to bristle at accusations of turning soft. He did not accept the premise. The republican movement was changing, evolving really, for the better, but the principles were the same.

"I do believe that the republican movement has developed along revolutionary lines. Now, it has not developed along traditional republican lines. I concede that Ruarí [ÓBrádaigh] can claim to be the traditional republican—"abstain from politics, remain pure." But that increasingly becomes a minority pursuit. It does not relate to ordinary people and their everyday lives and their struggle: education of their children, the health services, work. It is just a mythology.

"The fact is that the struggle needed to branch out and take on the enemy on the enemy's grounds—which is politics. It is okay fighting the British Army—in fact the IRA could fight on for another thirty years—but that is not the same as achieving something or showing something for all the sacrifices and all the deaths, including those of your enemy.

"And that is where Ruarí and other dissident republicans do not respect their comrades. They do not respect the fact that the people who have been on hunger strike, who have been on the blanket protests, who have done life sentences, who have killed soldiers—the majority of these people agree with this strategy. So they are actually anti-republican in that respect; they do not follow the consensus. People who have fought recognize changed circumstances. They see this as a wise way forward. Ruarí has no respect for that."

Morrison had been involved through the heady days of the struggle, when the IRA campaign was relentless and politics was a novel experiment. However sordid republicanism looked from the outside, it was a noble adventure for Danny Morrison. The battle was on and it was immediate. There was hardly time to think. That had all changed with Morrison's conviction. Years in prison gave him time, infinite time, to think about his life and the cause.

Morrison has a passion for writing. It spread beyond his politics, and just weeks before he was arrested, Morrison's first novel, *West Belfast,* was published. The prison sentence became Morrison's catharsis, and he spent much of his time there writing. He was alone with his thoughts, a rickety desk, and a pencil stub. In his reflective moments, Morrison realized that the republican struggle would have to be transformed. He was a realist, not an ideologue. He could see that there was room for compromise.

"The world is changing in such a way that some of our ideas of sovereignty and nationhood are being overtaken by new concepts," Morrison noted in a prison letter to Gerry Adams, the Sinn Fein president. He pointed to the fight against apartheid in South Africa, and saw parallels there. Morrison quoted ANC (African National Congress) member Albie Sachs in *The Soft Vengeance of a Freedom Fighter,* who said, "We might find ourselves confronted with hard decisions, whether to hold out for generations if necessary, until we are finally able to overthrow and completely destroy the system of apartheid, or accept major but incomplete breakthroughs now, transforming the terrain of struggle in a way which is advantageous to the achievement of our ultimate goals."

After five years in prison, Danny Morrison would be released at over forty with no wife, no house, and no job. When Morrison was young and just beginning his involvement that would not have troubled him. He expected to either be long dead or living in a united Ireland by the time those concerns crept up. But at the pace it was going, the revolution would outlive the revolutionary.

Danny Morrison was no fainthearted coward. He had witnessed the slow, grinding attrition of the IRA campaign and the bloody wake it had left. He had survived decades of living under the threat of death. He had faced bouts of despondency and doubt. He had endured all of that because he felt a conviction of conscience. Now Morrison's conscience was telling him the fight was over.

"I think there is some disillusionment, but I don't think that the object of the disillusionment is with the republican leadership. He told me that day, I think people are saying, 'Unionists and the Brits are still the same; they have not changed.' But I don't think people are saying, 'Let's get out the gear and get stuck back into them.' People who are responsible know that fighting and dying and killing is not worth it at this point. That is a fact. This is what is incontrovertible. There is no way any dissident republican group will be able to replicate the tempo of the IRA campaign. And if that IRA campaign led to a military stalemate, that is what we are heading back into. Even if they are able to bomb hotels, even if they are able to kill soldiers, even if they are able to plant a bomb in London or kill a soldier in Germany, it ain't going to change the balance of political power, and that is what you fight a war for. Unless you can change that, you are fighting for the sake of fighting and for the sake of your own ego. And it is wrong."

I was unconvinced when I left Morrison that day. Wasn't everything he said just a matter of opinion? "My brother did not die for this," Bernadette Sands McKevitt, Bobby Sands's sister, reportedly said after the Good Friday Agreement was signed. Her husband, Mickey McKevitt, a former quartermaster for the IRA, was a leading figure behind the

Real IRA. Who had the authority to speak of Bobby Sands's sacrifice? His former comrades? His sister? If Bobby Sands or Patrick Pearse were alive today, would they still support the use of violence or would they back the Good Friday Agreement? How could one objectively judge Josephine Hayden's outlook against that of Danny Morrison? Each of them had gotten involved in the republican movement for the same reasons. Each of them claimed the same history and venerated the same martyrs. If the principles were the same, why did some people feel they had to fight, die, or go to prison in the name of the struggle and others thought the violent struggle was over? In the end, was the difference anything more than a capricious personal conceit?

Idealist or pragmatist? Patriot or traitor? Who could judge? It is often a narrow ledge between the two, and the difference is often only settled by time and chance. In the end, it is the victor who makes the rules and writes the history. I find that judgment rather unsatisfactory, but there is no other way to explain it. Danny Morrison was sure that he was right. But the dissident republicans were just as sure of their own position. Each felt that they would be vindicated in time.

My mind drifted back to Anne, one of the few women I had met in the Republican Sinn Fein offices. She was young but acutely preoccupied. She told me a common, melancholy story.

Her family was driven out of their home at the beginning of the Troubles—just like the McConvilles, just like so many other families—and they moved to the Twinbrook housing estate of west Belfast, which was quickly becoming an IRA stronghold. Soldiers on the streets, army checkpoints, security searches, gunfire, and bomb scares shaped Anne's formative years. Many members of her family were arrested or imprisoned for IRA involvement. Anne took a cue from the world around her and got involved with the republican movement, helping with street collections and playing in a republican band. "Whatever they needed, I done because I thought they were doing the right thing," she said. But then the IRA called a cease-fire and Anne was dismayed.

When Anne was eighteen, she had a companion named Pearse Jordan. His mother owned a clothing shop around the corner from where Anne worked in Belfast city center, and the pair would often meet for lunch. They had a lot in common. Having survived a searing childhood in west Belfast, they had both turned to the republican movement for a sense of stability and purpose. Anne was involved in the softer side of the struggle; Pearse was an IRA volunteer, though they never spoke about it. And while there were just three years between them, Pearse was older and so Anne looked up to him a bit. When Anne felt intimidated at work, which was often because she worked near the bottom of the Shankill Road, Pearse would give her support. "He was someone I could talk to and cry with," Anne said. "He was just always there."

Just before five o'clock on Tuesday, November 25, 1992, Pearse dropped by to visit Anne at work. She saw him again a half hour later, lying dead under a forensic blanket on the Falls Road.

Pearse had been driving alone and unarmed in a red Ford Orion when he was rammed in the rear and side by two unmarked police vehicles that forced his car onto the pavement. Stunned, Pearse got out of the car and started to run. Without warning, according to witnesses, the police opened fire. Pearse Jordan was hit several times in the back, and he died while a priest from the nearby St. John's chapel gave last rites. There was no official explanation as to why Pearse Jordan was targeted, though several other IRA activists had been ambushed in similar circumstances around that time in what many called clandestine security force "shoot to kill" operations.

Anne was devastated. She left the country to grieve on her own for a while, but eventually came home. "It took a while to get over it after a lot of crying and moping around the house," she told me. And while there was no hope of finding solace, Anne at least took modest comfort knowing that Pearse had died for the cause. He knew that he could be killed or imprisoned; the IRA was honest with their volunteers about that. But the IRA also promised that no matter how many volunteers fell, the struggle would continue. That was the vow that sealed the commitment. It was a certainty that a volunteer could carry unto death. But then, the IRA called their first cease-fire less than two years after Pearse Jordan was killed, and the struggle, at least the one that he joined, was over.

"To me, if they were discussing a cease-fire, why did they let him die? Why not just hold back? To me, he was used," Anne lamented. She said that it was dishonest for the IRA to change the rules. What if Pearse had known that there would be a cease-fire? Would he have joined? Would he have been in the car that day? Now there is no way of knowing.

Anne was doing street collections for Republican Sinn Fein when I met her, and she had joined their marching band. Former friends and comrades in the mainstream republican movement were now strangers. They would turn their backs on her and throw her out of republican clubs. "I don't think people ever thought that the IRA would give up the struggle. I don't think people thought it would really happen. Now if you go to bars at night, they don't allow people to sing rebel songs— you know, songs about dead volunteers. They try to stifle that. They think it riles people up, that it brings back memories and gets people emotional. If people get emotional, they start questioning things. But you can't block it out that way. You can't get rid of it that easily."

And in another example of cascading misfortune that made me wonder if, somehow, tragedy in Northern Ireland was contagious, Anne had been plagued by many ordinary hardships. In the years since Pearse's death she had lost a child at birth, had had ovarian cysts removed, and had been diagnosed with diabetes. Volunteering with Republican Sinn Fein was an added stress that endangered her health. "I don't know where things will be in the future, because everything I have planned has gone wrong. I have lost a friend, and my health has suffered. So now, I just take one day at a time. Friends of mine get so frustrated, they might say, 'What will we do this weekend?' I tell them to wait until we get closer to the time. Things in this life can just turn so quick, you never know."

For Anne, involvement with the Republican Sinn Fein was Pearse's retribution. She was getting back *at* them *for* him. "But don't get me wrong," she said. "I don't want a return to violence." Yet she was involved with a group that was still committed to a violent campaign. The values she was expressing did not add up to the life that she was living.

Anne was angry and lashing out. Republican Sinn Fein was able to exploit that emotion. But it takes more than resentment to build a movement, and the number of idealists was dwindling.

One rainy morning I went to visit Tommy Crossan. He had been convicted for his part in a Continuity IRA gun attack on a Belfast police station and was expecting to be sentenced any day. Prisoners who supported the peace process were being released, and the ones who opposed it, men like Tommy Crossan, were being held in Northern Ireland's remaining prison for male inmates, Maghaberry. There, all of the privileges that Bobby Sands had died for in the Maze were revoked. Crossan had to wear a prison uniform, cooperate with prison work, and was held on the same wing as his counterparts from dissident Protestant paramilitaries. One of them had recently thrown a cup of scalding water in Crossan's face. Twenty years earlier, if word had gotten out that a republican prisoner was being held in such conditions, Belfast's Catholic ghettos would have erupted in protests and riot. But few people cared or even knew about Tommy Crossan's plight.

I traveled to the prison with Crossan's family, sitting in the car between his wife and mother. Through most of the ride, the women sat smoking in near silence. Crossan's mother was cradling a parcel of fresh fruit and some buns in her lap. Anne, Crossan's wife—thin, dark-haired and attractive—was holding some newspapers and trying to conceal the latest edition of the Republican Sinn Fein newsletter, *Saoirse,* inside a copy of the local *Irish News.* "Sometimes they don't look inside the papers," she said in her dulcet Waterford brogue.

We drove deep into rural County Armagh where Maghaberry, a sheer gray fortress, was situated alone in a desolate valley. The prison was so remote, it felt like it could burn down tomorrow and no one would find out for days. If it did, would anyone even have cared? The building was modern and soulless; the guards were just as cold. We were escorted into the belly of the building through a maze of air locks. Tommy Crossan was already seated at his side of the table when we reached the visitor center, and I was once again facing one of the last Irish rebels. But unlike Josephine Hayden, Crossan was young, twenty-nine. And his time in prison had just started while Josephine Hayden was about to get out. For the next half an hour, giving scant attention to his family, Tommy Crossan and I talked about the next phase of the republican struggle. He was cocksure and had an answer for everything.

The Continuity IRA was preparing a new campaign, he said. They were ready to fight on. He dismissed the group's shortcomings—lack of arms, cash, and volunteers—with an assuredness bordering on the delusional. Continuity IRA ranks were swelling with disaffected IRA members, he told me. Money and arms would soon follow. Informer leaks were being plugged. The organization was getting stronger, tighter, more disciplined. Violence was still the answer, and they were prepared to carry on with the campaign.

"During the early nineties, the IRA had the British on the run. Bombs in the center of London were destroying their economy. They were on their knees. Then the IRA decides to stop? The only language the British understand comes from a five-hundred-pound bomb. If the IRA are not prepared to get rid of the British, they should hand their weapons to the groups that are."

Crossan spoke with a mixture of bravado and jocular friendliness that seemed indifferent to the prison sentence that surely loomed. The abortive gun attack that had landed Crossan in jail had been pointless. It was never going to destabilize the peace process or advance the republican cause. Crossan was a maverick who carried all the glorious defiance and tragic naïveté associated with that term. He had committed a lonesome act, and that loneliness was only accentuated in an isolated prison wing. He had no friends in prison and did not dare dream of a future life when this would all end.

Although Tommy virtually ignored his wife and mother, I noticed that they were watching him with a fixed, somewhat mesmerized stare. They were not concerned with what he was saying—the casual description of bombing and shooting—but only that he was present, in good spirits, eating well, and not being mistreated. The political movement that abandoned Tommy Crossan in prison did not interest them. They just wanted to know when the system would loosen its grip and return him to his family. "Talk to them," I wanted to say, growing uncomfortable with his attention. "Because they are going to see you through this."

"He is still in a state of shock," Anne told me the day after the sentence was read. "He had been hoping for eight years or under, maybe even just six. He never thought he would get ten years. But the judge said that Tommy tried to break the peace process and so he was going to give him a stiff penalty. The judge tried to make an example of him."

Just as Tommy Crossan was beginning his life in prison, Josephine Hayden was getting used to life on the outside. She was released in the late summer of 2000, and we had a drink in a Dublin pub several months later. We had both read a recent story in the newspaper about Nicola O'Connor having just had a baby. It seems that she had been so stressed about Joseph's murder that six months had passed before she realized that she was even pregnant. It was a boy, and she named it Joe. Josephine and I talked about that for a while. "It's terrible, isn't it?" she asked. "What the IRA did to that girl. Oh, I will have to remember to write Tommy Crossan a letter. He's a young lad. He can get through it all right."

As for herself, Josephine was still getting adjusted to a normal life. Having moved back into her old house, Josephine was getting reacquainted with her children. She was taking some sociology classes and working part-time stocking shelves in a grocery store. Every couple of weeks she went to see her partner, Michael Hegarty, in Portlaoise Prison. Would the relationship last? Josephine did not know. She was getting tired of running back and forth to prison, especially since she had just left one herself. But what about the movement? Was she getting tired of that too? "Well, I'm not saying that I want to get back involved, but I will if they ask me."

Saint Patrick

❐　　　❐

"We have a special guest tonight," Lee Reynolds said, surveying the small crowd in the East Belfast Methodist Mission church hall. "Saint Patrick!"

On cue a bald, stout man dressed in what appeared to be a tailor-fitted potato sack entered the room. Holding a wooden staff and with a coarse rope tied around his waist, he was a plausible rendition of a fifth-century cleric, but for a pair of sneakers peeking from below his frock.

Saint Patrick took a seat.

"Are you Irish?" Lee Reynolds asked, in a mock talk show format.

"No," Saint Patrick gravely answered.

"Where are you from?" Reynolds followed.

"I am from Britain," Saint Patrick replied.

"How did you end up here?" Again, Reynolds.

"I was taken into slavery." And for several minutes, the two men continued the stale interview.

In the audience, a few gray-haired parishioners and the minister looked on curiously. Two haggard women from the neighboring drug and alcohol treatment center abruptly left. A folk singer strummed a few tunes. A historian lectured about Saint Patrick's message. A local flute brigade, outnumbering the audience, squawked for Protestant Belfast's Saint Patrick celebrations.

A few days later, dozens of Saint Patricks dressed in elaborate green robes, full cotton beards, and sandals led a march through Belfast. School-aged children glided in on floats, marching bands advanced in formation, and thousands of revelers pulsated to the beat pumping from a makeshift stage erected outside the city hall. Everyone there was happy, and Catriona Ruane, the event organizer, dashed among the raucous crowd with satisfaction.

Only the bust of Queen Victoria, standing on the grounds of the city hall, looked uneasy. It had been erected a century earlier to celebrate the inauguration of the city hall, but the crowds gathering at its feet were less than reverent. A few youths mounted the pedestal, scaled the pleats of the British monarch's dress, grasped her scepter, and stuck an Irish flag in her hand. The gathering, almost entirely Catholic, howled their approval.

In most cities, Saint Patrick's Day celebrations are about as controversial as sunshine but how, or even if, Belfast should commemorate the ancient saint has become an insuperable issue. Not wanting to get dragged into controversy, Belfast City Council refuses to fund any official celebrations. That leaves local community groups—Protestants and Catholics independently—to organize their own events and antagonize one another in the process. In a country where nothing is neutral, Saint Patrick is one of the few icons that has yet to be appropriated.

Catholics honor the men who tried to end British rule. Protestants honor the men who tried to preserve it. Names like Patrick Pearse, Michael Collins, and more contemporarily, Bobby Sands, belong to the Catholics. They are part of the tapestry of the rebel. Lord Carson, who signed a blood vow to resist Irish independence, is held in esteem among Protestants. King William of Orange, who defeated the Catholic King James in 1690, is revered for the same reasons. They were all men of flair and conviction who, most importantly, chose a side.

It's a safe bet that if one side venerates someone as a hero, the other side loathes him or her. But there are some exceptions, the rare occasions when both Protestants and Catholics want to claim the same hero. When they do, some revision is usually in order.

One such hero is James Magennis, who won the distinguished Victoria Cross—Britain's highest wartime honor—after leading a three-man "midget submarine" team on a perilous mission during World War II to plant bombs on the hull of a cruiser blocking Singapore Harbor. After the Japanese vessel was sunk, the British navy launched a full-scale attack on the Malaysian port. Though Magennis had been born in Belfast, it took over fifty years before the city council considered honoring their native son. When they began to debate a possible tribute, no one quite knew which side to take.

Magennis was a Catholic, which appealed to Irish nationalists, but he had served in the Royal Navy, which they were less enthusiastic about. Protestants had the reverse feelings—they wanted to honor a loyal soldier, but felt ambivalent because of his religion. In the end, local councilors crossed their fingers and voted unanimously to erect a monument honoring Magennis, knowing, in their own minds, that it was for their own conception of the man.

Saint Patrick offered an even more complicated problem. He died centuries before the Protestant reformation, so technically, he was part of a shared Christian ethos. But no one was going to settle for that. Catholics see him as theirs—Ireland's patron saint. Protestants rebut on technical grounds—Saint Patrick was originally from modern-day Britain or Wales. More than that, Protestants recognized something in Patrick's evangelism and defiance against church authority.

So, while most of Ireland's heroes have been divvied up, St. Patrick is still available, and each Saint Patrick's Day in Belfast, Protestants and Catholics fight for him.

Before I met her, I had already heard many opinions of Catriona Ruane. The most generous descriptions were that she was opinionated; the more grudging said she was a rabid republican. But all agreed that she could be a charmer and warned me to be on guard.

When we met in her office along the Falls Road, the "charming" description seemed to fit. Originally from County Mayo, her lilting Irish brogue was a welcome change from the gruff Belfast accent. And she was welcoming. Although clearly swimming in work, she was friendly and helpful.

It was late January, two months before St. Patrick's Day, and preparations were well under way. As we walked up the stairs to her office, Catriona carried a large plastic bucket. A few hours later she would use it to hustle west Belfast for money. Once again Belfast City Council had refused to fund her Saint Patrick's Day celebration.

"It's ridiculous," Catriona told me in a fit of pique. "The city council spent seventy thousand pounds on a fireworks display on Halloween. They spent nearly half a million pounds on New Year's Eve celebrations. They give money to rugby, parades—every major event in this city.

"We are demanding that Saint Patrick's Day be celebrated. That is a very reasonable demand. Now, without the city council's money, we have to go out and get money from the local people. That means they have to pay twice. They have to pay their local rates and put their hands in their pockets for this. No matter what the city council says, what we have here is anti-Irish discrimination. They can dress it up in all their fancy words and all their fancy excuses, but the bottom line is that it is anti-Irish discrimination."

Catriona had served as a human rights worker in Nicaragua during the eighties, while the war was on there. When she returned to Ireland, she came to Belfast and began investigating alleged security force abuses. Righteous indignation seems to come easily to her.

But Catriona is also an inveterate organizer. West Belfast Catholics used to commemorate the introduction of internment—when in August 1971 IRA suspects were rounded up in mass arrests—with riots, carjacking, and lawlessness. That does not happen anymore. Ten years earlier, Catriona brought her administrative flair to organizing the West Belfast Festival—a local event featuring Irish dancing, traditional music, and homegrown artists. After Catriona culled money from America, Europe, and reluctantly, the Belfast City Council, and after she spent years promoting and marketing the event, the West Belfast Festival drowned out the street protests.

Catriona is proud of that—of turning a mindless event into something constructive and enriching—but not everyone feels welcome at the West Belfast Festival. It is an unapologetically Catholic and nationalist affair, which does nothing to endear Protestants.

So, when Catriona organized Belfast's first Saint Patrick's Day celebration in 1998, Protestants took cynical notice. There were floats, bands, costumes—but few Protestants. Political speeches and revelers waving Irish flags put them off. But the city council gave modest funding for what over fifty thousand attendees called a success.

The next year, Catriona planned a bigger extravaganza and asked for—well, demanded—more money from the Belfast City Council. But if the council was reluctant to give her money the first year, they were downright hostile the second. Having one of the most preposterously lavish council facilities in the British Isles rarely inspired statesmanship among local councilors. Their ornate hall served more as an arena than a debating chamber, where Protestant and Catholic representatives postured, pontificated, and wrested for control of the council's meager budget.

It started back in the eighties, when Sinn Fein started fighting for, and winning, seats on the council. Back then, spirited debates occasionally turned into physical altercations, and it was not uncommon for police to forcibly remove members from their chamber. It hardly mattered that cemetery maintenance and pest control were the council's two main responsibilities.

Pressure eased over the years, and some councilors even started speaking to one another. But there was always a chance for one side to try to score points against the other. As the Protestant majority slipped, those opportunities became more available. Saint Patrick's Day funding was a chance, one of the last, for Protestant councilors to flex their muscles. Or at least that is the way Catriona Ruane sees it.

"Unionism, elements of unionism, saw the potential for this and saw that we were serious about organizing and began to block our parade. They have been using every excuse in the book not to fund us. First, it was 'there were Irish flags at the last march' and then it was 'there were children attacked'—it is just total lies about the event. There were a few councilors leading the opposition, but Sammy Wilson and Nelson McCausland were at the fore."

One of the more colorful, and surprisingly clever, members of the council, Sammy Wilson will probably best be known for an ill-considered naked frolic he took with a holiday companion among the fields of France several years ago. If he engaged in that sort of thing customarily, he had managed to keep it a secret until a Sunday tabloid got their hands on some photographs. The companion was female, luckily, so Wilson's puritanical electorate could pardon the lapse, though the story, and its accompanying mental image, lingered, much to his embarrassment.

"The council has certain rules," Wilson explained, putting the emphasis on formalities rather than on his personal antagonism towards Catriona Ruane and her Saint Patrick's Day parade. "We have to be careful not to support an event that is party political or supports only one group. Now this is all public record, but in past marches there have been political speeches, and IRA supporters organized some of the floats. We were not prepared to fund that. We would support a parade if it was cross-community [Northern Ireland–speak for involving both Protestants and Catholics]. We even put that to Catriona Ruane, but she would not have it."

Catriona reluctantly admitted that this was true. After the first funding was approved, the city council included one caveat when it granted £50,000 for the following year's parade: It had to be cross-community. That meant Catriona had to work with Nelson McCausland, who organized the Ulster-Scots Heritage Council which housed the Saint Patrick's Heritage Association, headed by Lee Reynolds. It's no wonder the whole operation fell flat.

Being Protestant in Northern Ireland, for many, is a struggle to be not-Irish. Nelson McCausland—an evangelical Protestant, a politician and historian—leads the charge in trying to preserve, even resurrect, what he says is a distinctive Protestant culture. In many ways it is a game of catch-up.

Catholics have the Irish language; McCausland says Northern Ireland Protestants—as descendants from Scottish planters—have a right to an Ulster-Scots language. It is an authentic tongue, McCausland argues. But with striking similarities to English (*lairne* is *learn*, *airm* is *arm*) some linguists say it is, at best, an overworked version of an antiquated country dialect.

"Parity of esteem," McCausland demands, and he has won some

support for his project. The Good Friday Peace Agreement gave Irish and Ulster-Scots equal recognition. A post to translate minutes of the Northern Ireland Assembly into Irish was quickly filled; a similar position to translate Ulster-Scots remains vacant—no one has proficiency.

Ironically, Nelson McCausland resents the Good Friday Agreement, even though it gave Ulster-Scots its endorsement. He also resents the European Union and their generous "Peace and Reconciliation" grants that help subsidize his Ulster-Scots movement. McCausland wishes he did not need their support; he wishes Protestant culture was self-sufficient. But it isn't.

Nelson McCausland and Lee Reynolds share a modest work space in North Belfast. Compared to Catriona Ruane's office, it is a cupboard. Sheafs of paper were carelessly piled around the room when I visited. On the walls were posters promoting Scottish heritage. Without more funding, Nelson McCausland and Lee Reynolds would both be out of a job, so they were not getting too settled.

When it comes to culture, Catholics raise more funds than Protestants—Lee Reynolds admitted it himself with more than a touch of jealousy. Years of neglect from a Protestant-controlled government forced Catholics to become more self-reliant. Combined with generous giving from America to Australia, their coffers are replete. And Catriona has one thing Nelson McCausland and Lee Reynolds lack: public support.

"It's going to take some time," Reynolds admitted in his office. "Protestants don't know enough about Saint Patrick yet, but we are going to keep spreading the word. Hopefully we can make him more acceptable in another year or two."

Reynolds was once militant in his beliefs. He led a radical unionist youth movement as a college student and even made an insolent bid for the Unionist Party leadership, but now he just seems dejected and tired of fighting.

"The city council agreed to give fifty thousand pounds for a St. Patrick's Day Parade, and I cochaired a cross-community planning committee with Catriona Ruaine. We spent about three to four months in negotiations and left all the hard questions to the end. When it came to the end, the big issues were still unresolved.

"We had a problem with actually holding the event on Saint Patrick's Day because the state school system does not recognize it as a public holiday. We wanted Protestants to be able to watch and participate in the parade—we even tried to get the schools to take a day off, but that did not work. We also were not happy with how the event itself was being managed in terms of flags and symbols. Basically, Catriona Ruane said everything should be allowed. But the way this town is at the minute, if you have thousands of people waving Irish flags and Union Jacks at the same event, there is going to be a riot.

"So, they did not want to move the day and they were not happy with our suggestion to control flags and symbols, so basically, things broke down. When it came time for the council to decide who was going to get the money, the council pulled all of it. Their attitude was basically: 'a plague on both your houses.' "

A lack of council support did not stop Catriona Ruane's parade, as she shrewdly raised nearly the total cost on her own. It was hard work, but it came with an added sense of pride and allowed her to sue Belfast City Council on charges of discrimination. Lee Reynolds had to cancel his Saint Patrick's Day event but called in a few favors and pooled some European funding to organize his short "Saint Patrick cultural tour."

On Saint Patrick's Day itself, I eschewed Belfast altogether and headed forty miles south to the small Northern Ireland town of Downpatrick where, it is alleged, Patrick spent most of his life. Northern Ireland did not exist in the fifth century, of course, when Patrick first arrived. Back then, Ireland was just a desolate island on the outskirts of a dwindling Roman Empire, and Patrick was a teen enslaved by Irish pirates. Punishment, Patrick would write, for his faithlessness.

Days of solitude spent tending sheep were also a time of solemn meditation and prayer for Patrick, and it was then that he found Christian penance. He eventually escaped, returned home to Britain, and underwent meager religious training before returning to Ireland to evangelize.

The river Slaney winds through Downpatrick to the Irish Sea, and it is on her banks that Patrick is believed to have landed as a missionary. *Saul* is the anglicized version of the Irish word for *barn*. In a town by that name, Patrick is rumored to have first put a barn to ecclesiastical use.

"Saint Patrick turned the right side of the stone up today," Anglican Bishop Harold Miller said with a smile, standing in the sun outside Saul Church on Saint Patrick's Day. "We say that whenever the weather is as good as this. Mind you, the sun always seems to come out today."

Through the doorway of the small stone chapel, parishioners arrived well dressed and orderly—as Anglicans do—and quietly took their seats. In the adjacent rectory hall, clerics fastened flowing green robes. Erected in the 1930s to commemorate the fifteen-hundredth anniversary of St. Patrick's arrival in Ireland, Saul Church is little used though it was standing room only by the time the service started.

Afterwards Bishop Miller, wooden staff in hand, led the congregation on the two-mile march to Down Cathedral, on whose grounds, it is alleged, Saint Patrick is buried. It was a walk between what some consider to be the two holiest places in Ireland.

"We call this our pilgrimage," Bishop Miller said. "There was a time, before the peace process started, that we just would not have made this walk. It would have been considered too controversial. This is a sign that things have changed."

Later that morning, I dashed over to Saint Patrick Catholic Church, Downpatrick, where Father Brendan Murray was reading a traditional Irish mass. "Now not many people in the service would be fluent Irish speakers," Father Murray admitted later. "But they would know enough to follow along."

In the front pews of the near-full cathedral, boys and girls from a local scout troop were looking singularly bored. After mass, they presented a clump of clover, which Father Murray duly sanctified. "Bless these shamrocks and all who wear them," he said, and then the scouts crowded around the pulpit for a quick photo.

There was a time when children did not join "uniformed organizations," as the scouts are known—another consequence of the Troubles. The discipline and apparel too much resembled paramilitary groups. That the scouts could gather together for worship was, as a scout leader told me, another sign that things had changed.

When the chapel emptied, many in the congregation headed for an ecumenical service at Down Cathedral. I rode with Father Murray, and along the way, we passed Bishop Miller and the Anglican pilgrims. When we pulled into the parking lot, a local cleric gave a wave. "Any space for me in there?" Father Murray asked.

"Aye," the minister answered jocularly. "Just cram it in there somewhere."

Down Cathedral stands majestically on a prominent hill with its own history of ecumenism—once serving as a Catholic friary, it burned to the ground before the Church of Ireland restored it. Clergy from the main denominations—Presbyterian, Methodist, Catholic, and Anglican—each robed in their own distinctive dress, joked and chatted on the way into the chapel. They had a community, if not a faith, in common. They were friends. Any dogmatic differences they had were nothing compared to shared experience shepherding their flocks.

"Now, it is only in recent years that the Church of Ireland has celebrated Saint Patrick," Father Murray said—emphasizing yet more change. "It used to be that they just did not recognize him. The attitude was: 'If another church is celebrating something, we won't.' It is just like other things in the past. There was a time when one church did not say the Lord's Prayer because the other did. And it was not that long ago that we did not worship together."

And some of the worst enmity had been among Protestant denominations, as Presbyterian Reverend John Dunlop described in his sermon. "Not long ago," he joked, "I would not have been welcome here because my ordination would not have been recognized. But now here we are having traveled across great frontiers, not always a distance in geography, but against the winds of prejudice. In obedience to God, we have overcome our misgivings."

After the service, clergy left the building and made their way among the headstones of the adjoining cemetery to the irregular stone slab into which the word *Patric* is chiseled. There, a wreath of carnations and daffodils was laid.

"But to be honest," the cathedral curator confided mischievously, "we don't know for sure if that is where Patrick is buried."

By then, Saint Patrick must have turned the stone over again because the skies had darkened. The religious commemorations had ended, and townsfolk wandered off the hill and into the streets of town, where the secular celebrations had begun.

An inebriated patron of Saint Brendan's Pub in the center of Downpatrick stumbled towards the exit, stopped, and looked up. "Your shamrock seems to be drying out," Dick Looby the proprietor said, fingering the few wilted petals pinned to the fellow's lapel. "Better get yourself into the same state." The two men burst into riotous laughter.

It was the busiest day of the year at Saint Brendan's Pub—a name chosen since 'Saint Patrick' was already taken—when a week's custom is done in a few hours. "Now, actually we would say that fella was drowning his shamrock," Looby said with a grin. "Which is something you will see quite a bit of around here today."

Outside the door, the Saint Patrick's Day Parade was under way. It had the feel of a country carnival. A cavalcade of antique cars led the procession. Floats and marching bands followed behind. There were men on stilts, unicyclists, jugglers, and miniature ponies. Across the street, local band Take It Easy broke up a set of traditional Irish music with a version of Neil Diamond's "Sweet Caroline."

Through it all, Looby stood in the threshold of his pub looking out on the procession and giving a running commentary. One eye was on the patrons filtering through the door; the other was on the march.

"Show me the way to go home!" one drunken man crooned, bracing himself on Looby's shoulders.

"That way!" Looby pointed into the street.

"All right, squire?" Looby asked an underage, would-be patron sheepishly trying to make his way into the pub. Back out the door he went. When I asked how long the pub would stay open, Looby looked at me with disappointment. "Until the money stops coming in." Obviously.

The *crack*, as locals call this species of banter, was contagious. It was easy to get caught up in the rhythm, and if you got flummoxed, you had better get out of the way. Otherwise, you would end up the target of some barbed jibes. Dick Looby served as the main jester and ringmaster.

Not a soul passed through the door without a word for him. Young women seemed to hit Looby's soft spot, and they all stopped to give him a hug or quick peck on the cheek. Little old ladies who just wanted to use the toilet were graciously allowed through. If a patron tried to leave with one of Looby's pint glasses he would, in one motion, lift it from the person's hand and pour the contents into a plastic cup, reminding such people that they had not been in his pub, then sending them on their way.

This was what Belfast's Saint Patrick's Day march was supposed to look like—Protestants and Catholics celebrating in harmony. Everyone was welcome. Families were strolling along the sidewalk. Music was in the air. The town council had organized the event themselves and used a simple formula to avoid controversy. All the marching bands and floats were carefully vetted. People could bring any flag they liked, but the thousands of neutral banners distributed by the council were sure to outnumber the ones that might spark controversy. Most of all, people were just asked to bring their common sense and respect for others.

It all went to show how much things had changed, I was again told. But I had been in Northern Ireland long enough to know that change was something embarked on reluctantly and with endless suspicion. Was this the best people could hope for: a pilgrimage march, kids wearing uniforms, a parade?

Dick Looby has owned Saint Brendan's for over forty years. If anyone could give me a straight line on all the talk of "change," he could. So I asked him, hopefully, about things getting better.

Looby gave me a patient, slightly patronizing stare. He did not want to dash my hopes, or sound like a curmudgeonly old-timer, but he had been standing in that doorway a long time. Maybe he was cynical, or maybe he had just seen too much.

"It is a sort of peace," he admitted. "People are not killing each other, and they are parading together here—that's nice to see. But there's a lot people don't see. Things have changed—ya they're better—but there's still a wee bit further to go."

Remembering the Roses

A n old, familiar story was unfolding when I arrived in Northern Ireland. It had to do with a fraternal, Protestant organization, the Orange Order, and their preoccupation with marching around the province in celebration of their faith. The problem was that Catholics tended to see the Orange Order's celebration of faith as a denigration of their own. Generally, Catholics objected to the Orange Order marching through their neighborhoods. The Orange Order's insistence that they could march anywhere and the Catholic residents' objections were customarily played out during the summer months in what locals called the *marching season*. I had heard that term used with a sense of foreboding akin to what Americans in the southeast know as the hurricane season. It comes every year. Nothing can stop it. Some years are peaceful and others are not—there is no way to tell what to expect until it has started, so it is best to prepare for the worst.

In Northern Ireland, the marching season had become an annual bloodletting. The Parades Commission, the official arbiter of controversial parades, ruled as to whether the Orange Order's most disputed parades could go ahead. Then Protestants or Catholics, depending on which side felt aggrieved, would take to the streets in protest. The most contentious march by far was held along the Garvaghy Road, in the town of Portadown, twenty miles south of Belfast. Catholic residents of the Garvaghy Road, emboldened in part by paramilitary cease-fires, started campaigning against the Orange Order march in the summer of

1995. Three years later, in the summer of 1998, the Orange Order was, for the first time, prevented from marching down the Garvaghy Road and they have not marched down the road since.

I arrived in Northern Ireland after the summer of 1998. It was a strange time. The Good Friday Agreement was only a few months old when Northern Ireland endured one of its most turbulent marching seasons. Disgruntled members of the Orange Order, loyalist paramilitaries, and disaffected Protestants went on a rampage. The violence was punctuated by a firebomb thrown through the window of a Catholic family's home, killing of three schoolboys: Jason, Mark, and Richard Quinn. It was difficult to know what to make of events. What was a true reflection of the mood in Northern Ireland: the peace agreement or the continuing tribal violence?

The Garvaghy Road controversy seemed incomprehensible and I had an impulse to disregard it. It seemed like an aberration, a disruption of the order and stability promised by the Good Friday Agreement. But after spending some time in Portadown, I saw how the events there distilled other issues. The Garvaghy Road was more than a place scarred by a sordid conflict. It was a state of mind, a moment in time, and an identity. It presented a familiar story. It was a story about changed circumstances. It was a story about the jarring moment of realization that a familiar past no longer charts the way toward the future—even worse, that the past itself is uncertain. There was intrigue, deception, moments of farce and tragedy. The Garvaghy Road controversy presented the elements in Northern Ireland so carefully in their natural state that it almost seemed a contrivance.

Harold Gracey's trailer was cramped, but it had most amenities. There was a sink and a cooker in the kitchen space. The living area had a television and a sofa. There was a dining table where a telephone/fax rested. Behind one narrow door was a bedroom. Behind another was a shower and a toilet. There were a few thin, square windows that let in light but left the cabin feeling drafty. The entire trailer frame was propped up on sandbags behind security cameras and a steel gate.

Harold Gracey had been living in the trailer for six months by Christmas 1998. It was positioned next to Drumcree Parish Church on a prominent, windswept hill at the far end of the Garvaghy Road.

This was not the life Gracey imagined for himself when he retired as a stock clerk with the Northern Ireland Electricity Board. He had worked hard all his life. He looked forward to leisurely afternoons in his garden and holidays with his family. The trailer he lived in was the sort of thing he might have taken to the beach if he were on vacation—but this was no vacation. Being confined to a cell was more like being in prison—but he was not being punished. Harold Gracey could leave anytime he wanted. His wife and family were at their home just a few miles away. They would have welcomed his return.

But Harold Gracey was the district master of the Portadown Orange Order, and that role came with certain responsibilities. On the first Sunday in July, Gracey would dress in full regalia and lead his brethren and some marching bands to Drumcree Parish Church. There, a special service was held to commemorate the Battle of the Somme, one of the bloodiest engagements of World War I, which took the lives of thousands of men from Northern Ireland. After the church service, Gracey would lead his brethren off Drumcree hill and make his way back towards Portadown along the Garvaghy Road. The whole event only lasted a few hours.

All that changed in the summer of 1998 when Orangemen were permanently halted. Harold Gracey took his responsibility as district master seriously and moved into his trailer on Drumcree hill. His aluminum home became the Orange Order's defensive rampart.

Gracey vowed to stay put until the Orangemen got down the Garvaghy Road, and through the early months of his protest, Gracey became a Protestant folk hero. He was standing by his ideals at the time when Protestants felt abandoned. Gracey's name was praised from pulpits and street corners. Rallies of support were held across the country. T-shirts and flags were embossed with the phrase "Here we stand, We can do no other." Martin Luther said it first; Harold Gracey made it famous.

But Gracey was a reluctant martyr. He did not relish the protest or the notoriety it earned him. When he first moved his things into the trailer, he naïvely hoped to be back home in a matter of weeks or months. He never expected to spend that much time on Drumcree hill.

Gracey was partly motivated by pride—he had made a promise and was going to keep it. He also felt a commitment as leader of the Portadown Orangemen, but there was something more. Living in the trailer was more than protest—it was a standoff.

Most days, Breandan MacCionnaith (pronounced McKenna) works from the Garvaghy Road Community Center. It is a small building about half a mile down the Garvaghy Road. There are just a few meeting rooms, a kitchen suite, and an office. From there, employment schemes, youth programs, mother/toddler groups, and Irish language classes are run. And before the Garvaghy Road marching controversy started, those were the programs that occupied MacCionnaith's time. But when the earliest opposition to the marches began, MacCionnaith emerged as a leader of the residents.

The people of Northern Ireland were introduced to MacCionnaith during media coverage of the first Drumcree standoff in 1995. There he was on the television screen looking defiant, speaking with indignation about "these marches local people have to endure" while his supporters stood in the background waving placards and banners. Who was he? What did he want?

Over the years people found out and developed one of three opinions. They either supported MacCionnaith—"it's about time someone stood up for the ordinary Catholics"; they opposed him—"for just trying to crush Protestant culture"; or they quickly grew tired of him and wanted him to go away.

Today, MacCionnaith's face is immediately recognizable. He is the acknowledged spokesperson for the residents, so whenever there are talks to break the marching impasses, Breandan MacCionnaith is there. He has met local businessmen, political and religious leaders, the British prime minister, the Irish premier, and political activists from around the world.

MacCionnaith grew up through the early days of the Troubles in Lurgan, a town near Portadown. Instilled with republican militancy as a boy, MacCionnaith joined the IRA, was arrested in a bombing raid, and served six years in prison. After his release, he assumed a low profile as a community worker. MacCionnaith acknowledges that he has no love for Protestant culture and that he wants the Orangemen to stay off the Garvaghy Road. He is the main obstacle in their way, and if the Orangemen ever do walk the Garvaghy Road, it will probably mean going over or through Breandan MacCionnaith. But MacCionnaith explains that he is also a socialist and a father. As a socialist, he thinks the marches are unjust. As a father, he wants the Orange Order stopped before his children grow up.

Being in the spotlight was new for MacCionnaith. He had no prior experience with television interviews, print reporters, and photographers, but luckily he was a quick study. Now he seems comfortable in the role—maybe too comfortable. If he enjoys the attention and his resentment continues to grow, will MacCionnaith ever agree to a compromise that allows the Orange Order down the Garvaghy Road?

That is what Harold Gracey asks. He also wants to know why one meddlesome Catholic like MacCionnaith is being allowed to step over three centuries of proud Protestant tradition. He wants to know what happened to the days when the Orange Order was welcomed everywhere it went. He wants to know when Protestants are going to wake up.

Harold Gracey's standoff with MacCionnaith became more than a provincial squabble. It became an indicator of the tensions still left in Northern Ireland and a measure of the Good Friday Agreement's durability. For many, the Orange Order and Harold Gracey were an anachronism, a throwback to Northern Ireland's ugly past. With the Good Friday Agreement, times were changing.

Forty years ago, before the Garvaghy Road went by that name, Orangemen walked the same route and affectionately called it "the walk." Portadown was just a small rural town at the time, and the walk was just a humble stretch of gravel. It was there that Sam McGredy, one of the province's largest horticulturists, grew roses. He ran a huge operation. The hills were covered in flowers, and the air was scented with their perfume. McGredy was one of the biggest employers in the town. He was a Protestant but not an Orangeman, and he was loved by the whole community. His flowers were renowned across Britain, and they were shipped around the world.

"I remember it well," Harold Gracey told me. "There were a few homes along there. My people are from that area—my grandfather and father. They were Orangemen too; I must be third or fourth generation."

But by the early seventies, Northern Ireland's Troubles had erupted. When the IRA started a bombing campaign in England; people there did not want to receive packages from Northern Ireland—even if they did contain flowers.

So Sam McGredy left for New Zealand, taking his rose business with him. The fields of flowers were developed into public housing—mostly for Catholics. "Rose Cottages" stands as the only reminder of Sam McGredy's enterprise.

More public housing is planned for the area, and so even more Catholic residents will be moving in among the fields around the Garvaghy Road. "Things change," Breandan MacCionnaith told me. "There are no more roses, only people."

When the 1998 Garvaghy Road march was first banned, thousands of demonstrators dug in at Drumcree hill.

It became the nerve center of the protest where Harold Gracey and a few supporters maintained a twenty-four-hour presence. The message to the Parades Commission was that the Orange Order was unbowed.

The Orangemen thought they could muster enough support to intimidate the Parades Commission, and they intensified their campaign around Christmas. They aimed to finish the march before the end of the year, and several large-scale protest marches were planned as a final push.

I visited Portadown a week before Christmas in 1998 on a day when the Orangemen promised ten thousand brethren would be marching to Drumcree Church for a carol service and one of their biggest protests.

"It doesn't feel like Christmas," a waiter at Bennett's Bar in the center of town said. "You would go to other towns and there would be a little bit of buzz. Here it's quiet. People are going about their shopping, but it is not the same."

Festive lights crisscrossed the streets and carols played, but falling drizzle dampened the mood. This was supposed to be one of the busiest shopping days of the year, but the shops were deserted. Business was slow at El Porto Café. There was a time when people would have stayed in town, the proprietor said, "now they just get their things and go home." When asked why, she responds evasively, "There has been trouble."

That afternoon, thousands of Orangemen arrived by the busload from all across the country, choking the streets. With them were hundreds of marching bandsmen and well-wishers. The Orangemen looked dignified, with neatly combed hair and clean-shaven faces. The bandsmen were a bit rougher—pimply faced and slack jawed. The Orangemen kept to themselves while the bandsmen swaggered about the place.

I started talking to Millie Sturgeon. She was a member of the Orange Order's female auxiliary, lived in Portadown, and had been protesting with Harold Gracey since the beginning. She knew what was really going on along the Garvaghy Road, she said, because she has Catholic friends. "And see the likes of Breandan MacCionnaith?" she asked. "Well, he is holding them people for ransom 'cause most of them want the Orangemen down that road."

And there were a lot of lies going around, Sturgeon explained. People were being given the wrong idea. Firstly, Catholics were not intimidated from coming into town. "Wait till I tell ye," she started. "There's nothing stoppin' them people from comin' into town. You can bet if there were, Breandan MacCionnaith would send a squad of the IRA in."

She remembered years ago, back before all this started, "before Breandan MacCionnaith stepped on the scene. Back then, community relations were good. Back then, people got along grand. Then MacCionnaith started to stir things up."

At around two o'clock, the march started. Barrel-chested drummers with arms like sewer pipes pounded out a steady beat. Sturgeon left me as she and the other marchers began to gather and assemble into formation. Banners rose like sails above the sea of people.

The security presence was discreet at the beginning of the march, mostly unmarked cars, but grew more pronounced as the marchers neared the church. As the march got closer to the Catholic enclaves around the Garvaghy Road, armored police cars were everywhere and soldiers were surveying the crowd through rifle scopes.

On the horizon was Drumcree Parish Church; its spire was a thorn in the sky. The procession turned towards the church and Harold Gracey emerged from his aluminum hut. Down a short path along a hedgerow, he walked erect to a makeshift podium fixed to the back of a flatbed truck. He was dressed splendidly: black pinstripe suit, gloves, and coat. He stood in silence with arms folded behind his back and watched in satisfaction as the mile-long march passed before him.

Orangemen tipped their hats to him: "Hey there, Harold." "Ya all right, Harold?" "You're doing a great job." Some occasionally shook his hand; others patted his shoulder or pulled him in for a quick word in his ear.

Brother Hugh Ross, an officer of the Portadown Orangemen, opened the proceedings in prayer. There were a few words of thanks for the glorious Christmas message; a word of blessing for those killed through thirty years of terrorism; a word of praise for the Protestant faith; and a final plea: that like Moses parted the Red Sea, so would God make a way for the Orangemen down the Garvaghy Road. Amen.

After a carol, Bible reading, and few words from other honored guests, Harold Gracey was congratulated for the peaceful vigil he had kept. "Hear! Hear!" the crowd said. And for his dignity. "Yeah!" they yelled. And too for his determination. "Harold!" they barked.

Gracey took the podium to thunderous applause and cheers. The sound of a security helicopter hovering overhead echoed across the grounds with its *chop-chop-chop*. Gracey gave the sky a disdainful look, then turned to the crowd with a grin. "Fellow loyalists," he bellowed, "welcome to Drumcree!" The amplifier crackled, then cut off for a moment. Orangemen looked at each other, perplexed. Then someone screamed accusingly, "MacCionnaith!"

Gracey put the microphone aside and continued. He was only audible to a few hundred of the gathered thousands—but if they had been standing with him since July, they had heard it all before.

"It's not about Harold Gracey on a hill," he said. "It is about our Protestant faith and our Protestant culture. It is time the government wakened up to the fact—that we are not going to be held for a ransom by anyone."

Through applause, Gracey reminded the brethren that he had made a vow. He promised to remain until the Garvaghy Road march was completed. "I can assure you," he said solemnly, "I will be here. For as long as it takes, I will be here."

Gracey invited the Orangemen to join his protest and then he was carried off the stage on a wave of applause.

The Star of David Accordion Band was warming up for the national anthem to end the demonstration when Hugh Ross got people's attention again for another announcement.

Gracey had received hundred of cards and gifts from well-wishers during the Christmas season, Ross said. They had all been a great source of encouragement, but for the card he had received the other day from the Garvaghy Road residents. "Wait till I tell you what is inside, for I don't think it's funny," he said.

The front of the card was a copy of a mural on the Garvaghy Road: Orangemen marching blindly in circles with the words: "Re-route Sectarian Marches!" The inscription read "Greetings from Garvaghy Road, Portadown—from the residents. Hope you enjoy Christmas on the hill."

"This just lets you see the people we are dealing with," Ross said, as the crowd hissed.

Earlier that afternoon, Breandan MacCionnaith had hosted a steady stream of journalists at the Garvaghy Road Community Center. He sat in the main hall, lounging back against a bench, smoking a cigarette.

"People have no idea what life is like in Portadown for Catholics," MacCionnaith said of the harassment many residents had faced since the protests started.

"Things could not have been worse in the last six months," he went on. "Catholic-owned shops have been burned; people have been killed; the town is divided. That is the ongoing cost of the Orange Order protests."

A few weeks earlier, MacCionnaith and the Orange Order had engaged in talks to end the dispute. One of British Prime Minister Tony Blair's top aides had flown in to chair the negotiations. Meetings lasted for several days before they collapsed in failure. When they did, the two sides could honestly say that they had not seen eye to eye.

Harold Gracey and his colleagues refused to sit at a table with Breandan MacCionnaith. It was a policy that they stuck to rigidly. "Proximity talks" allowed the Orangemen and residents to negotiate without ever speaking to one another. The two sides would agree to a venue and take positions at two separate wings of the building. Each side drew up an opening proposal and handed it to a facilitator who would courier it across the hall and come back with a response. Proposals were read and replies were made with facilitators bouncing back and forth like tennis balls. As time went by, proposals often turned into demands to which one side invariably took offense and walked out. When they did, they met the press and pointed to the other side's intransigence.

The great lengths taken to prevent any chance encounter—separate toilet facilities, timing of breaks—increased the perception of farce. Nothing was achieved at the proximity talks, according to Mac-Cionnaith, and he participated only reluctantly—suspicious that Orangemen were using the process to give the false impression that they were good-faith negotiators.

But what was there to talk about, anyway? I asked. The Orangemen wanted to walk; the residents said no. There did not seem to be much room to maneuver.

There were issues to discuss, MacCionnaith told me. The number of Orange marchers that passed through town, the number of bands, whether music would be played. And, in recent times, MacCionnaith had skillfully opened the scope of any possible settlement.

The Garvaghy Road march was only a symptom, MacCionnaith argued. Employment, housing, discrimination—those were the real roots of division in Portadown. Through some crafty negotiating, MacCionnaith insinuated those issues into discussions about the Garvaghy Road march. "Nothing will be agreed before everything is agreed," he warned.

So before MacCionnaith would even consider the Orangemen walking down his road, he wanted to discuss how European peace and reconciliation money was spent, training and employment funding, grants for new businesses. MacCionnaith had the attention of top bureaucrats and politicians; he was going to make the most of it. He wanted money—lots of it—to improve life for Catholics living along the Garvaghy Road.

MacCionnaith was interrupted for a phone call. At the other end of the line, someone played the Orange anthem, "The Sash," into his ear. MacCionnaith chuckled, then hung up. "Let the British government deal with the march in the words of the Good Friday Agreement," he said. "They should be putting an end to the sectarianism in this community."

The Orange Order's Christmas effort ended in failure. Only half of the expected ten thousand Orangemen attended, but their campaign continued through the winter and spring. Every week, the Orangemen tried to march down the Garvaghy Road. Each time, police turned them away. Through it all, Harold Gracey sat on the hill.

But Gracey was not alone. Across the country, Protestants held rallies and marches of solidarity. Just up the street from my apartment in east Belfast, a group of women, mostly wives or daughters of Orangemen, supported Gracey with a "peace camp" from a vacant patch of grass at a major traffic junction. Their numbers varied, but there were usually fewer than ten. Around dusk, they came out with folding chairs and a

Thermos of tea. They sat and chatted in front of a sign that read *Honk if you Support Drumcree!* At around ten or so each night, they went home.

Paula Savage, a young mother, had been at the peace camp since the start. She phoned Breandan MacCionnaith when the protest started. "I rang him from that phone box over there," she said, pointing down the street. She argued with MacCionnaith for a bit about the march before she lost her temper and hung up the phone. "He put my head away," she said, exasperated.

About a month after Christmas, the Portadown Orange Order spokesman, David Jones, was invited to address a major rally at the east Belfast peace camp. In fact, Harold Gracey had been invited to speak, but Jones was there in his place. A few hundred people had gathered. Among them was Millie Sturgeon.

"It may take ten to twenty years," Sturgeon said, "but as long as I can breathe I will keep fighting to get down the Garvaghy Road."

But the protests were losing momentum. Sturgeon's determination notwithstanding, sporadic protests were not enough to get Harold Gracey down Garvaghy Road. The Parades Commission was determined to enforce their ruling. The Orange Order needed more support, but people were losing interest. Most people felt there was nothing they could do. Others just did not care anymore. David Jones took the microphone that night with an earnest message. If things did not improve, if there was not more involvement in the protests, they might as well give up.

The Protestant people were under threat, Jones said. Gerry Adams, the British government, the British secretary of state—they were all against Protestants. He scorned the editors of the major papers, who called for compromise, and the police, whom he accused of being heavy-handed. Jones even scolded Orangemen, too many of whom were "prepared to sit at home and let our civil and religious liberties go."

Others had capitulated, but, Jones reminded people, Harold Gracey was standing tall. He would never surrender. Gracey was invoked as proof that Protestants could withstand treachery.

"My message to you all from Harold Gracey tonight is to go back into your own communities and let people know about our protest going on here tonight," Jones implored.

Jones and Gracey knew they might have to stand alone. As July approached they had burned every bridge and alienated almost every ally they ever had.

MacCionnaith knew he was winning, but the cost of victory was constant vigilance. Blocking the march was like catching a tiger by the tail, and he dared not let go. MacCionnaith believed he had to keep a watchful eye on the Orange Order, their tactics and strategy. He also had to continue the seemingly pointless negotiations. In the meantime, he was mindful of his own safety.

A few months before the planned July march of 1999, Rosemary Nelson, a prominent human rights lawyer from the town of Lurgan, was killed when a booby-trap bomb exploded under her car.

Nelson and MacCionnaith had grown up together in Lurgan and campaigned together around the Garvaghy Road march. For MacCionnaith, it was a blow for having lost both a friend and a colleague. "Of all the people who would have been involved in this," MacCionnaith said after the murder, "Rosemary would have been the one who I worked with most closely."

Nelson's murder also reminded MacCionnaith that his life was in danger. He had been the original target, it was rumored, and Nelson was only the bomber's second choice.

MacCionnaith is part of the government's Key Persons Protection Scheme. The program distinguishes five levels of danger. MacCionnaith started at level five (the least threatened) but climbed to level two, which means, among other things, that his home is installed with security cameras and bullet-resistant glass. But that might not be enough.

MacCionnaith is a public person. Certain events are scheduled like clockwork, and his address at the Garvaghy Road Community Center is well known. People breezed in and out of the building all day long. Loyalists have already tried to attack him there, but he was not in the office at the time. "I have asked them to put security around this place, and I am still waiting for a response from them," MacCionnaith said, with a chill of foreboding.

■　　■

July approached like a gray horizon. No one knew what to expect at Drumcree, but the outlook was not good.

Loyalist terror groups were attacking Catholic homes around the province. It was an attempt, security sources suspected, to raise tensions in the run up to the Garvaghy Road march. In the most serious attack, Elizabeth O'Neill—a Catholic grandmother living in a Protestant estate in Portadown—was killed when a pipe bomb was thrown through her living room window. Meanwhile, on the streets of Portadown, skirmishes between Protestant and Catholic youths were becoming more frequent.

More proximity talks again ended in failure. The rhetoric from both sides was still strident, and without any agreement, it was once again left to the Parades Commission to make a ruling on the Garvaghy Road march.

Days before the march, Parades Commission Chairman Alistair Graham held a press conference at the Stormont Hotel in east Belfast to announce the ruling. Considering the previous twelve months of Orange Order activities, most observers knew that there would certainly be another ban.

No sooner had Graham made that announcement than the hotel's fire alarm began to squeal. It was a bomb alert. Graham and his colleagues briskly left the building and continued the press conference from the parking lot.

The day of the march, Orangemen gathered at the Orange Hall in the center of Portadown as usual. They gave every signal that they were going ahead. David Jones said Orangemen were "bloodied but unbowed" by the Parades Commission ruling. Despite Jones's defiant words, there were rumors that the Orangemen were tired of the protests and were looking for an honorable way out. They wanted to cut a deal that would end the campaign and, if possible, save a shred of dignity.

The march set off that afternoon and wound past Portadown's scenes of violence: Edward Street, which had been destroyed by republican bombers; Woodhouse Street, where a loyalist gang kicked Robert Hamill, a Catholic, to death; Corcraine Street, where Elizabeth O'Neill was killed by a pipe bomb; Charles Street, where Frankie Gallagher, a policeman, was killed while policing a riot. As the march moved along, there was no trouble. Even when it passed Saint John the Baptist Catholic Church, there was hardly a stir. A few hundred Catholic residents stood by and watched the marchers pass.

Even if they were squealing for confrontation, the two sides would have found it hard to get to one another. The army and police had launched one of the most elaborate security operations ever seen in the history of the Troubles. The RUC chief constable, Sir Ronnie Flanagan, warned the press that the security measures would look awful. He was right.

The army built a moat at Drumcree hill. They dug a twelve-foot-wide ditch, flooded it with water, and used a helicopter to keep it full. Then mud was piled high along the banks of the moat and the surrounding fields were turned over. Lines of barbed wire were strung through the fields like a chicken coop, and dozens of armored cars lined the other side. Drumcree Road, part of the banned route, was blocked with a seventeen-foot steel wall topped with more razor wire.

When the march finally reached Drumcree Parish Church, the Orangemen filled the hall. Gracey was already waiting and took the front pew. The mostly male congregation was a bit gruff on the hymns, but they sang with vigor. The Old Testament lesson was original sin. The New Testament lesson was the prodigal son. The men heard the scriptures, and then they prayed. They prayed to be guided by God's governance—that they should not fall into sin but become one with Him.

After a few more hymns, Reverend John Pickering—tall, slender, and thin lipped—stepped to the pulpit. The Orange Order's Drumcree service was Pickering's inheritance. His predecessors had held it for generations and Pickering was expected to do the same. He was happy to do so, but was less keen to get involved in the controversial protest.

Harold Gracey was a squatter on church property. Although Pickering had to practically step over him on his way into church, he tried to distance himself from the controversy.

"I have been encouraging people to pray to almighty God that there would be a change, and we are trusting that it will all be over," Pickering had told me weeks earlier. But, he said after a pause, "We don't see a way how that can happen right now."

In recent months, Pickering and the Church of Ireland leadership had clashed. Pickering was reluctant to rebuff the Orangemen for their protest since many of his parishioners supported it. By holding the Orange service, he was defying a church directive.

With the dainty hands of a country parson Pickering arranged his notes and began the sermon. His theme was division: how thirty years of violence had divided people and how, looking across the fields that surrounded the church, people were divided still. It was a picture of the whole country, Pickering said. That was not what God, the lover of concord, wanted. He wanted harmony. "It makes me sad," Pickering lamented. "It make us all sad."

The sermon went on about being separated—divided—from God. If that division is not bridged, he said, then people will be separated from God forever. "When we are one with God," Pickering said, "then we are one with other people, and divisions are taken away."

No one expected the Orangemen to carry the lesson any farther than the church's vestibule. A standoff was under way, after all. The media and public were ready for a repeat of scenes from the previous year, when Orangemen and their supporters faced down the security forces.

Hundreds of Protestants congregated in the fields and waited. A few had binoculars and were peering across the moat and no-man's-land to where residents and the police were peering back. Harold Gracey was to serve the first volley by leading Orangemen to the seventeen-foot steel wall, where he would deliver a letter of protest.

But something unexpected happened. Before Gracey marched to the wall, Pickering came down into the fields with a bullhorn. "Could you please move away?" he pleaded with the crowd of supporters. "Could everyone please move back?"

Orange Order marshals herded people away from the moat banks and steel wall. "Please, folks, we are not going to have a protest until people move back," they said.

Most people resisted. They had been waiting all day for this. Some muttered in discontent and tried to stay, but eventually the area was clear. Then Harold Gracey and just eight other Orangemen—not the hundreds that were expected—marched down to police lines. The steel wall folded back, and a single officer emerged. The protest letter was handed over, and the Orangemen left the hill.

Most went to Pickering's house adjacent to the field. There, Gracey gave an address. They were not giving up, Gracey said, only continuing the dignified protest that they had started. In a speech attacking ecumenicism, Breandan MacCionnaith, and the Parades Commission, Gracey swore he would stay until the march went ahead. "But if it is not peaceful," he warned, "Harold Gracey will not be here."

He was going back to the hill, he told the crowd, and "if you come back to join me on the hill, you are very welcome."

They would not admit it, but the Orangemen had backed down. Northern Ireland sighed in relief.

The security presence remained in place for another few days, but the hundreds of extra personnel had nothing to do so they played cricket and volleyball in the sun among the armored cars. At the local shop, fatigued soldiers casually wandered in for biscuits and tea with their berets folded in their back pockets. Life was getting back to normal.

I stopped by Drumcree Church a few days after the dust had settled. The seventeen-foot steel wall topped with razor wire was about to be dismantled. The security forces were packing up. A few tourists and curious locals wandered around the fields while some of Gracey supporters huddled in a makeshift lean-to next to the church.

The wooden structure had been built months earlier to give protesters a place to escape the elements. Inside were a few benches, a space heater, and a small cooker where a kettle was constantly on the boil. It was a small but cozy alternative to standing in the rain. Like everything else about the protests, what began as temporary was becoming permanent. A weather-beaten sign counted down the days that Harold Gracey had been "incarcerated at Drumcree."

Sipping cups of tea and chomping on biscuits, talk among Gracey's supporters turned to the prospects of a future march. They were optimistic. "Oh, it would not be long now!" some mused. Others had heard tell that the prime minister was about to scrap the Parades Commission—a reward for the Orange Order's restraint.

Up at the trailer, Gracey, too, spoke with aplomb. He was sitting with a few friends, waiting for a fax from the prime minister's office. It was all very confidential, Gracey said; big news was on the way. Breandan MacCionnaith was on the run now for sure, he said.

We chatted for a few minutes, and then he invited me to sign his guest book—the second volume. Maybe when the whole thing was over we could sit down for a long chat. Maybe.

Down at the Garvaghy Road Community Center, MacCionnaith was glad to see me. The hundreds of reporters and photographers that were covering the march had left, and he seemed to miss the attention.

The Orange Order's decision not to escalate the protest showed some PR savvy, MacCionnaith was willing to admit, but he was more skeptical than Gracey that it would lead to an early march.

"This time last year the Orange Order said they were going to get down the road by the end of July. July went past. They said they would get down before the end of August. August went past. Then it was September. Then it was by the end of the year. Then they swore they would get down by Easter, and they are still up there," MacCionnaith reminded me.

No, he did not think the Orangemen would march anytime soon, and he doubted the Parades Commission would be scrapped. That was just a bit of Orange fantasy, he said.

More likely, MacCionnaith thought, the Orange Order—perhaps including Harold Gracey—and he would meet to discuss the issue. Then, after the Garvaghy Road residents had been granted the dignity of that meeting and after the Orange protests were called off, after agreeing to conditions on the march itself *and* after the government dealt with the community's social and economic issues, the march could go ahead. "If the conditions are right," MacCionnaith said, "there is no reason why the Orange Order cannot march down that road."

But what would MacCionnaith even say to Harold Gracey if they did meet? "It's long overdue, Harold, isn't it?" He grinned.

■   ■

More marching seasons have since passed. Harold Gracey eventually left Drumcree hill—not in triumph, but in surreptitious visits home for a hot meal. When the press revealed that Gracey's protest was not permanent, he dropped the pretense and took a vacation. And that seemed to capture the mood among Orangemen at Drumcree—they were getting tired of the fight. Along the way, many of their former supporters had abandoned them. "Decent Orangemen must stand up and proclaim that what has happened at Drumcree is shameful," Reverend Brian Kennaway, a former member of the Orange Order's education committee, told me. Kennaway led eight members of the Orange Order's education committee in resigning. More and more, despite sporadic violence committed in the Orange Order's name, the organization was falling into the past.

Sometimes when it was quiet, I walked through the centuries-old cemetery cascades down the front of Drumcree Parish Church. A few hundred headstones fill the grounds. Some are new and polished. Others are too old to even get a rubbing. Near the church walls, on the first tier of the cemetery, stands a granite tablet inscribed with the name Emma Jane Gregory. She died in 1903. She was only twenty-one.

Her entire family survived her, so when they buried Emma Jane Gregory and marked the spot, her name was etched across the top of the memorial. The other family members were added over the years. First, it was Emma Jane's grandmother. Her parents were buried next. Then it was her sister. Finally, six decades after Emma Jane Gregory was interred at Drumcree Parish Church, the names of her younger brother and his wife were added to the old stone marker.

Across a brook and over some fields, the name Mary Fearson is chiseled out of another headstone. She died young, too. She was twelve when she was buried in the graveyard adjoining St. John the Baptist Catholic Church. Mary Fearson, her parents, and the rest of the family are buried in the same plot and their names too stretch over the stone.

Whenever I was in the one graveyard or the other, I thought that I saw the headstones shrug at each other in mutual dismay.

On the Beat

◻   ◻

A few hundred local residents had gathered in the Poleglass Youth Center one spring evening in 1999 to offer their opinions to the Patten Commission on police reform. Chris Patten, the last British governor of Hong Kong, silver haired and exuding English decency, was chairing the commission that would recommend changes to Northern Ireland's police force: the RUC. Before issuing their report, the commissioners held months of public meetings around Northern Ireland. They hoped to hear thoughtful suggestions about the future of policing, but more often they were berated, insulted, pleaded with, or dismissed. The meeting in Poleglass promised to be eventful.

The roughly two thousand homes in Poleglass, west Belfast, were built in the early eighties while apartment towers in the center of town were being demolished. Planners hoped neighborhoods like Poleglass would somehow dissipate the misery and bring back the sense of community lacking from the soulless high-rises. For all their efforts, Poleglass was still situated on the outskirts of the city in an area of notorious blight and neglect. The whole development was eventually swallowed up by an expanding Catholic ghetto controlled by the IRA, and with a level of security higher than almost anywhere else in Belfast. The residents' experience with police authority usually involved searches, arrest, intimidation, and harassment. They had one suggestion for the police commission: Disband the RUC.

Still, the meeting was civilized at the beginning. At the front of the auditorium, behind a folding table, sat three commissioners. Facing them were rows of seated residents. The commission members were ostensibly impartial; the residents obviously were not, as a quick glance around the room revealed. A black-and-white photo collage that ran along the walls traced the allegations of RUC abuse through thirty years of the Troubles, including collusion with Protestant death squads, torture, and intimidation.

"Serving the Community RUC Style," one section was sarcastically headed, and it featured pictures of police in riot gear beating protesters with truncheons or dragging them off the street. In one frame, John Downes stood unarmed among a thin crowd of protesters. In the next, Downes was lying shirtless after being hit by a plastic bullet from short range. Those photos were mounted next to a copy of the police directive that plastic bullets are to be used "whenever it is judged the minimum and reasonable force."

"It is my pleasu— It is my duty to present the commissioners." The local moderator opened with this ambivalent line. And so the commissioners introduced themselves without embellishment or fanfare: Kathleen O'Toole, a former Boston police officer; Sir John Smith, a deputy commissioner of the London Metropolitan Police; and Dr. Maurice Hayes, a director of Belfast's Mater Hospital.

The crowd hated the police, and the tension was palpable. It was important for the commissioners not to become proxy targets for that loathing, not least for their own safety. If the crowd thought that the commissioners were police apologists, they might find themselves lifted from their chairs and thrown out the door. The commissioners were allowed to be there because they were recognized, however cynically, as people who had the power to make a change. Though the residents dared not believe it, there was a chance that the commission might even be sympathetic to their plight.

Nobody had ever actually asked Poleglass residents what they thought of the police, and thirty years of resentment had accumulated. They were sick to the teeth of hearing other people talk and were eager for someone to listen for a change. The commissioners knew that and kept their mouths shut. They were sitting on a cork, and every word they spoke would only agitate the crowd. So they sat silently, nodded occasionally, made studious notes, and listened intently. Dr. Hayes looked exceptionally taciturn. He was from Northern Ireland and knew exactly what was ahead. His head dropped into his chest through much of the presentation.

"The RUC have perpetuated the conflict because they have no respect for this community," opened a local woman in a five-minute statement on behalf of thirty-two community groups. "They are not a representative body," she continued. "They have failed to represent the people. None even live in this community. They have been involved in abuses and are a totally discredited force that has to be replaced."

Then the floor was opened for comments. A fourteen-year-old girl told of her generation's disillusionment growing up with a police force that seemed to do nothing but harass them in the streets and sight them in rifle crosshairs. Worse than harassment, said Tony McCabe of a local residents' association, the community was completely ignored when they raised road safety problems. One local man accused the police of colluding in his son's murder. But, he asked, didn't the police have a hand in the murder of plenty of Catholics?

As the microphone made its way through the crowd, each person sounded off. Few of the comments were constructive. Most were anecdotes of dissatisfaction or suspicion. The commissioners sat with their hands clasped solemnly. "Thank you for your presentations," Kathleen O'Toole finally said. "It is the most important part of the process."

The meeting was about to close. The crowd had subdued their anger long enough to express themselves with composure and dignity. They knew, like witnesses before a court hearing, that emotion often diminishes the facts. All the speakers had managed to contain themselves, and it looked like the meeting was going to stay bottled up when Daniel Groves stood up and pulled the cork.

He uttered what every single person in the room had restrained themselves from articulating since they sat down: "I have no faith in this commission," he began softly. Soon he was riding a wave of cheers and whistles. "This is nothing but a British government whitewash!"

He barked insults and invectives barely intelligible over the din of cheers. He railed against Chris Patten, the British government, and every official who had ever heard the reports of police abuses and did nothing. They were all conspirators to the injustice, Groves said. Every member of the establishment was indicted, and the only solution was to throw the whole lot out and start over.

Dr. Hayes looked up. He had had enough. He had served as an administrator in one of Belfast's most distinguished hospitals for years, and he had chaired the committee that drafted rules for the police. "I have been a civil servant here for thirty years, and I am not going to take this!" he shot back.

Dr. Hayes tried to defend his profession and his colleagues who had spent their careers trying to change the system from within. But he was outmatched. He was facing a crowd that wanted nothing of it. "How dare you!" Groves was bellowing. "How dare you! You were a civil servant and allowed this brutality to happen? You were a civil servant for thirty years and never tried to stop it?" he sputtered.

Dr. Hayes wisely restrained himself and gave no reply. The crowd eventually settled, but their true feelings were out. They were feelings shaped by experience that eroded Catholic faith in the police.

"Robert was beaten up! The police were there, but they did nothing!" That was how Diane Hamill heard that her brother was in a coma. The words came from her mother in a frantic phone call to the Royal Victoria Hospital where Diane worked as a nurse. Diane was shocked by the news. Twelve days later, when Diane saw grim-faced doctors leaving her brother's hospital room and she heard that Robert was dead, her shock was giving way to outrage. But that was in the spring of 1997 and much has happened since. Now, after years of campaigning for the truth about that night and justice for those who were responsible, Diane Hamill is rarely shocked and outrage is hard to muster.

That night Robert had been at a dance held at Saint Patrick's Hall in Portadown, with two cousins, Joanne and Siobhan Girvan, and Joanne's husband, Gregory. There was a time when Catholics lived in the area around Saint Patrick's Hall, but that was before the Troubles broke out. Now Saint Patrick's Hall is in an isolated corner of town.

No taxis were available that night so the four decided to walk home. It was only about a mile, but they would have to pass a dangerous junction in town—the corner of Thomas Street and Market Street where Catholics leaving Saint Patrick's Hall would often meet Protestants leaving The Coach nightclub. When they got to that junction, they hesitated. They could see some Protestants gathering at the end of the road but they could also see a police car. Robert said that they should be all right and he stepped out into the street. It was around one-thirty in the morning.

About twenty yards away, four police officers were sitting in a three-ton armored Land Rover. They were armed with handguns, plastic bullet equipment, and CS gas spray. They wore flak jackets and headgear. Their vehicle radio and their individual radios were in working order.

As soon as Robert Hamill stepped out into the street, a crowd of about thirty, maybe fifty, Protestant youths attacked. The two men were separated from the women, dragged to the ground and beaten. Robert was hit in the head with a bottle that must have knocked him unconscious because he did nothing to defend himself after he collapsed to the ground. "Kill him! Kill him!" The crowd shouted as they took turns stomping and kicking Robert's head. "Kill the bastard!" For blocks around, people could hear the women shrieking. No one in the Land Rover stirred.

After about five or ten minutes, one of the witnesses ran to the Land Rover and literally pulled Constable Alan Neill, the driver, out of the vehicle. "You sat there and did nothing," he shouted. "You sat there, watching that happening and you did nothing."

Finally, police got out but none of the officers attended to Robert Hamill. The first request for assistance was received at Portadown police station, situated about two hundred yards away, at 1:45 in the morning. When the ambulance arrived a few minutes later, the crowd of Protestants was still unruly and showed no signs of dispersing. Instead they beat and shook the ambulance when it took Robert and Gregory to the hospital. After the ambulance had gone, the police left. No one was arrested that night; no one was even questioned. No crime scene was declared and no forensic evidence was gathered. Police returned to their barracks, ended their shifts, and went home without even filling out an incident report.

Police accounts of the attack varied over seven, often contradictory, statements issued in the days after the attack. Within hours of the beating, police said that twenty-five-year-old Hamill, a "youth," was injured in a "clash between rival factions." Three days later, with Hamill still in a coma, police released another statement describing how officers "were alerted to a disturbance and immediately intervened," but "became themselves the subject of attack." By the time that Robert died, more disturbing facts about the police's handling of the incident had come to light. Minutes before the attack, a pedestrian had approached the Land Rover. "Be alert," he told the police, "some young people are coming from Saint Patrick's Hall." Police took no interest in the warning. Constable Clare Halley, one of the officers on the scene, apprehended one of the Protestant gang. She took his name but then let him go.

Within two days after Hamill's death, six men were in custody facing charges for murder. Within six months, all but one of the defendants, Marc Hobson, were released. Constable Alan Neill was the prosecution's main witness against Hobson. He described how the lighting was good in the street that night. He was only standing about ten yards from where Robert Hamill lay on the ground when he saw Hobson—described in some detail as a young man in his twenties, five-foot, eight inches or so, with a goatee beard and a round face—approach and draw back his foot as if to kick Hamill in the head. Neill described all of this, but then said that he did not know whether the blow landed on Hamill's head.

Marc Hobson was acquitted of murder and convicted of causing an affray, a misdemeanor. He had already served half of his four-year sentence while he was waiting for trial, so it was not long before he was back on the streets. Diane Hamill has seen him on the streets of Portadown. He laughs at her.

Diane Hamill's campaign for criminal charges against the police has not met much success. The Independent Commission for Police Complaints expressed its satisfaction with the investigations into Robert's murder. Diane approached David Trimble, leader of the Ulster Unionist Party and the family's local Member of Parliament, for assistance. Later, Diane saw a copy of the letter that Trimble wrote to the police superintendent of Portadown on her behalf. "Further to your telephone conversation with my wife," Trimble opened. "Could you confirm if I am right in my understanding that the police patrol on the scene attempted to intervene [in Robert Hamill's beating], but were prevented from doing so by the crowd?"

Diane decided to launch a civil suit. Rosemary Nelson, the Hamill family lawyer, requested copies of the security film from the center of town on the night of the attack. The police refused, saying that they had already checked the videotapes. When Rosemary Nelson pushed the police on that and other matters, she was threatened. The last time that Nelson requested the tapes was two weeks before she was killed in a car bomb.

Diane Hamill has not given up her campaign, but she is growing weary. She does not know whether the people responsible for Robert's murder will ever be punished, but she will not stop fighting. "When my mummy and I are in town and we see the police, she starts to say things. But I can almost make them vanish; I don't see the RUC. I try to make her like that; I don't want them to make her twisted inside."

Across town, on the night after the meeting in Poleglass, a smaller, more civil crowd assembled in Sir Robert Wilter Hall at Queens University at a further meeting of the Patten Commission. The campus, on the edge of salubrious and affluent south Belfast, offered a different setting and a different tone from Poleglass.

Most attendees were Protestant; they had last been in the hall as students and now lived in the area. They were employed, well educated, and arrived poised and neatly dressed. While the front rows at the Poleglass meeting were the first to be filled, people in the spacious Wilter Hall seemed reluctant to get that close to the commissioners. They scattered in clumps around the room.

People had no gripes or complaints. Their few encounters with the police were cordial words exchanged at the occasional security checkpoint through which they briskly passed. Most people held the police in high regard. The police were their fathers, sons, friends, and neighbors. Attending such meetings was unseemly but necessary because if people did not stand up for the police the outrageous allegations and advice of the previous Poleglass meetings might go unchallenged.

There were no posters along the walls at Wilter Hall, and there were no formal submissions. People came to assert the principle of law and order and defend the status quo. In Poleglass people were angry. In Wilter Hall they were afraid. They were afraid that the commission would upend the system they trusted and arbitrarily replace it with something foreign just to appease a few Catholic antagonists and troublemakers.

Chris Patten sat at the head of the table with five commission colleagues. He had convened enough of these meetings to gauge his audience in an instant. He also knew something about Northern Ireland, having served as the province's minister for housing twenty years earlier. Patten knew how the night's meeting was going to be played out before a single word was uttered.

Most people would steadfastly defend the police and cast aspersions on those calling for change. A few would give guarded criticism, and at least one would call the whole process a sham. Many people at this meeting were suspicious that Patten's report had already been written. They believed the final plan to scrap the RUC was sitting in his office, waiting for a rubber stamp once the public meetings were concluded. These meetings, they thought, were just to give the appearance of a community caucus.

Patten's remarks spoke to the community's concerns. "We are genuinely interested in hearing people's views," he said. "We are not in anyone's pockets, and we are nobody's patsy."

But the crowd was also defensive. The media was already guessing what the reforms might look like, and none found broad favor among Protestants.

"It would be scandalous!" one man said of the suggestion that the *Royal* prefix from the Royal Ulster Constabulary be dropped. "I believe most people would be totally opposed to that."

"No," said another critic. "It would be like spitting in the faces of those police who were killed."

"Some people seem to believe people in uniforms are perfect," one man explained of past police scandals.

"But you can't expect everybody to be angels," a woman finished.

"Sure, there are bad apples in any police force."

Endless investigations into police behavior had "left the police force completely demoralized," said retired officer Donald Millikin. It was difficult enough for police to maintain order in a deeply divided society without constant scrutiny into their methods, he continued.

As the meeting was concluded, Millikin warned, "If you get this wrong we will see twenty years of trouble."

Patten nodded acknowledgment.

In 1952 Donald Millikin took stock of himself. He was nineteen, through school, and looking for a vocation. Twenty years earlier, a man in his shoes would have been sent into a factory or shipyard. But those industries were gathering dust, and, besides, Millikin was looking for a bit of adventure and a break from his family. Joining the police was not a calling, just the closest thing to a suitable job. Pay was poor and living conditions were basic, but Millikin was young, single, and up for anything. After six months of training he got his first post.

Millikin had never heard of a place called Armoy. He had to consult a map to find the speck of a town along Northern Ireland's rugged Antrim coast. The town was little more than a fishing village less than sixty miles from Belfast, but in days when people lived their lives a few meters from where they were born, Armoy was a world away.

The people he was sent to serve were known as "Glen Folk" for the

Glens of Antrim around the town. They had unfamiliar country cus-
toms and an accent Millikin found almost unintelligible. The first traffic
accident he attended to was between a bread truck and a tractor. Millikin got out his notebook to take a statement, but the men were speaking in their broad Antrim dialect and it was like a foreign language.

The Armoy police barracks was called a "four-in-one station": four
constables and one sergeant. The men lived and worked there. It was
appalling, Millikin says, but most of his day was spent out in the field.
There were no police cars; instead the men patrolled on bicycles. Millikin enjoyed those peaceful rides through the countryside. Wherever
he went, he was welcome.

"Especially among Glen Folk," Millikin remembers, "there was a
traditional Irish welcome. If you were a stranger at the door, even if you
were there to give them a summons, you had to have a cup of tea. They
gave you a drink. That was your business; you did your business, and
then they had to give you a welcome."

The town was well ordered and barely needed policing. Everyone
had his or her role and pretty much stuck to it. The police played arbi-
trator and responded whenever something serious did occur, but they
spent most of their time getting to know the community.

Officers like Millikin had so much time on their hands that in the
spring, they took an agricultural census. Millikin surveyed farmland and
recorded how many acres were used for barley, corn, livestock, and
potatoes. It kept him busy and gave him an insight into people's lives.
That was important because the police were not just there to investigate
crime; they were wardens and caretakers.

Life in Armoy was too rugged and difficult to be muddled by political differences. People needed each other too much. If there was a poor
crop, people turned to each other for help. If there was a personal problem, they trusted each other's goodwill. Petty animosity was not a
luxury they could afford. A simple country life would not sustain it.

"At that time I had no conscious realization of Catholic and Protestant divisions. I had not been brought up with divisions, and when I got
there everybody was the same. They were all very friendly people," Millikin remembers.

After almost ten years of retirement, Millikin looks back on his callow youth with nostalgia. When he started work in Armoy, the serious violence of the seventies was still a generation away. He was doing normal police work in a stable society. He had no notion of the violence that was to come, and even if he had, he could have done nothing to stop it.

When he left Armoy, things were beginning to change. It happened slowly, sometimes in spurts, but the kind of policing he was accustomed to was over. In the late fifties, Millikin served in Lisniskea, County Fermanagh, on the border with the Irish Republic. He was married by then, so he no longer lived in the barracks but in a thatched cottage a mile from town with his new wife and their young child.

It takes about five years of work and training, Millikin told me, before men start to think like policemen. Eventually, it becomes the only way they think. A veteran officer like Millikin sees almost every problem as a policing problem. And if not a policing problem, then a dilemma that could use police reasoning.

Security, criminal profiles, motives, suspects—that is how he sees the world. When he was in Armoy, he used this knowledge to great effect. If there was a robbery, he knew immediately who to pull in for questioning. There were only a few people in town capable of it, and eventually, after asking the right questions, he would get a confession. He realized that there was a discernible criminal pattern that was being followed. The behavior was always the same. Once an officer cracked that behavior, he cracked the case.

But the pattern was different in Lisniskea. Days before Millikin arrived, the police barracks had been attacked. The old IRA—the small group of bandits that operated before the Troubles—had begun a campaign to take over border areas like Fermanagh. The barracks were sandbagged and heavily guarded against further attacks.

Millikin knew his life was in danger, but he did not know from whom. During the day, he felt safe. People from both sides of the community greeted him cordially, but at night he knew he was vulnerable. That is when ambushes happened. When he got home he slept with his revolver under his pillow.

"See, the secret of police work is identification," Millikin confided.

"Crime is committed by people who think they will get away with it." But this was not ordinary crime. It was not easy to identify people. When they were identified, they became martyrs and heroes. Millikin had not been trained for that. It worried him.

When Millikin was transferred to east Belfast in the late sixties, the police capacity to patrol both communities was nearly at its end. He worked mostly from the Mountpottinger police barracks in the Short Strand, the same building that I had jogged to on my first trip to Belfast. Catholics were hemmed in—Protestants bordered the small enclave on three sides, and the Lagan River was on the fourth side. It was an isolated area with a history of past sectarian skirmishes. There had once been a barrier at the junction of Seaford Street, the main thruway where the two communities met. A sandbag wall had been erected there in the twenties to prevent people shooting across the divide. In the years before the Troubles started, Millikin and the other officers used to laugh at the notion: a barrier between the communities? That sounded ridiculous.

Yes, there was communal tension, but no violence. Even when local Orange Order marches annoyed the Catholics, there was no real confrontation. The police did not allow it because they "would have been in a queer bit of trouble with the head constable if a person so much as raised a shout [at an Orange parade]," Millikin said.

No stones were thrown? I once asked. No bottles?

"Listen," Millikin answered emphatically. "There would have been a whole inquiry and policemen would have been hauled over the coals if a bottle had been *allowed* to be thrown."

When violence did erupt in 1969, the police were unprepared. They had neither the training nor the equipment to deal with widespread civil unrest. Millikin remembers police lines—hundreds of men—sent to put down riots. They made impressive numbers, but they had no order. There was no strategy. Police would stand under a downpour of stones until one of the officers got fed up, yelled '*Charge!*' and led an advance. The rioters would retreat a few yards, and then it would start again. Soon the police got frustrated and started throwing stones themselves. They did not know what else to do. "It was mayhem," Millikin remembered. "One side was as bad as the other."

It was around that time, when heavy rioting erupted in Derry, that Millikin got fed up with how bad things had gotten. He was working dispatch on his own. Most of the Belfast officers had been sent to deal with the riots when a call came in. There had been a routine burglary. Customarily, a unit would have been sent right away. Officers would interview the householder. Neighbors would be canvassed. The missing items would be logged and suspects questioned. But no officers were available. They were in Derry, and Millikin had to explain that to the caller. He had to tell a citizen that the police could not answer his complaint because they had been stretched to the limit. Until things settled down in Derry, Millikin told the caller, there was no telling when someone would be available. When Millikin put down the phone, he knew that the police were in trouble. "We always believed," Millikin said, "no matter how rough things would get, we would win. We would restore order."

Uphold the law and maintain order. That is a policeman's job. That is what Millikin was trained to do, but nothing had prepared him for the position he was now in. Order was breaking down, and no one seemed to know how to stop it.

He was not trusted by half the community. Many hated him. Some wanted him killed, and a few had tried. The pressure was immense, but the frustration was worse. He had joined the force to do good and serve the community. For many years, he felt that that was what he was doing, but the feeling was robbed when the violence started. There was no chance to serve when he was under attack.

Millikin had had the community's trust for so long that he had taken it for granted. Now that Catholics no longer wanted his kind of service, there was nothing he could do. His uniform was always going to stand in the way, and he was never going to be able to do the work that he once did.

Millikin is not naïve or simpleminded. But for the chance of birth, he might have been throwing bottles at the police instead of wearing their uniform. Still, society needs laws, and those laws need to be enforced. The police do not make the laws; they only enforce them. They cannot decide which laws they will follow. Millikin knew the politicians had no idea how to restore order and he could see that the police were being thrown at the problem. He resented that, but there was nothing he could do. Particularly in the early years of the Troubles, the police were given impossible orders and denied the tools needed to carry them out.

The Irish flag was a divisive symbol, the government said, and whenever the police saw one, they were to remove it. Police with guns strained community relations, the government also decreed, so the force was deprived of weapons. Enforcing the first order was provocative. Obeying the second was reckless. But when Millikin learned an Irish flag was flying atop a telephone pole in the heart of the Short Strand, he led four unarmed men to take it down.

A crowd of residents had gathered at the scene. Millikin knew many of them well. He tried to break the tension with a little friendly banter. He was only enforcing the law; it was not personal, he told them. But the faces in the crowd were wooden. The time for civility had passed. It was personal, and they did take offense. The crowd began to grumble and stir, and one young man stepped directly in front of Millikin with his hand in his pocket. He had a gun, Millikin was sure, so he grabbed the man's wrist like a vise, holding it in the pocket. They stood like that for a minute, staring at each other. Eventually someone moved forward and grabbed the man around the waist, pulling him away. Millikin also stepped back and left, but policing the area had forever changed.

Catholics in the Short Strand started to taunt and jeer at the police. Coming out of shops, they would throw bottles of milk at passing patrols. The force began to look more like the army than the police. They were heavily armed and wore bulletproof vests. Millikin often shuddered as he walked the streets, feeling himself caught in a sniper's lens. His friends and colleagues were being killed daily. There was nothing he could do.

Millikin would think back to the early days. He used to ride his bike through the streets of Armoy, welcome everywhere he went. People trusted and respected him, turned to him with their problems. That was police work, he believed. That was why he had joined the force.

Now he was riding behind the reinforced steel of a Land Rover fearing assassination. How had it all gone so wrong?

Through thirty years of violence, the RUC had been stuck in the middle. They were one-half civil police force, one-half army auxiliary. While they tried to carry out normal policing duties, they were under the threat of assassination. Over three hundred police officers were killed while working one of the world's most dangerous police beats.

Police reform was an inevitable consequence of the peace process. The only question was what would change. Like so many issues in Northern Ireland, there was a slender space for compromise. With the terrorist threat gone, the police would have a new civil role. The total number of officers would decrease, but more Catholics would have to be recruited and the force would have to gain the confidence of both sides of the community. There were some symbolic changes to come: a new name, uniform, badge. And there was an entirely new structure for oversight and complaints. But would the changes go far enough to win public confidence? Well, the new police service ended their recruitment drive in the spring of 2001—ahead of schedule and with an abundance of applicants.

Sharon and Kevin

❐　　　❐

When they first started going out, Sharon swore that she would never tell her parents about Kevin. There was no way that the relationship could last, she felt, so there was no point in upsetting them. Sharon is Baptist and Kevin is Catholic. No matter how they felt about one another, Sharon kept insisting, there was no way to work things out. Still, they would meet and talk. They talked a lot about faith and their upbringings. It was spiritually dangerous, Sharon thought, for her to be seeing a Catholic. It might even be a sin, but she did not know for sure.

Desertmartin is a situated about halfway between Derry and Belfast—a rural town that interrupts the rolling green hills of pasture and farmland. That is where Sharon grew up. Her family is part of the Protestant farming stock that has been part of that land for generations. They live in a world of communion with the land and God. They measure work according to how much they sweat, and they mark time according to the seasons of sowing and reaping. Their lives run according to that simple, trusted cycle, and they set their existence according to its rhythm. There is wisdom to that life that is passed down over generations, just like the land. So when Sharon was a little girl and her parents would say "Don't trust Catholics," they were not really being bigoted. They were just passing on the sort of prudent aphorism that was so long-tested that it no longer bore questioning.

But even as a young girl, Sharon was prone to asking questions.

Her mother found that difficult, and their relationship was often stormy. Sharon's mother had been taught that it was improper for a lady to ask questions; it was either a sign of ignorance or bad manners. Words that came from the Bible, the pulpit, or her husband's mouth, in particular, were to be flatly accepted. But Sharon asked questions; in fact, she seemed to have a question for everything and everyone: her parents, teachers, and even the minister. It was part of the independent streak that her mother found so difficult.

Sharon had been leading a sheltered life in Desertmartin; she would be the first to admit that now. Of course, no one who leads a sheltered life knows it at the time. When she left Desertmartin at eighteen, she started studying at a college in the seaside town of Bangor. At first, she came home most weekends, but, then, suddenly and without explanation, she started to spend more of her free time in Bangor or in Belfast.

Sharon met Kevin while working as an intern at a youth center in the spring of 1997. He came from a small town just a bit farther west of Desertmartin, but like Sharon, he had started to leave the rural life behind. Kevin was most everything that Sharon wanted in a boyfriend and they had a lot in common. They both wanted to see some more of the world. After a few weeks of spending time with him, Sharon did not know what to do, but she suspected that her parents were curious about her absences from home.

Sharon's mother knew that she was hiding something, and she could guess what it was. It had to be something about a boy; that much seemed obvious. What else could there be to make Sharon slink around the place and run off to Belfast all the time? But it was not like Sharon to keep a secret about a boyfriend. There had to be something about him that Sharon did not want her to know. Sharon's mother had her suspicions. She asked her other daughter if her suspicions were true: Was Sharon dating a black man? When Sharon heard that one, she laughed out loud. Still, it was getting too difficult to keep a secret, so she confessed. Sharon remembers that day. She was standing in the kitchen, and her mother, who was sitting in the living room, got hysterical. "How could you do this to me?" her mother cried.

That was a hard time for Sharon. Living at home meant being close to everything that she had ever relied on or trusted. Now all of those things seemed strange. She was upsetting everything in her world. Sharon had expected her mother to react as she did, but she was not prepared for how others behaved. What you're doing is *wrong*, everyone told her. To a woman of strong Christian faith, there was no firmer rebuke.

Her friends from church were scandalized. They would read Bible passages to show her why dating a Catholic was *wrong*. Be sure you don't turn into one of them, they warned. More than that, it was her father's quiet disapproval that cut her.

Then she grew concerned about her safety. Not long after Sharon and Kevin started dating, a Catholic girl was murdered as she lay in the arms of her Protestant boyfriend. She and Kevin split up twice in those early months. Sharon just could not handle the pressure. Each time that they got back together, Sharon was still sure that it could never last.

Everything changed when the couple left Northern Ireland. Sharon started a course in northern England, and Kevin was doing a further degree in sociology a few hundred miles to the south. They saw each other every weekend for a year, and then Kevin moved up to live with Sharon. Their relationship thrived. Sharon found more support from her friends in England than she had at home. Over the next three years of her study, she and Kevin were able to sort out their problems. Still, Northern Ireland was where they belonged, and they wanted to go back.

When Sharon saw her parents again, she told them that she and Kevin had gotten engaged and that they were living together. Sharon's family had secretly hoped that the couple would split up. Sharon's sister got engaged around the same time to a Presbyterian friend of the family. Things had been so easy for her. Why couldn't Sharon have done that? Word would spread about the engagement. What would Sharon's mother say when people asked, "And how's your Sharon, then?" How could she possibly tell someone that Sharon was living with a Catholic? It was hard to say whether explaining that they were engaged would make it better or worse. Once the news was out, at least no one would have the temerity to ask the next question—"Do you approve?"—which was just as well, because she did not know.

Things would be awkward for Sharon's father as well. He is a member of the Orange Order, and some of his brethren were bound to ask about Sharon. The ones who had young, unmarried sons of their own probably had an eye on her. Sharon's father was not sure, but he thought he might be forced to leave the Orange Order if Sharon married a Catholic.

The people of Desertmartin are deeply observant Christians, but their reliance on something as uncertain as the land has made them somewhat superstitious. Marrying a Catholic would be a transgression; it would invite something on their family. Sharon would be turning against the faith that she had been raised with. Desertmartin is a town that demands a strict observance of the rules of convention. It is also a town with a long memory. Protestant families that have sold their farms to Catholics have been known to lose every friend they ever had as a result.

These matters began to vex Sharon's wider family circle. An aunt, her mother's sister, sent a card congratulating Sharon on her engagement—she did not approve of what Sharon was doing, but not to send a card would have been uncharitable. Inside was a small, handwritten note: Couldn't Sharon see what she was doing to her parents? They had a reputation in the town. Her father was a pillar of the community and one of the elders of the church. Sharon should respect them. Couldn't she see that what she was doing was *wrong*?

The next time that Sharon saw that aunt they were both standing beside the hospital bed of the aunt's daughter, Nicola. Nicola was an assistant in a local nursing home in the area, and she had been secretly dating a Catholic who worked in the kitchen. One evening, after the two young lovers had parted, Nicola was driving home and her car verged off the road. Nicola was thrown out of the windshield and seriously damaged her spine. Doctors did not know if she would survive. Nicola's mother met her daughter's lover in the hospital. Somehow, after the accident, the aunt's perspective changed a bit.

So where does the story of Sharon and Kevin end? Well, they are married now and taking things one day at a time. They are a young couple, after all, who will know a lot of joys and hardships. They have stopped dwelling on the peculiar set of challenges that they face since they know so many ordinary challenges lie ahead. But it seemed to me that it was only a matter of time before their family and friends would see how courageous they are.

The Old Neighborhood

t is hard to say how such things start because the reasons are lost when the revenge attacks begin, but three Australian tourists were beaten up in the Short Strand in the early hours of Saturday, May 13, 2001, and things escalated from there. The young men had been walking from the center of Belfast when they passed through that neighborhood and were attacked by twenty youths. One of the three Australians nearly lost an ear; the other two were not too badly injured. It was the sort of event that happened almost every weekend to anyone foolish or daring enough to walk past that religious interface in the small hours, but because the victims were tourists, almost universally recognized as a neutral element to be shielded from Belfast's brutality, the media seized on the story.

I was trying to get some work done at a friend's house in rural Northern Ireland when I read about what was going on. Before long, I would be leaving the province, and I was still hoping to find some positive story on which to end my trip. I just wanted to get an eyeful of some heartening image, an anecdote that I could tell my friends and say: See, things are getting better. That I was still anticipating some sign of closure showed how much there still was to learn. The peace process was not moving forward according to some trajectory; it wobbled and gyrated so that everything that looked like a good omen was followed by something of a disappointment.

Still, I headed back to Belfast to see how things were going in my neighborhood. The Australians had not been part of Belfast's Protestant community, but the Protestants took offense on their behalf. Twenty-four hours after the three tourists were beaten, a hail of bottles and stones came raining down over the peace wall and onto the Short Strand.

"It went on through the morning, and these streets here looked like something from Beirut, and that's not one word of a lie," George "Pee Wee" Lundy told me.

Lundy lives in a small house on Bryson Street, the road running parallel to the peace wall, a position that means he gets a fair bit of the trouble when it comes. After he heard the first of his windows crash at about four in the morning, Lundy woke his four adult sons, plus his wife and daughter—they all share the same four-bedroom house. They went downstairs to the kitchen, where they sat smoking and drinking until the attack subsided sometime after dawn. All of the front windows, about fifteen of them in varying sizes, were smashed.

"I've been living here for fifteen years, and I've never seen anything like this," he told me. That was three days after the Australians were attacked, and the contretemps were ongoing. There were nightly skirmishes, and during the day Catholics were attacked when they ventured out of the Short Strand. If I wanted to hear about that, Lundy suggested, I should go see the McMullans around the corner.

Just past the breach of the peace wall, where Madrid Street cuts across the neighborhoods, there is a row of houses. The ones at the end might as well have a bull's-eye painted on the side because they are the closest, most obvious targets for Protestant rioters. The McMullans lived one house in from the end.

I did not know Brian McMullan's face when I went to his door, but I knew his house well enough. From my place on the end of Madrid Street, the Protestant end, I had often pitied the poor souls that lived at that address. Brian's fingers were stained brown like his teeth. I noticed this when he brought his cigarette to his mouth. He had graying hair and a ruddy face. He ushered me into the living room where his wife, Sharon, was sitting. Brian had to be in his forties, and Sharon looked to be about ten years younger than that. They had six children—three girls and three boys.

The McMullans described what had been happening, how "our ones" and "their ones" had been going at it for the past few days. It did not have anything to do with the Australian tourists, they said. The Short Strand had been under intermittent attack for years, Brian McMullan explained. "And the wall only makes things worse. They might as well turn it into a starting line. It protects the people that are throwing stones, gives them something to hide behind. What they should do is tear down the wall and the houses in between so that there is a big gap. But they won't do that. Just look at the Great Wall of China. That's been there for years, and this wall will be here for just as long."

On the previous Sunday morning, the first morning of the latest attacks, some of the Protestant youths shouting down Madrid Street had warned the McMullans, "We'll get youse at the post office!" There is no post office in the Short Strand; the nearest one is located just a few hundred yards across the religious divide. On Monday mornings, Sharon would collect the family's unemployment benefits there. It made her uneasy, going into the Protestant area, but there rarely was trouble. Peter, the man who owned the post office, was decent. It would have been easy for him to disdain his Catholic customers, but mostly he seemed to empathize with them, and that helped ease Sharon's anxiety.

The unemployment checks were late that week, so it was not until Tuesday morning when Sharon and Michelle, the McMullans' sixteen-year-old daughter, went down to the post office. As they stood in line, a gang of about six Protestants stormed the building shouting insults and pelted Sharon and Michelle with eggs and flour. The women just stood there. What else could they do? The gang eventually fled, and the women ran back to their neighborhood in hysterics.

I asked Sharon how she felt about what had happened. She said that she was not too bothered and was just trying not to think about it. After all, this sort of thing happened all the time. Their windows had been broken more times than they could count. Their car was regularly vandalized, and the kids had taken their share of abuse from the people on the other side of the wall. There was even one time when some Protestants came through the front door of the house and started wrecking the place before Sharon repelled them by throwing flower-pots. She was getting used to it all.

Then Sharon and Brian started to laugh. It was an unsettling laugh, sort of dark and hopeless. It was a laugh that was heard only from people who stopped believing that they could change their misfortune. "Ya, I know this is crazy," it seemed to say. "But if you'd only accept it, you could laugh too." But to accept it, you had to understand it, and that meant living through all the everyday horrors until you were utterly despondent. One of the most offensive things about the Troubles was that it could take any sense of indignation or umbrage and turn it inside out so that nothing mattered anymore. I had been in Northern Ireland long enough to start realigning my understanding of words like *disappointment* and *desperation*; that was as close to the madness as I cared to go.

Sharon said that she was tired and that her head hurt, so she excused herself to lie down. I left the McMullans for a while and returned that evening as a crowd of about thirty Protestant teenagers gathered at their end of Madrid Street. Brian was leaning over the sofa that was pushed against the front end of the living room: knees on the seat, elbows perched on the windowsill. Above his head, the reinforced windows were cracked but still holding.

"See that?" Brian beckoned me over. "See that young fella there? He's always getting things stirred up." It felt a bit as if I had been invited to observe wildlife from some secret blind in the Serengeti. The Protestants were a pack of restless lions prowling around in their tracksuits, sneakers, and baseball caps. Brian kept a pair of binoculars on the floor next to the sofa.

On our side of the wall, there was a small crowd of Catholic teenagers and a few adult chaperones. The girls would walk towards the corner, shake their hips at the Protestants, and then turn away. Occasionally, one of the really young Protestant boys, maybe seven years old, would run forward and throw a stone. Each of these gestures was met with whoops and cheers from their own side. Brian barely spoke a word as he peered up and down the road. All I could hear was the low din of the crowd and the steady ticking of the clock mounted on the wall.

"Are you not scared to go down there?" Brian abruptly asked. When I left that afternoon, I had walked directly down Madrid Street and across the divide into my neighborhood to see David Clelland. He had not been in, so I turned around and came back down Madrid Street before I left the Short Strand. It might have been imprudent considering how tense things had gotten, and I sensed that Brian judged me as being dishonest or even disloyal for having gone to the other side. I suddenly felt very ashamed, even a bit intimidated by his question. "You don't know who to trust," he said. "You don't even know if you can trust me."

I thought that comment deserved a reply, and I wanted to explain myself or even apologize, but Brian was already back in position on the sofa peering up and down the road. As night fell, the crowd of Protestants suddenly gathered into an irregular formation and began to sway in unison, darting around like a flock of starlings. I feared that this was some sort of ritualistic gesture, a preface to the Protestants storming directly down Madrid Street. Just then, three armored police cars came squealing down the road and blocked the junction between the two sides. The crowds dissipated, and everyone began to wander away.

Brian turned around on the sofa to face me. "This might be a quiet night." He shrugged. When things had settled down, we sat there in the living room and talked about life in the area. "You lived over there. You must have seen what it is like," Brian said to me with a slightly accusatory tone. He still seemed suspicious of me having crossed the religious threshold earlier that day, but after a few cigarettes and a cup of tea, he relaxed. Brian cannot read, so I thumbed through the newspapers and told him what they were saying about recent events. Michelle had come in by then, and she sat in the living room with us.

"If things are so miserable," I asked, "why do you stay?" It was a question that I often put to people like the McMullans, and they often responded as if I were being facetious. I might as well have asked "Why are you Catholic?" This was their home; it was part of who they were.

The family could move across town to another Catholic ghetto or maybe deeper into the Short Strand and away from the flash point, but that was it. Neither of those options appealed to Brian McMullan. He did not want to leave the network of friends that his family had developed, and he was too defiant to be forced out of his house. It was this same stubbornness that explained why Brian did not follow his neighbors' lead and protect his windows with chicken wire. He was not going to live like an animal.

Brian told me that he could handle the abuse, but he worried about his family. Michelle was sitting right next to her father, and Brian touched his daughter's hair as he spoke. "This child here, she's been through a lot growing up in this house. With what happened the other day and plenty more over the years . . . She's always been a great support to her mum and her brothers and sisters. There were times when her mother was not very well, and she took care of her. If I could do something to get her away from this, I would not be too long in doing it. Living here is just something that we have to deal with, but I know that when she grows up she will do more with her life than I have ever done. She will be able to move out of this place and make something of herself. You see? It's the young ones. They'll grow up and things will have changed—maybe not in a place like this, but away from here things will have gotten better."

Everyone in Northern Ireland seemed to have a quick fix for dealing with the Troubles, a formula that would sort it all out. "My solution?" the Catholic plumber who once came to fix my leaky boiler offered solicitously. "The governments should say, 'Look, we are giving this until about 2005, and after that it's gonna be a united Ireland. Anyone who wants to stay, you're welcome. Anyone who wants to go, we'll buy your house and give you some money to start somewhere else.'"

Some Protestant friends offered the same solution, but in reverse: help the Catholics move to the Irish Republic and let the Protestants live in the north in peace. But maybe that is how the word *peace* had become so loaded. I often heard it used more as a verb than a noun: something that someone might do to you. More than once, I heard people hiss "peace" as the most venomous invective. Either that, or it was a trite word drained of meaning. A multicolored PEACE sticker was visible through a child's bedroom window out my back door. In a sense, it was encouraging to see that someone had bothered to put that message in the child's window, but it also made the word seem rather impotent. People had grown so cynical of the word *peace*, it was often noted, that before it could be achieved they would have to call it something else. Maybe that, too, was a trite observation, but it seemed to be getting close to the truth.

Peace might be an unrealistic standard because it is both so idealistic and so relative. Anything measured against it is bound to be unsatisfactory. Sitting in the McMullans' living room, it was easy to become disheartened. But taking a step back and surveying the landscape from a distance, the subtle shifts of life in Northern Ireland came into view. Brian was probably right; the peace wall in the Short Strand would be there for a while. But across town, the Whiterock army barracks—one of the most detested army installations in Northern Ireland—had been leveled to make room for residential housing.

Peace was coming, I was sure of that, but it was taking its time. That Brian McMullan talked about a better future for his daughter showed that he believed it, too. If it did not come in Michelle McMullan's generation, then it might come in the next when the daily normality of life has pushed all the grievances and bitterness out of people's memories. When peace comes, it will not announce its arrival. Few people will acknowledge it, so it might last.

ACKNOWLEDGMENTS

I am deeply indebted to many people. First, to those who appear in this book. Their trust in me may be the greatest compliment I ever receive. My dear friends in Northern Ireland provided kindnesses and company that made life there such a joy. In particular, Jim Rea's interest in my work and well-being was a constant comfort. My friend Richard Good has seen my earliest interest in this story unfold. John Wonnocott will surely remain the kindest, most decent man I know.

At home, two mentors and friends, Steve Nash and Richard Couto, gave me endless inspiration and support. To Gail Ross, my agent, who saw my vision for this book and for Tracy Brown, my editor at Ballantine, who shared that vision too. And finally, darling Orla, for your love and support.